The Technology Machine

HOW MANUFACTURING
WILL WORK IN THE
YEAR 2020

PATRICIA E. MOODY
RICHARD E. MORLEY

THE FREE PRESS

THE FREE PRESS
A Division of Simon & Schuster, Inc.
1230 Avenue of the Americas
New York, NY 10020
Copyright © 1999 by Patricia E. Moody and Richard E. Morley
All rights reserved, including the right of reproduction
in whole or in part in any form.
THE FREE PRESS and colophon are trademarks of Simon & Schuster, Inc.
Designed by Kim Llewellyn
Manufactured in the United States of America
10 9 8 7 6 5 4 3 2 1

Library of Congress Cataloging-in-Publication Data

Moody, Patricia E.
The technology machine: how manufacturing will work in the year
2020/Patricia E. Moody and Richard E. Morley.
p.   cm.
Includes bibliographical references and index.
1. Production engineering—Technological innovations.
2. Manufactures—Technological innovations.   3. Industrial
management.   I. Morley, Richard E.   II. Title.
TS176.M64   1999
670'.9'05—dc21   99-26716
CIP

ISBN 0-684-83709-9

For the Nissitissitt River,

"many small stones,"

that rises from Potanipo and flows

ten miles to the Nashua,

which flows to the Merrimack,

down to the sea.

Patricia E. Moody

To the memory of my son,

Robert Edward Morley.

1963–1995

Richard E. Morley

CONTENTS

PREFACE   ix

INTRODUCTION   1

1

How Manufacturing Will Work   7

2

One Hundred Twenty-seven Wild Cards—
Who We Will Be, and What We Will Do   35

3

WHACK, Why You Can't Get There from Here   67

4

Technology Rules! The PLC Breakthrough   95

5

Intelligent Systems that Will Get Us There—
Chaos, Complex Adaptive Systems, and Other Enabling
Technologies   119

6

The Big, Big Wave—Four Software Meta-Systems
that Will Transform Manufacturing   157

7

Managing the Technology Machine   185

8

Two Meta-Systems: The Bullet Train and Plastics!   211

9

In the Land Where the Engineer Is King   235

10

Silicon Life on a Carbon Planet   261

NOTES   303

BIBLIOGRAPHY   305

ACKNOWLEDGMENTS   307

INDEX   311

ABOUT THE AUTHORS   319

When I turned four, my father took me on a tour of the St. Regis Paper Mill: We saw the steam power plant, the cutters and rollers, and the finished paper rolls in the mill yard. He lifted me up to see over the edge of the pulper, a huge tank that ground sheets into pulp. The machine noise made it impossible to hear his explanation of the paper-making process—but I tried to take it all in.

I smelled the river and the pulp paper; we lived by the mill whistle, and we noted when we crossed the covered bridge on the way to school what color the Nashua River was running, often green-blue, occasionally red. The water was never clear.

Mill Street

Manufacturing is an addiction that runs in my family. Since I was little I have hung out with engineers and factory workers. I too love machines, technology, and manufacturing. My family lived with the hope, the boom, and the decline of both a mill town and an industrial city—we came to understand and expect the strain the swings produced across the town. Schools ran to very lean budgets, new cars and new homes were rare, and overtime was a necessity. During shutdown the parking lot at the swimming hole filled up and Main Street was quieter. Our lives ran to the rhythms of the mills.

Vassar Street

Anyone who has ever walked down Vassar Street in Cambridge, Massachusetts, a dirty, well-used side street running off Mass Avenue and parallel to the athletic fields, in the heart of MIT, will remember the excitement of ideas on the move. Here new companies make their first appearance, renting temporary space in anticipation of growth—from the Dome of the academic community, to the leased concrete row of spinoffs, some of which make the jump to Route 128's golden acres, many of which fold and are re-created in a different incorporation. Vassar Street is one of a few technology birthing spots, like Steve Jobs's garage, and the Hewlett-Packard garage, and Henry Ford's shed. These are holy places that drive the Technology Machine.

Patricia E. Moody

The Barn

Andover Controls . . . Modicon . . . Flavors Technology

When I was six I learned how to drive a tractor, and when I was eight I did my first engine job. I made it to MIT, but got bored with the routine and took a forty-year sabbatical punctuated by the creation of many new devices and about twenty new companies, raising twenty-seven kids along the way, making continual forays into new technologies.

On New Year's Day in 1968, hung over and tired of deadline-driven holidays, nights and weekends spent designing single-application automation devices with a six-month shelf-life, I made the decision to change the way factories work. I knew that we would soon reach the limits of custom, hard-wired automation solutions, and because I was bored and tired, I created the Programmable Logic Controller (the PLC). We were at the very beginning of the mini-computer revolution—standard computer programming fare was punch cards and tape.

Factories were wired up with thousands of unique switches, relays, and human technicians. But I knew my PLC design would have an impact on factories at least as big as what was coming in computers.

Thirty years later, the industry spawned by the PLC represents $5 billion of technology growth and wealth and jobs, extending into dozens of process applications, from paper-making, to chemical processing plants, to steel refineries and bullet trains. For that innovation alone I was presented in 1997 by the Franklin Institute with the Prometheus Medal.

Technology has been my compass, and the journey has been a good one, punctuated by lurches and fresh starts, never smooth, but always exciting. Hundreds of fellow travelers to our technology base, a unique idea factory back up in maple tree and stonewall country of New Hampshire, The Barn, have shared the excitement of our journey.

I have been joined at The Barn by other technology gurus, and we have taken our belief in the power and the hope of new ideas into the money world. Our Breakfast Club has reviewed the business plans of thousands of hopefuls, a few dozen of whom won our blessings and our venture capital support. My approach to evaluating a good idea's potential for real impact and real profit is contained in this book. As always, we continue to feed the Technology Machine.

Happily, because we have eyes—we are gurus and seers—the opportunities will continue to appear on the horizon, as one thing leads to another, and another and another. . . .

Richard E. Morley

Everybody's got a bumper sticker—"Live free or die," "Honk if you love engineers," and "Repent, reboot and re-enter." We have one too, and it is "The Technology Machine makes $$$$$$$$$$$$$." That's what this book is about, and it's what drives us. Anything else—stock prices, mergers, acquisitions, life-cycle studies, MRP, the T word (teams)—is embroidery.

We love technology and engineers who make it. Our heroes are guys who make things, and who discover new ways to make things better or different.

We know that manufacturing professionals feel that they are living in the fading twilight of their profession. And it's true, they are—manufacturing, like trains and agriculture and the U.S. Postal Service before it, is going away. Fewer people and fewer plants are required to satisfy demand.

But the Technology Machine that will run replication centers (manufacturing sites) in the year 2020 will be created and managed by an incredible group of technology kings. We know these geniuses, and we believe in them. We want you to know that very few of the professionals running the show now will successfully migrate to the new era; "the others" will wander endlessly, road warriors armed with a laptop and an open-ended employment contract, like Moses in the desert, waiting for the old ones to die. We wrote this book for anybody in manufacturing today who feels the darkness coming on, and who is so active surviving that he has not stopped to breathe and put together the pieces that form a picture of his world twenty years out.

We want to help, because we have manufacturing in our blood. We grew up bending and grinding and polishing metal; we are happiest wearing white socks and oily shoes. We like to take things apart, and maybe put them back again, but always one part different. We walked to school past brick mills and rivers that once powered a thousand water wheels. Our parents worked to the rhythm of the noon whistle. We *always* wear safety glasses, and the second language we learned was BAL.

We want to tell you what it is going to be like, and who the good guys are, and how to get ready. If you are listening—and only the guys that we love, the ones who hold the future of manufacturing in their hearts, the Technology Kings, are—we will tell you the stories that will take you there.

Patricia E. Moody and Richard E. Morley

INTRODUCTION

BILL HASTINGS

Listen to me, college boy, you can

Keep your museums and poetry and string quartets

'cause there's nothing more beautiful than

line work. Clamp your jaws together

and listen:

It's a windy night, you're freezing the teeth out

Of your zipper in the ten below, working stiff

Jointed and dreaming of Acapulco, the truck cab.

Can't keep your footing for the ice, and

Even the geese who died to fill your vest

Are sorry you answered the call-out tonight.

You drop a connector and curse

Take to the air like sparrows who freeze

And fall back dead at your feet.

Finally you slam the SMD fuse home.

Bang! The whole valley lights up below you

Where before was unbreathing darkness.

In one of those houses a little girl

Stops shivering. Now that's beautiful,

And it's all because of you.

—BY TODD JAILER.
COPYRIGHT 1997 TODD JAILER,
REPRINTED WITH PERMISSION.

When politicians and executives talk about a healthy economy and growth, they usually speak in *numbers*—ROI, bottom line, cash flow, LBOs, stock splits, margins. But when company creators and technology fanatics talk about growth and economic prosperity, they speak in *ideas*—how to increase the communications bandwidth to accommodate millions more bits flying into your system unit, or how to simultaneously launch satellite payloads that govern linkages between design centers in New Hampshire and production centers in China, or how to take the complexity out of inbred production scheduling systems, or how to hit the next level of thin-wafer technology.

Not every one of our beloved technologies has found a practical application. Intelligent agents were, just five years ago, one of those early technology winners that fascinated software engineers, but whose practical, controllable applications eluded them—like the GM Paint Shop, installed and deinstalled a few years later, a walk-on part in the evolution of complex systems factory applications. The Fort Wayne installation was a huge breakthrough whose long-term value proved itself more in the eventual impact its trials and proofs had on later installations in other industries than in the savings GM found from painting cars a better way.

Some new technologies continue to circle the field, defying our ability to predict their exact touchdown time. Motorola's Iridium project, for example, long in the design and planning stage, as it neared launch time, was shadowed by dozens of copycat, more competitive communications and more profitable mega-projects.

Technology Is the Driver

Technology and knowledge are the drivers in manufacturing, because technology creates wealth and fuels growth. Technology, or machine intelligence, combined with individual excellence and integrity, will rule the future. *The Technology Machine* is a guide to the accelerated changes in manufacturing and the technologies and people that will drive them. The authors challenge readers to stretch beyond "isms" to the core drivers of growth—technology and spirit.

Learning to See

The Technology Machine will be built on intelligence, simplicity, and pure process, a new way of building distributed manufacturing production networks. Essentially, technologists and manufacturing experts are learning to see, making new connections between customers and suppliers, and establishing information and process flows where none could have connected before. By not focusing on the lean enterprise, stripped-down entities whose technology skills are minimal and whose focus is still an obsessive attention to workforce issues, technology pioneers are constructing a flexible, responsive system capable of applying intelligence and speed to manage and generate growth and market dominance.

Armed with fresh insights—simple truths and clear visions—the readers will know the right questions to ask to rebuild our fractured, downsized enterprises. Watch for Wild Card predictions on the winners and the losers in the technology games.

Technology breakthroughs—examples include 3M's Post-It notes, Visicalc and the Apple—must meet four criteria:

FIGURE I.1

FOUR TECHNOLOGY RULES

Breakthrough Technologies . . .
1. Increase productivity.
2. Enable functionality.
3. Enable the user.
4. Enable postinstallation optimization, survivability, market
   share, and user lock-in.

Technology shams, such as GE's inflexible and unfixable Factory of the Future, Lotus Symphony, a composition never written to be played, OPT, an overly complex software "solution" seeking the right problem, were all commercially questionable technology applications whose creations were heralded as breakthroughs. When weighed against the Four Technology Rules, they failed the test. The Factory of the Future quickly ran afoul of changed aircraft customer requirements, leaving the complex machine to build spares. OPT, software imposed on sloppy and out-of-control production systems, got lost in its own algorithms. Hewlett Packard's two-pound calculator wristwatch, for example, an intriguing idea years ahead of its time, failed Breakthrough Rule Number Three, although it met Rule Number Two.

Current manufacturing approaches range from completely technology-driven, distorted visions of the future, to oversimplified team approaches that co-opt excellence. Not every production facility will be inhabited by self-managed work teams, and not every successful production facility will use machine intelligence to run every operation.

The Technology Machine will continue to spit out premature and inappropriate "solutions"; as managers and user/victims, you need to pick the winners, as investments, and as a means to carry your organization into the next millennium and beyond. If you can understand the technology, see its application, and answer yes to all four checkpoints, buy the stock, wait for the growth and payout.

Put on your helmet and get ready, because we are taking you for a *ride.* You are going to see some incredible manufacturing sites—the

Fort Wayne Paint Shop, Falcon Cold Forming, the Shinkansen Bullet Train, Gene Kirila's Greenville, PA Company, the Blackbird, the Java-hoe, and more. You are going to understand what manufacturing will look like in the next millennium, what technologies and what kinds of people will work there. You will see the process from a glass-walled booth two stories up, and you will see the products slipping quietly out the door. We will connect the dots to show you how to get there from here—which technologies have the power to take the true course, and which management fads and pitfalls to avoid. Here we go!

1
How Manufacturing Will Work

Chaos, Pain, and Transformation

When Francis Cabot Lowell, through a supreme act of industrial espionage, memorized the guts of the English power loom systems he had seen in 1811 on an extended stay in Great Britain, he launched a two-hundred-year run for American manufacturing. Lowell pulled together all the disparate functions of the textile production process—carding, dyeing, spinning, weaving, bleaching, tasks that had been contracted out to rural farmwives and small shops—and arranged them in sequence in a single site, a new four-story mill on the banks of the Charles River in Waltham, Massachusetts, the prototype for thousands of factories that followed. The first experiment was successful beyond the incorporators' dreams, a money machine; 200 percent profits fueled more and bigger mills—Lowell, Lawrence, Lynn, and Manchester, New Hampshire's Amoskeag complex, the biggest cotton plant in the world—more innovation, and urban communities of mill workers. The golden era for manufacturing had begun.

A DEDICATION TO BRICKS AND MORTAR

But process innovation and dedication to scale did not come without some pain. Complete vertical integration of the textile process led to captive company workers, Taylorism, piece rates, and huge profits. The brief utopian era of the mill girls—educated Yankee farm girls who left the countryside for an average of two years' work in the mill city of Lowell, where they attended concerts and lectures and shopped for machine-made items—gave way within less than ten years to cheaper immigrant labor. And within fifty years, the promise of complete vertical integration of the textile process had led to strikes and work stoppages, lung diseases, disinvestment in machinery, and a litany of excess and inflexible profit production whose aftereffects have lingered long beyond their usefulness.

TECHNOLOGY OVERTAKES MANUFACTURING

Manufacturing progress has always been limited by technology and human factors—availability, training, wages—but we must learn to apply the two main components of every production system, machines and people, in different ways. In the coming decades, manufacturing professionals will be technology partners, rather than servants to machines. The future isn't about bigness, or powerfulness, or economies of scale. It's about smartness, values, supreme technical mastery, and constant innovation: the Technology Machine.

Most of us survived the hard marches through the computer crusades of the seventies, the eighties' lighthearted flirtations with excellence overlaid on rigid hierarchies, and the nineties' over-the-hill-but-can't-quite-see-the-bottom struggle toward an enlightened industrial enterprise.

"Leading edge" in the nineties was about people, systems, and communications. Companies like USX that grew successful by building bigger operations had to learn to think small and light (Nucor's electric-fired mini-mills, for example); they needed to reach outside their walls to find suitable teammates (Japanese steel producers, for example). Still, it wasn't enough.

Manufacturing excellence alone will not carry good companies into the next millennium. Simple manufacturing excellence has become, as has quality, merely the ticket to the big leagues. What does this mean for manufacturing pioneers and survivors right now?

TRANSFORMATION IN THE NINETIES

The nineties will be known as the decade that witnessed final dissolution of all entities we grew up with—our churches, schools, families, government, businesses, health-care systems, music, maybe even our tax and currency systems. The bad news is that this unraveling will continue, but the good news is—for only another four or five years. Manufacturing professionals should expect to feel great discomfort, many surprises, big highs and lows, and confusion, and to be generally "off balance." Coping skills and pharmaceutical solutions—Prozac, stress-reduction clinics, and natural mood levelers—will be perfected and stretched to their limits.

RECOVERY FROM CHAOS AND PAIN

We want to put the pieces back in order again. We refuse to continue in this uncomfortable, "disorganized" state, so it seems only reasonable, and painfully natural, that we will reassemble the pieces. The glorious product—for a *few* companies—will be a true re-formation, a rebuilding into new entities.

And, as usual, business—not government or education—will lead the way, because it is those of us in business who are responsible for designing, making, and shipping *things,* who need effective structure to live.

It is a dangerous time. With the stock market soaring and lurching uncertainly, many companies feel that they have already been reengineered, empowered, and reborn. Why change, why anticipate the difficulty of any more distractions from returning to the happy business of being successful? Why now?

Lotus, Bowmar, Apple, DEC, Data General, Apollo, NeXT, USX

(formerly USSteel), NCR (National Cash Register), General Motors—the long line of at one time equally happy, busy, and successful companies stretches across a landscape we all occupy. We're stepping around the detritus. Each of these companies made one or two strategic errors—perhaps depending on proprietary software or sloppy manufacturing, or not listening to customers. And each failed to recognize and anticipate, and to be ready for big technology swings.

Motorola's Six Sigma initiative, for example, and the Baldrige Award have led many lesser organizations to attempt excellence. But in fifteen years, the long line of troubled corporate contenders will lengthen to include companies that *only* concentrated on manufacturing excellence, that *only* perfected that slim area of opportunity, production. *It's not enough.*

THE NEXT FRONTIER

The biggest areas of opportunity lie ahead of and after manufacturing (see Figure 1.1 on the next page). Look at the areas that feed and draw on the manufacturing function—all the places where idea transfer and development barriers stand in the way of ultimate customer fulfillment. These circuit breakers include traditional purchasing, MIS, order administration, accounting, middle management, senior management, possibly human resources, logistics, trucking, warehousing, design, design engineering, perhaps manufacturing engineering, returns, customer service, quality control, even teams—all areas where time is used up with no payback. And these waste areas lie especially thick at the second, third, and fourth tiers of the extended enterprise; the small- and medium-sized producers are one level—but a world away—from final assembly operations.

Just as Motorola proved that quality is a given, that you can't even be in the game with less than Six Sigma quality, so must we accept the inevitability of lean, perfect, agile, laboratory-like manufacturing processes. We already know how to do this. We know how to lay out efficient lines, how and when to introduce automation, and in what

FIGURE 1.1 *Opportunity Areas*

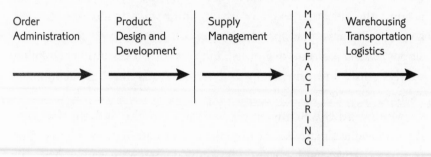

The Manufacturing Continuum

Order
Administration

Product
Design and
Development

Supply
Management

M A N U F A C T U R I N G

Warehousing
Transportation
Logistics

Opportunities = time, quality, cost, flexibility

degree. We know how to select and develop and train and motivate our workforce. And we know how to measure—boy, do we ever measure! Any number you want, we've got.

THE LAST FRONTIER

Manufacturing, as this linear representation of the process from request to shipment shows, is the thinnest slice of the process, because in the past twenty years smart managers have taken much waste and labor out of the process. Indeed, the current focus on lean manufacturing is an obsession to drive waste and layers of complexity out of manufacturing, to strip it down to its bare essential processes for what is to come, apparently leaving few opportunities now for tweaking.

Further adding to the integration challenge is the fact that as manufacturing grew from Lowell's semi-automated textile mills, to Intel's clean room, robotic plants, various separate management areas—especially engineering, supply management, and production—developed their own noncommunicating systems, philosophies, metrics, and even career paths. These pieces will need to be reintegrated into a technologically complete process—not eliminated. They offer wide-open and unique opportunities for innovation and custom, intelligent solutions that manufacturing innovators have not developed. In the 2020 enterprise, such functions as order administration, product development, and cash farming will blur into a single order communication process. Every bit of information that can be maintained for correct billing and product specification will be transmitted electronically in parallel to actual material processing. In effect, the opportunity time line will compress into a single input and output flow circuit diagram. With no more linear systems flows, the computer that moves the intelligence becomes transparent—what remains is innovation in design and clean, fast replication.

What we don't have across our industrial landscape—including and especially along the extended value chain—is consistent, predictable, integrated *easy* excellence. That's where the Technology Machine takes its rightful, advantageous place among the winners, carrying them to unthinkably high levels of performance, at unimaginably low costs.

Excellence must characterize every member of the entire value chain in metrics like 10X, a time-to-market improvement objective that drives organizations, particularly electronics, to develop and launch new products the way that grocers handle fruit that has a shelf life of three days, and Six Sigma quality. Look to the second, the third, and even the fourth tier for enterprise excellence in different technology areas.

Does that mean that customers must certify, "Baldrige," or otherwise demand excellence out of their excellence partners? No, because we do not have time to wait for the inevitable result of that approach. It means, as our friends at Honda say, "Go to the spot." Take excellence on-site.

EXCELLENCE IN THE YEAR 2020

Let's extend our definition of excellence to enterprise excellence. Concentrate on the front end of the system—design and procurement, logistics, packaging, and customer service. These are the areas

FIGURE 1.2 *Islands of Excellence*

Excellence in 2010

The Islands of Excellence, and

"The Others"

---

where the Technology Machine will take huge chunks of time and money out of the system, where it will make the biggest impact on product design and introduction, and where product design will become customer design.

ISLANDS OF EXCELLENCE

In the year 2020 there will be two types of enterprises: the Island of Excellence, and all the rest. The Island of Excellence organization will do many things extremely well—manufacturing, real-time customer design of product and simultaneous production, or customer fulfillment. The workforce on the Island will be very special—specially selected, trained, motivated, and aware of their position as an elite corps. The organization at the Island will be deceptively simple—a lot happens with few ripples on the water, quietly and smoothly.

You might notice that things are in balance—functions that were, in previous decades, functionally siloed all seem blurred, or integrated, into a smooth flowing unit.

And the people are *different*. Diversity is not an issue. Although we see both sexes and many racial and ethnic "colors," the overall pattern of the fabric of this organization—a well-selected, well-constructed, and simply laid-out quilt—is one of integration. From not too great a distance all personal differences blend into the overall design.

We do not see plaques bearing plastic corporate mission statements here. Instead, each inhabitant of the Island will have experienced a holistic, two-year apprenticeship program—where they learn to *live* the mission—for it would be a mistake to expect new members to find themselves quickly in this simple, but strong culture. People need time to adapt, and the security of knowing that they are trusted and expected to behave appropriately.

And what of the spirit? Well, it's reassuring to know that the generation that followed self-indulgent Boomers and Generation X—the Reformation Generation—has returned to basic values. This generation will have none of their parents' irresponsible neglect of the whole human entity—mind, heart, soul, as well as intelligence. The distinguishing characteristic of working on—rather being a member of—the Island is its integration of spiritual energy with physical and mental capabilities.

Inhabitants of the Island wear uniforms. The first fifteen minutes of each day are spent in light exercise, a form of Tai Chi. Sometimes associates sing or participate in an island-wide assembly. Many workers are engineers and many are "technicians," but all have an integrated, common vision of how their daily work fits into the Island's business. The icons and the myths of the building of the Island are well-known to all—for each trainee hears the stories and repeats the words and legends of the founders, who are soft-spoken, wise, and ethical.

Associates of the Island stay connected in various ways, for many years. Indeed, workers, once accepted, are encouraged to rotate into a few pivotal positions. Discipline and termination mean exclusion from the Island. And what could be worse than being cast off to feed with the Others?

THE *OTHERS*

Let's look at the nonelite group. A "Mad Max" bunch, these guys make things, all right—commodities of little intelligence, twisted metal components, flashlight switches, broiler pans, vinyl dog collars, and an occasional custom cable order. These workers have an edge to them—their skin shows the pock-marked and fluorescent-lighted reflection of days, years, decades spent in a war zone. They twitch, they scramble, they kick and stumble; periodically their eyes recapture a common   focus—teams / quality / certifications / quality / communications / productivity. But it all passes, worn down by a lurching, erratic corporate attention span that makes attention deficit disorder look like the company's single unifying theme.

Take your choice—The Island of Excellence, or The Others.

2020, The Vision

The challenge is to form a new enterprise vision for the entire extended enterprise, one that is technology-based and driven. Your most difficult job, however, will be to define and prepare for the human role. That vision reaches beyond manufacturing excellence into three key areas—value-chain excellence, organizational excellence, and the knowledge worker. *The challenge—to re-form an extended enterprise, encompassing second-, third-, and fourth-tier producers—will require many hands, but one mind.* For all these challenges, the Technology Machine provides the muscle *and* the brains.

Value-Chain Management

Partnering? An overused word. Supply chain? Too mechanical. The virtual corporation? Smoke and mirrors. Value chain? Yes, that may be as close as we can get now, but in MMXX there will be islands, archipelagoes, and networks of excellence.

The Language of the Extended Value Chain

When GM's Jack Smith addressed the Stanford Manufacturing Conference, there was irony in his talk, not in what he said—improved financials—but in what he did *not* say. The conference theme was partnering. Smith spoke only indirectly about partnering and demonstrated exactly why our sleeping giants cannot take places in the MMXX lineup. Where in our current system of financial metrics do we read "Return on Partnering," or "The Total Accumulated Value of the Extended Enterprise," or "Return on Innovation"? In a company that values single-entity performance—stock prices, for example—this long-term measure is missing. A few enlightened enterprises—Motorola did once—have broader vision, if not the metrics to support it. "These enlightened few" recognize that astigmatic attention to a single, narrow area of performance, or dependence on size to win, or more of the same, even a proliferation of supplier awards and Baldrige applications, is not enough.

2020, THE VALUE-CHAIN VISION

By the year 2020, the Island of Excellence Enterprise Partners will have achieved excellence in customer fulfillment. They will have created a perfectly balanced, socially integrated entity that translates customer ideas or wishes instantaneously into perfect product. The Enterprise Partners will conduct their transactions ethically, profitably, and in a way that protects the common good.

This vision will be outlined and supported by excellent communications.

The value chain will be driven by simplicity. The vision will be mirrored in many forms of partnerships, the ligaments of the Island of Excellence's extended enterprise body. It will be stretched and extended to include all the "last frontier" opportunity areas around manufacturing, the spots where customer fulfillment happens—design, logistics, and procurement.

In 2020, the value-chain vision will have achieved the re-formation in which simple, elegant systems will ensure integrated data channels and rigorous information transfer throughout the value chain. The wish of Gene Richter, former HP procurement head, now IBM purchasing chief, for a buyer at every engineer/designer's elbow will be realized. Second-, and possibly third- and fourth-tier suppliers will continuously run to customer demand data. Simple visual systems will overlay hard numbers ("hernia reports"). The Technology Machine, centered on autonomous agents and complex adaptive systems

FIGURE 1.3 *Value-Chain Excellence Models*

EXCELLENCE MODEL	PRACTICE
Hewlett-Packard's Deskjet Printer Plant	Value-chain integration, enterprise-wide design, tooling.
Nypro	Entrepreneurial growth; real time on-line systems; strategic, global vision; quality personified.
Honda of America	Japanese/American innovative spirit.
Nucor	Compensation system direct link to strategy; "cowboy steel"; innovation.
Solectron	Quality, strategic growth, and acquisitions.
Gregory Associates	Outsourced strategies, adaptive work-force. Technology tiger.
Valley Logistics	Small stuff, big ideas. Smart.
Asea Brown Boveri	Global, organizational innovation industry leadership.

software, will replace and augment complex current user protocols, such as top-down driven software and central planning cycles.

Supplier development will be a corporate dictum. Dave Nelson, head of John Deere's worldwide supply management organization and former head of Honda's award-winning purchasing program, feels that this supplier development approach, and others, such as Chrysler's SCORE, set the pace for preparing suppliers and customers to meet all their demanding customer needs. By 2020, supplier excellence will have exceeded big original equipment manufacturers' capabilities, but at this point, progress is erratic and scattered, so much so that Nelson asks, "If supplier development programs like BP have such great value in monetary payback, as well as long-term relationships, why don't North American companies rush to implement them?"

VALUE-CHAIN EXCELLENCE MODELS

No companies now perform all the best value-chain practices. Some, like AST, have pioneered systems; some people development; some supplier development; and some, like Lexmark, the printer producer that survived and built a new business based on an IBM castoff, have attacked development in commodity markets.

But many companies continue to struggle with the arrangement of people—focusing on *where* in-plants (supplier representatives stationed on-site with customers) work, for instance, rather than on *what* they do. They worry about what percent of travel works best and how many hours of training keep an employee alive and productive. However, in the re-formation of the value chain, we can look to a few excellence models. Although these pioneers use approaches that are not universally applicable—one size does not fit all—they tend to be geared to work at all levels of their enterprise. In 2020, everything you do to achieve the 2020 vision must advance the entire enterprise; anything less will leave you standing alone—brilliant, fortunate, but limited, and in a Darwinian sense, doomed.

VISIONARY LEADERS

The 2020 vision is being created by visionary leaders who stepped out of line, bringing a mirrored organization with them. The best technology companies reflect the best wisdom, ethics, and management styles of their heads. Their best leaders—the Galvins, Packards, Olsens, and Jobses, created a culture that outlived their own individual usefulness. Certainly Nypro, for example, would be only in the plastics business, not in the customer fulfillment business, without chief executive Gordon Lankton. Likewise, the personas of Motorola's Bob Galvin, DEC's Ken Olsen, and Al Decker of Black and Decker permeate their corporate cultures long after their daily involvement has passed.

This short list of visionary leaders is a source of *selective* inspiration. They are not perfect beings, but they share huge strength and forcefulness: Ken Iverson, chairman of Nucor Steel, a technologist who changed the way steel is made and launched a new technology from a single German electric furnace that archrival USX soon co-opted; Gordon Lankton, Nypro, an engineer who understood how to use real-time in-line process control to make very high-quality plastics, and changed and recast the plastics industry; William Hobart, Hobart Brothers, Troy, Ohio, a giant who continues to be enthusiastically supportive of workforce improvement from the ground up; Gregg Ekberg, president of Highline Controls, an engineer/entrepreneur who sees beyond the physics of an engineering problem to big business solutions; Gene Kirila, president and founder of Pyramid Systems, Greenville, Pennsylvania, another unique and energized entrepreneur who creates technology solutions where none existed before; Milt Gregory, president of Gregory Associates in Santa Clara, California, another pioneering technologist who understood how to put competing customers under a single roof, and how to give them expert, outsourced design help.

2020 METRICS

Jack Stack of Springfield Manufacturing, author Richard Schonberger, Tom Johnson, author of *Relevance Regained*, and many small companies have developed new metrics to track performance. Developing the right metrics to perfect the process continues to be one of technology managers' biggest challenges—too much data, and the system overwhelms the human mind; too little data, and human intervention destroys the systems. Shewhart Award winner Dorian Shainin's recommendation is to *"let the data lead you"*—first learn the process and its expected performance parameters, then follow the exception signals to perform midcourse corrections. The implications of this measured approach are that in the year 2020 there will be fewer measurement systems and disputes as technology innovators run to real-time feedback and control systems. Decision parameters will constantly adjust for changes, and pioneers will be more concerned with the *direction* of process performance—capability bandwidths, for example—than absolute, digital single-point metrics. Remember, the vision requires simple systems, some trust, and predictive performance.

The Technology Machine will move us toward fewer numbers understood simultaneously by more people at all levels of the value chain.

2020 ORGANIZATION

> The world is getting smaller . . . but it is not
>
> coming together. We are all participants in an
>
> unprecedented political and economic happening,
>
> but we cannot make sense of it.

—Richard J. Barnet, *Global Dreams*
(Touchstone, 1994)

Within another year or two, companies will have tired of the "teams fad" that proposes a one-size-fits-all process for human asset management. Sun Hydraulics, a Sarasota, Florida-based innovation leader in hydraulic valve technology whose human resource policies are remarkably progressive, even iconoclastic, refuses to use the "T" (teams) word! Instead, founder Ed Koski focuses on the Technology. Koski, an engineer/visionary, understands the value of individual, expert contributions and supremely agile information systems, above the structure associates use to work together.

Within another five years, a half-dozen of our better companies will have found a comfortable level of teaming and partnering, along with strong technical grounding with all associates. These innovators will look very different from our transitional organizational structures.

By the year 2020, in advanced enterprises, functional lines will have blurred and been redrawn, especially among design, supply management, replication (production), and traditional engineering functions. One associate (the title/work description most likely to replace our complex job grading systems), with a simple intelligent systems "associate," will perform customer fulfillment; in some Islands of Excellence, customers will replicate their own custom designs, specifically in clothing, recreational, entertainment, and communications products. Intelligent systems will supplement the combination of human management decision-making and fragmented software hierarchies and individual tools that we use now to run manufacturing. One aspect of intelligent systems, autonomous agents, can take very complex problems and allow distributed decision-making to dominate over rule-based approaches.

AUTONOMOUS AGENTS IN 2020

You are a passenger in a Boston Yellow Cab cruising Logan Airport at 7:00 P.M. Friday, looking to pick up one last fare before heading home. Your driver, a part-time bricklayer from Southie, fills the time waiting to move with "colah-ful" comments on local heroes—the Kennedys, a "tattuh'd sorry group," and the Red Sox, the eternal clutchers. You begin to wonder, in between stories, how this shuttle runs its pickup schedule. In 1965, an operations research model would have cranked Eniac-sized chunks of traffic pattern history, queue times, gas prices, baggage load, air traffic patterns, and dozens of other variables into a complex, long-running algorithm. But you smell the scent of simplicity here in this cab game, a real-time autonomous agent, running lean and light, always moving, no two jobs the same. This cab's driver maintains constant input-output communications as he moves. There is no central all-knowing dispatcher back at Central. The cabbie runs his own show. He is an autonomous agent, empowered with the independence and information he needs to make sensible decisions that keep the meter running. His limits run to the airport and downtown Boston and selected suburbs. Running to a traditional bucket-driven schedule, a schedule centrally derived and managed, with all its accompanying change-order headaches, would put him out of the Boston Cab business, right into the unemployment line.

You have just experienced an autonomous agent, simply served by a two-way radio and a supreme knowledge of the Boston back streets, two simple tools to get him through the day. The 2020 manufacturing/design/procurement specialist must be as fast, smart, and flexible as a Boston cabbie.

A word of caution: We are not calling for an extended enterprise replacement for the old vertically integrated organization, complete with hierarchically driven planning cycles and top-down thinking. And we are not describing a warm, fuzzy business unit whose happy workers empower themselves, however slowly, into "the right decision"! Everyone and no one is the boss, flextime rules, and we enjoy endless attention to individual foibles. Time and patience—and the world market—preclude this self-serving fantasy.

This Utopia, like most, won't be warm and fuzzy. The era of American-led rugged individualism will give way to an ethic that protects the common good, what Thomas Jefferson called the common weal, as well as that of the individual.

The winning organization will be smaller, but more like a SWAT team fed by common and very movable production resources, all members of the Technology Machine. Of course the workforce will be empowered and self-managed, a complete understatement considering the high level of training and technical skills and the speed of market shifts that they must pursue. In some electronics industries the perfect analogy for this structure is the police scanner—tuned in, filtering noise, always processing, and absolutely always on the prowl.

It is now clear that by 2020 traditional hierarchies or fragmented, loosely woven, ragged companies—independent operators not aligned for the common good or optimization of profits, false partners—will not be able to mobilize quickly to capture, defend, or move markets. IBM learned this. The first Gulf War (1984), in which massive troop and materiel movement—speed and mass—won over localized advantage, and current military simulation initiatives confirm it.

THE WORK OF THE NEW ORGANIZATION

When new organizations and enterprises form, new leaders appear. How will today's innovators become tomorrow's enterprise leaders?

They must first find the structure because it is the infrastructure that counts. The systems integration of all single-point technology—single innovation breakthroughs, like those of Francis Cabot Lowell,

Henry Ford, the Duryea brothers, Frederick Taylor, the Gilbreths (using film for motion studies to study motion and time)—must be connected to build waste-cutting industrial machines. These early innovators' desire for double- and triple-digit profits drove the scale of their enterprises exponentially upward. Later, immigrant labor, which reached a peak in the United States around 1917, fueled the Technology Machine. In the United States, unlimited resources and a pre–income tax economic climate fueled big dreams and big profits. The organizational structure that led to incremental technologies building exponential profit machines will change.

In 2020 the organizational structure will resemble a multilayer printed circuit board, whose success hinges on those critical contact points, or Touchpoints® between organizations or partners, where information transfer occurs. A good circuit is a combination of smart design and perfect deposition—too much or too little solder and the circuit is broken or unreliable. Manufacturing's job between now and 2020 is to build good circuits (organizations) and make their connections perfect (the extended enterprise). Technology provides the board, the current, and the chips. Further, we must pack more capabilities and even open slots into smaller units. Each component—each associate and his accompanying intelligent system "associate"—will be better and better prepared.

The image of manufacturing as an electronic circuit implies a vast network of independent, sometimes connected, sometimes circling, sometimes re-forming enterprises like what we see from X-ray astronomy of the galaxies. Suns form and burn out, taking their planets with them, or sometimes they in turn spin out new formations. The customer will be the sun and your partners' orbits will maintain perfect alignment for as long as they feel drawn to you.

COMPENSATION AND REWARD SYSTEMS

Since the late eighties compensation and reward schemes have become more complicated, to achieve complete accuracy and fairness

FIGURE 1.4

CREATIVE COMPENSATION

Do you want to reward individual performance or team performance?

$$ ⟶ Recognition
Time ⟶ Goodies

and to stimulate more than simple production requirements among a diverse workforce. Further, before companies began experiments with teams, group compensation tended to fall into the categories of either Improshare or executive profit-sharing schemes. Little had been done to dismantle primitive piece-rate systems that arose during the Taylorist era. Where piece-rate systems may have produced volume at the expense of quality and flexibility, systems of the nineties are intended to reward team goals, skills acquisition, and various short-term objectives. But companies that have attempted to build reward schemes based only on monetary rewards have found severe limitations on their plans for workforce flexibility and growth. New technologies don't introduce well if the organization is solidified around an outdated compensation and recognition system.

THE REWARDS OF HUMAN DEVELOPMENT

In the year 2020 your company, one of the Islands of Excellence, will want to reward some workers for patient and deliberate skills acquisition in a number of complex and challenging areas—languages, design and database use, simulators, partnering and cross-enterprise communications skills, as well as specific and changeable technology-driven knowledge. Less tangible requirements in the year MMXX, such as loyalty and demonstrated dedication to the team, will offer managers, of whom there will be far fewer, fuzzier compensation elements to factor into the formula. You should assume that most 2020 companies will be inhabited by knowledge workers, many of whom will carry no title or very descriptive, long technical strings of portfolioed capabilities, for example:

Simulation-expert, Web Master, high-level manufacturing/sourcing professional, trained physicist, Master's degree in computer science Red Team: five-year Island technical SWAT team, rotations completed to Level 5, trilingual, Canadian-born, technical/analyst, pro league shortstop, relief pitcher

EXCESSIVE ENVIRONMENTAL NOISE

Sounds excessive? That's the transition calling, sounding every one of its message-relayed, unfiltered communications capabilities. But by the year 2020, your enterprise will have discovered how to reconstruct the old hierarchies, allowing the best of the knowledge workers to emerge. Further, if you are aware, you will understand that these technologists will not believe that they work for you. They will be members of the corporation, or the network, but they will know they are technology drivers above all—not servants of accounting, or finance, or purchasing.

Knowledge workers will occupy very special homes on the Island of Excellence, the new world of work. People with these hard skills and supportive "ergonomic" behaviors will be found on the Island. The Others, the inhabitants of what we nicknamed the Territories of Mad Max, may talk like them, or try to look like them, or even produce mass entertainment vehicles—sound chips, movie cubes, files, paper—that simulate the knowledge worker's workday and his tools, but they aren't the "real thing." Without the basic skills and brilliant innovators, this packaged world becomes merely a reflection—for entertainment value only—of the exciting world of the knowledge worker. They will only come deceptively close to capturing the technology processes that create wealth and growth.

IDEAS BECOME THE KNOWLEDGE WORKER'S CURRENCY

Robert Reich calls knowledge workers "symbolic analysts." He describes them as brokers, or traders of ideas. His long list of jobs includes, with some paraphrasing, research scientists, design engineers, software engineers, civil engineers, biotech engineers, sound engineers, public-relations folk, financial banks, transactors, lawyers, real-estate traders/developers, some accountants, management consultants, energy consultants, agricultural consultants, MIS gurus and specialists, organizational development specialists, headhunters, systems analysts, film people of all varieties, writers, publishers in all forms, editors, and poets.

What are the most common words running through this list? *Engineers, consultants, or designers, fixers, talkers,* and *traders.*

> When I started out, they paid me for what I *did.*
>
> Then they started writing checks for what I *said.*
>
> Finally I got paid for what I *thought.*
>
> —ROMEY EVERDELL, SENIOR VICE-PRESIDENT
> (RETIRED), RATH & STRONG, AND
> THE FATHER OF MASTER SCHEDULING

IDEAS WILL BE YOUR CURRENCY—TIME YOUR ONLY COPYRIGHT!

Ideas will be your currency. You will shift, sell, hoard, hammer, share, and steal ideas. You will attempt to protect new ideas—new data pathways, for example, or niche manufacturing tricks—with intellectual property laws, but there will not be enough intellectual property lawyers, or enough court clerks to file and protect your claims to IP ownership. The best guarantee of intellectual property protection—retaining "ownership" and control of your idea currency—comes not from the courts, but from successful domination of markets and enterprises, faster, faster, and yet faster.

In the era of the Technology Machine, time will be your only copyright, along with your strong, shared ethical values on the Island—such characteristics as loyalty, trust, honesty, and devotion to the group will reappear as approved traits.

KNOWLEDGE WORKER MODELS: FOUND ONE!

Friday, 10:00 P.M., in a shuttle headed to San Francisco Airport. Most folks have already kicked back a beer and are dissolving into the weekend, a long commute, and dozens of unanswered voice-mail exchanges left in the ozone. A young man gets into the van, mumbles his airline destination, and pulls out a cell phone. Chattering away in Japanese, he punches in three or four calls in a row—occasional electronic English jargon slips through. Finally, the driver asks him to keep the beeps down—a traffic distraction—and she asks what we all want to know. Who is he and what is he doing?

His name is Clark. He is a semiconductor trader, a young American engineer, raised in Ohio, who spent two years in Japan, has a Japanese wife, and is on his way to a morning in Boston, followed by his return to the West Coast and Singapore the day after. Last week he hit four cities. He's armed with all the expected tools—laptop, cell phone, scanner—totally digitized. The only missing pieces are two Pratt & Whitney engines nailed to his Nikes! Clark is not rich. We picked him up at an "OK" apartment complex, not Palo Alto or a mountaintop lair. But he's *it*. A knowledge worker for the nineties. What he's missing is more of a lock on the Island (he travels too much and forgets where he is sometimes, another symptom of the transition), and some idea of his ethical or cultural bent (for he does have one, even if it's not as immediately visible as a white uniform).

We know that your current, transitional knowledge worker is a victim of the information age, looking forward to retirement, to "shutting off the bubble machine." The real challenge is to describe the skill set, the goals, recognition, and reward for the world of Mr. Clark in 2020. Today's knowledge workers tend to be overworked and misused, riding out the uncomfortable transition from the Machine Age to the Island of Excellence.

Remember the vision of the Island we presented several pages back. At this point we can declare that many "siloed" functions have blurred—procurement, design, production, and customer fulfillment—driven into alignment and reformation by technologies that remove the interdepartmental function barriers and create a smooth flow. The worker profile, therefore, will be someone comfortable with many functions, someone capable of satisfying occasionally conflicting objectives.

FOUND ANOTHER ONE . . .

This plastics producer roams the second tier, competing with hundreds of other Big Three auto component suppliers. Privately held, quick to latch on to technology boosts, loaded with over thirty suites of various CAD/CAM design systems, this company shows facets of the 2020 knowledge-worker environment. Upstairs, in a glass-walled room, sit clusters of blue-blinking terminals, wheeled racks of thick component sourcing books, and very quiet engineers barely moving as they flash from one screen to another, to phones and teleconferencing hookups. One in particular, Glenn, a twenty-seven-year-old veteran of both Rockwell and TRW, now happily progressed to the second tier, looks intriguing.

Sitting on Glenn's desk are the usual two terminals—one large display for 3-D design work, one for data transfer and review. Glenn explains how his Katia connection allows him to tie in to the Big Three platform team; he points to a pile of engineering drawings in process and a stack of printouts relegated to a box under the desk. But in between the two terminals sits an opened box of Pentel colored pencils, sharpened and laid in correct color sequence in a foldback cardboard holder.

FIGURE 1.5

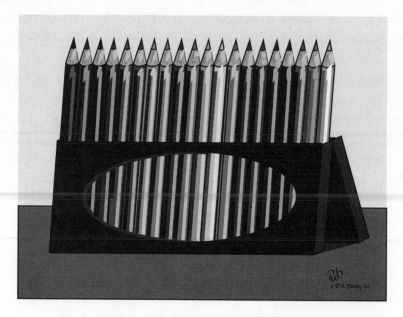

ENGINEERING TRANSITIONS

What Glenn does is bridge the gap between the stylists—the supreme gurus of auto design, who work with paper, pencils, and clay and create a gorgeously saleable design—which is then hand-carried to other engineers, who measure, transfer, modify, and generally nudge this creation closer to manufacturability. The stylists and the engineers don't talk. Politically they are separate; they speak different languages, use different tools, and worship different gods. And the serial nature of the process, combined with repeated setup times and measurements, accumulates the months into years. Small wonder it takes Chrysler, one of the fastest platform innovators, years and hundreds of engineers to produce a new design.

But Glenn, a transitional knowledge worker, has bridged the two worlds—one serial, politically captive, lumbering, and frequently crisis-driven; the other creative, and isolated from the production and sourcing processes.

So we have just added another line item to the knowledge worker's

FIGURE 1.6

THREE BASIC KNOWLEDGE-WORKER CHARACTERISTICS

1. Technical Base
2. Communications
3. Creativity
   And a fourth...
4. Ethics

job profile—cultural bridger, communicator, translator, integrator, artist.

THE APPEARANCE OF ETHICS

The fourth character trait of a knowledge worker is an ethical approach to work transactions. Ethics, the value set that truly dictates our business interactions, will be more important as we become more dependent on partnering, and interenterprise activities. A person's reputation—whether "his word" means anything, and other "fuzzy" characteristics—will travel with his technical portfolio, and it will determine not just with whom and how he forms alliances, but also where he lives and where he works.

In supply management, for example, it's clear that "ethical purchasing" is a code phrase for practices to be avoided—gifting, special favors, and so forth. But ethical transactions in 2020 extend beyond issues of business etiquette to technology management and group loyalty.

Each of these organizations has created a new organizational structure, as well as supplying innovative and advanced approaches to its market. Sun Hydraulics, for example, a precision hydraulic valve equipment producer, has no organizational charts and never uses the "T" (team) word. Pasadena Design Studio, another home to somewhat iconoclastic designers and engineers, has the key to redesigning the auto design process itself. NeXT, Steve Jobs's expensive, but

FIGURE 1.7

KNOWLEDGE-WORKER MODELS

Sun Hydraulics	System Software Associates
CNN	Vassar Street
Drew Santin	Santin Engineering
Pasadena Design Studio	Vermont Organ Works
Ross Valve	Flavors Technology
NeXT	Story's Boatyard

doomed, black-box computer company, proved that extremely high-quality, automated assembly processes could become "the machine that makes the machine." And Story's Boatyard, a two-hundred-year-old shipyard in Essex, Massachusetts, with a history of wooden boat production, through its careful protection of generations of wisdom about the magic of boatbuilding, is rediscovering ways to produce long-lost indigenous coastal designs with modern materials.

THE INTEGRATION/SPECIALIZATION DILEMMA

But how many skills can a knowledge worker accumulate in one portfolio? Or how many tasks can a multitasking professional deploy? In the year 2020 electronics suppliers, for example, will lead an enterprise serving primarily information/entertainment products. This task, therefore, will not require its front-line customer fulfillment teams to be proficient at mini-mill steel processing, but they must understand how their second- and third-tier associates select those sources, and what drivers affect mini-mill markets, and where the technology is headed.

Eventually human resource management may catch up with these evolving job descriptions, but the best 2020 organizational design model will come from current best practice models laid on the enterprise product objectives. Expect that most technology workers will be engineers or technicians; their personal assistants may be digital (such as expert systems) or "humanoid," such as writers, researchers, and commodity experts. Workers will be good talkers and writers and superb presenters, skills that already put talented engineers among the elite. Their rewards will be reasonable financial security, benefits, and the ability to partner with "the best" internally and externally.

2020

Prediction is a lot like physics. We can predict the future with 80 percent accuracy, provided we don't give a time scale on the predicted events. But if we try to establish the time scale, although we are inaccurate with the events, we will be correct in saying that there will be changes every day of every year. Stretching our vision to the manufacturing landscape twenty years out, we offer a vision of the manufacturing world in 2020, a world sharply divided between the successful technology-driven enterprises and the Others. Manufacturing processes will resemble laboratory-like environments—clean, quiet, and smaller—that turn out machine-made products in great variety. Autos, clothing, appliances, electronics, pharmaceuticals, chemicals, plastics—all these very different products will be designed off-site, perhaps even by the customer, and produced in small, fast replication centers.

The portrait of the knowledge worker is very important here, because rather than offer an impossibly high-tech vision of a future devoid of humans, isolated in an asphalt landscape, we predict that the way the manufacturing enterprise is organized, and the managers who run it, will be remarkably different from even the best groups of the nineties. We know that the changes experienced by manufacturing as it learns to produce more goods in fewer sites will be mirrored by similar changes in the landscape around it—ethics, education, factory villages, work habits, and the preparation of the knowledge worker and the technology king. In the best of enterprises, the human element will be protected and in control; in the worst, Mad Max will reign. Stretch your vision to the manufacturing world twenty years out. Come see what your home, your school, and your factory will look like.

2

One Hundred Twenty-seven

Wild Cards—Who We Will Be, and

What We Will Do

All of us can be successful in the future, provided that we admit the future will happen. And the driver for all the changes that will carry us there is the Technology Machine. Technology will form not only manufacturing, but social structures and communications as well.

In the year 2020, only twenty years from now, the systems that will "control" manufacturing and the people who inhabit the world of product design and replication, as well as their communications protocols, will be different from even the most advanced examples of today's extended enterprise. They will be faster, more powerful, and completely integrated, with more functions per pound than the most feature-packed boxes we have experimented with commercially.

Distributed, Localized Manufacturing

Global competitors will market, design, and produce locally. In the 1990s Hewlett Packard, Flextronics, AST Computer, Motorola, Solectron, Nypro, and Honda of America all put into place a global business strategy that broke down inherited economies of scale and their centralized manufacturing functions. The objective is closer, quicker customer contact and lock-in; the expectation is faster cash generation and cleaner, cheaper product flows.

Money flows, capturing payment as soon as a customer requests a product or as soon as the customer designs it—"harvesting cash"—will be enabled in Internet electronic currency exchange. Current unpredictable and cumbersome manufacturing practices, however, have held back the implementation of closed-loop payment services. By 2020 most businesses will have come to realize that they are in the business of harvesting cash—and products, whether they are assembled, poured, cast, or knitted, are simply the medium of trade. At that point they will have built on-line tracking to replication and shipment.

Manufacturing becomes replication of two product types—creative, on-line customer designs and standardization of specific products. Process intelligence, of course, marks the intelligent property boundaries of creative production; standardization marks the pure process performance. There is much untouched treasure in the creative design and replication area.

But Toyota, Hewlett Packard, Motorola, even two-time Baldrige-award-winner Solectron, and other models of manufacturing excellence have not figured out how to make a three-day car, or how to custom manufacture *in your kitchen* home communications and entertainment systems, or even how to offer self-designed, self-assembled color printer/copier/fax/TVs at the low, low price of one hundred dollars or less.

We know that the accelerated technology movement will change the way we work and how we live. But we do not envision a utopia in which absolute cultural and economic equality rules, or one in which every global citizen comes onto this earth equipped with a Ph.D education voucher, a universal cell phone, and a guaranteed livelihood.

WINNERS AND LOSERS

In the year 2020, there will be winners and losers. And the spread between the growth companies and the stragglers will be huge. Just as

FIGURE 2.1

Windows today is like Cobol was 20 years ago—Very pervasive,
but not something you would want your kids to learn.

—MOODY/MORLEY, 1999

640k ought to be enough for anybody.

—BILL GATES, 1981

There is no reason anyone would want a computer in their
home.

—KEN OLSON, 1977

I think there is a world market for maybe five computers.

—THOMAS WATSON, 1943

Heavier than air flying machines are impossible.

—LORD KELVIN, 1895

Microsoft's life cycle will inevitably lead Bill Gates to look for new avenues through which to funnel excess cash (the "Microsoft Bank"), so will new ideas carried on younger, stronger legs take their place, however briefly, in the winner's circle.

Wild Cards

Five years from now changes in the industrial landscape will not be as distinctive as twenty years out. The movement of progressive change will be almost indistinguishable on the landscape, a faint blurring along the fences as outlines of companies blur, some pulled down by gravity, others propelled by the momentum of a few profitable quarters.

But by twenty years out, in the year 2020, significant technology advances will have restructured entire industries—automotive, plastics, aircraft and personal transportation, communications, genetic engineering, education, and entertainment—so much that the contrast will be very clear. If we could lay the process flow map of Chrysler's 1998 design process, for example, on its 2020 map outline, there would be no overlap. The process itself will have been reconfigured—clay models and Katia design packages will be gone, and the Technology Machine will have compressed time-to-complete from months into days.

And not all technology success stories will take place in first- and second-tier nations, because technology advances will walk through, around, and under what had been economic boundaries. Software development that can now be performed as easily in India as in Redmond, Washington, illustrates the change that is coming. Steel manufacturing that could only be performed in Cleveland will be everywhere. Autos produced only in Detroit's mile-long factories will emerge from knockdown garage assembly shops in the Amazon and East Eighty-sixth Street in New York City.

Third World countries with emerging technology power, such as China and Pakistan, will be sources of high-tech profits. The Population Reference Bureau, a Washington-based research group, projects that by the year 2010, world population may reach six billion, up from 1.6 billion at the beginning of the twentieth century, with *most of the growth occurring in poor countries.* The bureau projects that China, India, the United States, and Indonesia will be the four largest countries, trailed by Pakistan (number five), and Brazil (number six).[1]

In less than one hundred years manufacturers defined and exhausted the principles of manufacturing engineering promulgated by Frederick Taylor. In less than ten years the influence of the Toyota Production System revolutionized global production and material delivery processes. We foresee equally powerful technology breakthroughs; we call them Wild Cards. One hundred twenty-seven mind stretchers follow.

Be forewarned—these Wild Cards may at first glance appear to be contradictory or shocking, or even a bit nutty. They do stimulate future thinking and challenge the Newtonian framework; there may even be some Wild Cards with which you cannot agree. The future deals the cards, and the best we can do is play them.

Time and Money

There are many excuses and a few good reasons for avoiding planning for the future. It's a funny thing about humans. They are one of the few animals capable of working into the future, and because of that gift, they refuse to acknowledge that they must. As always, the means to achieve the vision—math, physics—is now heavy, expensive, and relatively marketless, but it *is* good science, and the makings of killer applications of the future.

New ideas are plentiful, but the conversion of new ideas into killer applications is where the blockage occurs. The blockage can be cultural—an intellectual embargo such as standards, or lack of adequate elbowroom in the marketplace fed by monopolistic threats. In the year 2020, we will finally understand how to manage the process from idea through innovation to killer applications. We believe that what we call catalytic management—dynamic management that grows innovation—will be the solution to take us into flexible yet robust processes. Manufacturing and innovation management, rather than adhering to a Teutonic approach to business, will be free to farm its ideas, a shift to hunter/gatherer organizations.

The predictions that follow have technology roots; some of them describe the condition of families, villages, careers, and education. But the good ones—the winners—are enabled by technology breakthroughs that create wealth and feed growth.

WILD CARDS

1. Technology will drive not only manufacturing, but also social structures and communications. Expect that technology linkages will replace geography and family and language affinities that now form "natural" boundaries and communication patterns.

2. Mass production will give way to fully distributed manufacturing and point-of-sale manufacturing (see Figure 2.2). Mass production and its complex hierarchy of management structures enjoyed a 150-year run. Watch for industries that uncover the key to localized sourcing, design, and finally, production and reconsumption of recyclable materials, by the consumer and his family, himself. Manufacturing will become replication at the point of consumption (and design). What counts are design, time to market, and diversification of type. Product industries to watch for this kind of process innovation include clothing, recreational equipment, communications gear.

3. The 2020 winners in fifteen years will be small unknowns, unheard of or unrecognized now. They will come from explosive growth businesses including hospitality resorts, health and health care management, specialized transport, salesperson optimization, food, small armaments, and security. These "new" industries' experience will parallel the lengthening of lifetimes and the expansion of personal wealth, and they will thrive on compact data structures. Instantly available "Personal Health" and "Safety" profiles, even diet preferences, will fuel these "mini-industries." Allowable performance envelopes on systems, much as airplanes have envelopes of performance, will be clear. Our limitations will be more expansive than expected!

4. The 2020 losers are big, insular companies in the United States and Germany. Obviously arthritic companies—GM and Xerox, for example—whose age spots are showing through their well-structured financials, are predictable casualties. Less obvious victims include companies such as Microsoft, StorageTek, and Seagate, whose clear technology limitations are becoming inflexible.

5. "Marginal operators"—uncompetitive producers populated by fewer high-skilled workers—desperately substitute volume for intelligence: Concentrating on staying alive in their own geographic areas, their approach to design, marketing, production, and logistics resembles the strategy of cast-iron stove producers in the mid-1800s.

FIGURE 2.2

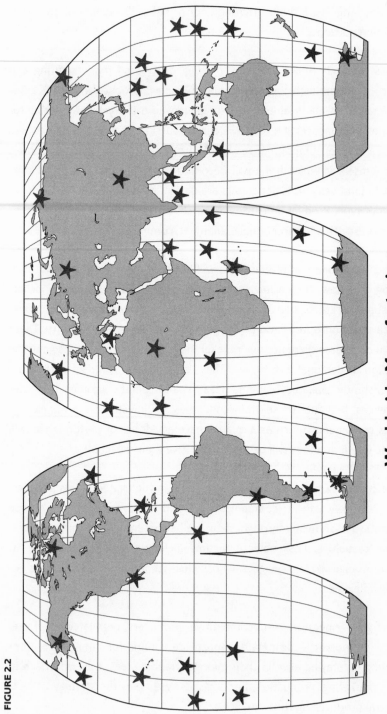

Worldwide Manufacturing

6. "Mini-industries," short-term, rapid growth and death, single-hit technology winners will replace mammoth industry sectors. Market segmentation will continue its downward-distributed trend. The former "computer industry" illustrates: computers have been niched into retail, research, industrial, and academic applications that differentiate their boxes. Watch for personal transportation industries, personal health, and personal security and entertainment ideas to "customerize," dominate, replicate, and die, all in less than six-month spans.

7. Remanufacturing. Cameras, motors, transmissions, paper, some consumer goods, will fuel a growth of the remanufacturing and retrofit industry. Sharp and fast technology adapters in the "reman" business, such as Williams Technologies of Summerville, South Carolina, whose entire strategic base is automotive reman, will prosper.

Junkyards. Junkyards for cars, appliances, and computer equipment have pioneered the recycling movement. They may look messy, but now that they are franchised, gated, and electronically catalogued, you need no longer pick through the bodies of rusted-out VWs to find a 1972 carburetor. The exact location of that assembly is available on-line; further, the parts may already have been cleaned and shelved for quick pickup and display.

At the extreme end of the life cycle, automotive shells feed mini-mills. Kenneth Iverson's creation of the mini-mill steel industry in Nucor's first electric furnace raised the prices for all junk vehicles to fuel steel commodity prices.

8. Japan will be a financial, not a manufacturing center. Pushing, tracking, investing, growing, and harvesting money will more suitable to Japan's lifestyle and cultural affinities. Software gurus who can solve money pipeline systems challenges will train in the United States and work in Japan. Expect to see a brain drain as more degreed computer scientists and engineers depart for Japan to develop advanced systems controlling the money pipelines in a country where computers have only slowly penetrated manufacturing and consumer markets.

9. Nuclear power will enjoy a renaissance.

10. Intellectual property law will boom and dominate Internet exchange and all other information media, because *ideas will be your currency, time your only copyright!*

11. Intellectual capital. The most important commodity will be people—not numbers of people, but *types* of people. Technical power will rule in manufacturing, in the medical community, in entertainment, and communications. Ph.D engineers and brilliant software and design gurus will take positions of management and corporate direction. Salaries of engineers go through the roof, and Dilbert awakens!

12. Commodity swings will drive system swings. When Honda pioneered the aluminum engine, resource limitations—the weight of steel and steel transport issues—dictated the new material's use in engine design. The first Honda aluminum engines, however, failed; repeated attempts to perfect the casting methods eventually yielded a series of blockbuster breakthroughs that led competitors to change their own technology within five years to aluminum casting. And in fact, in 1998 the Oldsmobile Aurora engine, all aluminum sump, block, and head, became the Indy racing engine of choice.

13. He who lives by the gas gauge always runs with an empty tank.

No successful company will be only "profit driven." The bottom line— profit, enjoyment, fun, societal benefit—is only the indicator of the successful creation of money, but money can only be created from raw technology and the ability to deploy it. The alchemy that creates killer apps from thousands of "good ideas" is the key element for growth in the next two decades. Being profit-driven only, however, won't drive innovation and growth, because being profit-driven means trying to drag the gas gauge from empty to full, hoping for the best. The alternative is to refuel, because when you have fuel, it does not matter what the gas gauge says.

14. We will see the return of lifetime employment—*for some.*

15. Raytheon. No engineers will want to work for the Raytheons, big dead institutions.

16. The U.S. Postal Service will abandon its marble, banklike monuments and roam the back roads and Main Streets. Post offices will sell stamps, cartoons, video tapes, CDs, and any remaining paper-bound communications. Electronic postal "clerks" will e-mail and service all plastic cards and currency exchanges.

17. Companies will get bigger and smaller. Factories will follow the life cycle of agriculture in the United States, which changed from small and medium-sized family farms to a mix of agri-giants and a very few small niche farms. In manufacturing, survivors will be very large, nondistributed enterprises and small boutique firms. "The guy in the middle," firms of about $100 million to $1 billion, will not be able to compete. Megacompanies will dominate some industries—the return of monoliths. In full-blown competitive markets, size reinforced with cash and innovation brains will battle extended enterprises formed from small, fast companies.

18. Crab skin and bone growth. New lightweight materials, like crab skin and bone growth, like the composites that revolutionized aircraft, skis, and tennis equipment, will change the way we design skeletal structures—aircraft, buildings, autos, trains. The material will be grown the way bone grows, to selectively put strength where the stress appears. Crab skin has two surfaces and layers. Both are smooth and sharp, and sandwiched in between are strong fibrous elements resembling a poorly installed fiberglass installation. Material can be eroded where no strength exists, or added where there is stress, just as in bones. A photolith on a stress basis will be a big material in 2020.

19. "Ink-jet" steel. Deposition (like the ink-jet printer) of molten steel and other metals will allow us to manufacture steel parts in three dimensions. In effect, using the splatter from a welding process and molten steel addition allows a buildup of steel product—like the three-dimensional printer—to make hard nonprototype steel-centered material. Applications include gears and complex parts.

20. Leather. Leather's live characteristics will make it perfect for high-end aesthetics; with a high price leather will fill its own niche.

21. "Invisible manufacturing." No consumer will be aware of manufacturing; consumers will take technology, embedded and stand-alone, for granted. (A hamburger is really a bite out of a cow.) Manufactured products are really a bite out of innovative replication; coupling the two images makes the concept much harder to accept. Uncoupled manufacturing and food make it more palatable for the environmentalists, capital investment, and consumer demand.

22. Wanted: aerospace engineers (and repair men). Thousands of communications satellites, carrying millions of payloads, will require feeding, maintenance, manufacturing, and service onboard. Satellite manufacturing, ground support, antennas, and communications and control will be big business.

23. Time travel. Experience the Renaissance or the Civil War through time travel—accurate simulation models—like Sim City, that transport users into alternative lives—the ghetto, college, even manufacturing.

24. Satellite manufacturing carried out onboard thousands of small satellites, costing $10 million each. Onboard space manufacturing, using solar power and high-bandwidth communications, will extend the boundaries of previously earthbound production.

25. No hands! Manufacturing sector shrinkage will follow agritech and electronics industries to eliminate hands-on labor cost. Computers and intelligent systems and few humans will manage manufacturing. Twenty percent of the cost of new facilities will be computers; most manufacturing labor costs will be for technical support—engineering, simulators, idea acquisition, just like the way movies and software were produced in the nineties. Less than 5 percent of the labor base will be working at hands-on innovative replication.

26. Outsourced design, manufacturing, portfolio advanced planning and scheduling, even marketing will be conducted on the Web and son of Web.

Stand-alone manufacturing automation technologies, like the PLC, robotics, and CNC (computer numerically controlled machines), will be compressed into embedded controls with variable software driven by JAVA-like real-time engines. The integrating software is the next generation Web with enterprise links to give the customer what he truly wants—market share, competitive advantage, and profit.

27. Big cost and speed opportunity areas lie in logistics and design to solve customer hyperneeds.

28. Expect the end of the commuter traffic jam, because people will live where they work, and work where they live—in factory villages, much as they did at the beginning of the Industrial Revolution. Business travel will be limited to replication site selection, or key-code controlled insertion of protected designs (burn-in) at the point of manufacture.

29. Manufacturing productivity standards will increase to the point where customers will contract for standard production costs. Productivity measures will follow industry standards; costs above labor and materials will cover the service differentiators.

30. Help wanted . . . technology personnel shortage. Higher demand for technology professionals results in shortages, especially high-tech males. Shortages drive more women into technology positions and all technology workers "stretch" retirement.

31. Television will be dead. Downloads and uploads through Internet communications boxes will produce customized entertainment/communications.

32. Personal tech. Everyone from the age of six months on will wear a "Batman utility belt," chips for power, memory, lifetime medical and education records, and enterprise documentation.

33. Computers will be ten thousand times more powerful.

34. Software will be dead—embedded intelligence rules!

35. The United States will not go metric.

36. Screwdrivers will still have funny heads.

37. Nuts and bolts will be replaced with glue and plastic and one-piece molded structures; manufacturing processes will focus more on injection molding versus component and assembly structures and their complex parts management systems.

38. Laser welders—buzz boxes—and cutters will be home tools, not just heavy industrial tools.

39. Smart everything! Smart furniture, smart tires, air filters, sunglasses, watch straps, faucets, speeding tickets, bank deposits, dictation, easy-fly choppers, gas turbine lawnmowers, nano toasters for nano toast, coffee cups.

40. Organizational structures will continue to undergo massive redesign. Task dictates organizational design.

41. Unions and guilds erode to the point of invisiblity.

42. The return of integrity. Integrity and value systems will determine enterprise and individual success. Ethics count, and everyone *knows*.

43. Quality time. Longer, tiresome work hours, "doing Dilbert time," will lead to frustration and demands for more quality time. Quality time will remain, however, undefined.

44. Welfare. Plastic welfare transactions will buy cars, homes, and food.

45. "If you cannot change the world, change yourself!" Drugs for every possible human condition and situation, from birth through reproduction and death, like plastic surgery, will be widely used among the poorer classes and the super rich. Drugs—mood changers, personality enhancers, elevators, levelers, violence inhibitors, uppers, downers, energizers, sex aids, death aids, aggression inhibitors—will replace cultural boundaries, church, and families.

46. Biotech. Headless bodies make great spare parts banks. On the day of your birth and your registration, your DNA scrapings will be catalogued for the Spare Parts Bank where cloned organs and tissues can be reserved *just for you*. What genetic manipulation and bioengineering cannot do, spare parts will. DNA catalogued to your identity registration number will prevent anyone getting "lost" or duplicated.

47. Virtual citizenship. Passports will be issued for your enterprise or satellite citizenship. Your legal addresses will enable you to enjoy all the satellite communications privileges of that star—banking, stock trading, messaging, info retrieval, contracting for protection, entertainment.

48. Extralegal banking. Satellite banks, above and beyond global regulation, like Swiss and Cayman Island institutions; pirate satellites will appear to take them out, either physically or with viruses.

49. 3-D faxes.

50. At-home ASICs (Application-Specific Integrated Circuits)—burn-it-yourself chips.

51. Enterprisewide laws will govern health issues. Per penalty of employment card withdrawal, you *will* eat broccoli twice per week, you *will* exercise for twenty minutes, you *will* take your daily mood leveler.

52. Africa—more wars and more famine.

53. "Irradiated fresh to you!" When you eat that sprig of broccoli, it will have been genetically engineered to grow hydroponically, irradiated fresh to you. New varieties of fruits and vegetables will appear whose names will be selected for the human appeal; they will actually have been created to contain maximum vitamins with maximum resistance to bruising and spoilage. "Old" varieties of apples, Macintosh, Northern Spy, and so forth, will satisfy high-price, high-"niche" specialty markets.

54. Disposable toothpaste/toothbrush.

55. Better bug zappers.

56. Ultrasonic torque wrenches.

57. Nano dung beetles, intelligent garbage collectors, will patrol your lawns and homes, looking for foreign objects in the landscape of uniformity.

58. Home Is Where the Intellectual and Entropic Closed System Is. Home septic and water recycling. Home septic tanks will process wastewater for reuse; the closed system technology will be provided by aerospace.

59. Wal-Mart wins. Volume product design, assembly, and sales centers win over high-cost specialty stores.

60. Local energy solutions—portable power generators in the form of fuel cells, batteries, mobile, back-pack cells, heart implants, lamps, and miniature gas turbines.

61. What am I bid? *Everything*—books, music, jobs, custom clothing, medical services—will be sold on the Web, a la Amazon. What am I bid? Jobs, stocks, airplane tickets, books, wives, kids, drugs, and gurus will be negotiated, paid for, and delivered, via the Internet.

62. Microchips. Each person in the United States now owns, whether he knows it or not, on average six microchips. In 2020, that number will rise to ten thousand micros per person, embedded in every salt shaker, every credit card, light bulb, each key on the keyboard, shampoo bottle, paperback book cover, and air filter.

63. Education. K–12 education systems will continue in turmoil; watch for megacorporations, tired of governmental social engineering experiments that fail to educate workers, to assume comprehensive, effective education programs, birth to death, that parallel the worker's employment cycle. Kids will work, adults will work, and seniors will work. Lectures and classroom experiences will resemble a rock concert more than a static pedagogical format (one teacher, thirty students, wood seats, and white boards). Universities will form and re-form around new issues, just as the Santa Fe Institute morphs to absorb new technologies.

64. The Americas will form new economic entities—New England and the Maritimes, Texas and Northern Mexico, Florida and Puerto Rico.

65. Killer computer applications, son of Netscape, son of JAVA, or Firefly or Push, will mutate into new wild beings that would be as impossible for us to manage now as nuclear energy was fifty years ago.

66. Bandwidth compression techniques will reduce the need for other communications vehicles, but bandwith demand will continue to explode.

67. Adaptive sensors will replace periodic diagnosis or maintenance. As wafer technology and miniaturization improves, opportunities to create very small sensors will change medicine, retailing, manufacturing, and many scheduling functions. Diabetics will use a supermarket-type scanner, for example, to check blood sugar levels. Detecting bearing life, maintenance requirements for other metal parts, process quality, paint and other coating chemistries, and the monitoring of retail sales or product movement will all be handled by intelligent sensors.

68. Weather forecasting will be easier and more accurate over a longer range, supported by emergent systems and data-rich modeling. El Niño's cascading pattern of Pacific storms, followed by southern tornadoes and East Coast hurricanes, for example, will be accurately predicted and simulated as to strength and behavior. "Instant gratification is much too slow!"

69. New forms of computers will proliferate, including quantum mechanical computers, biological computers, and optical computers. The new classes of computers will be embedded and wirelessly connected; they will discern sets or behavior patterns, filter for desired requirements, and make decisions and predictions. Supported by ultra-high-bandwith wireless links, small intelligence units linked to each other for very fast communications will form and re-form new systems as needed. Their connectivity design and control algorithms will be internally self-building, not even touched by wetware (wrinkled humanoids).

70. Voice recognition systems will dominate computing, banking, security. Although the cost of development of today's primitive voice recognition systems was billions and early systems took years to develop, next-generation systems will be richer and more flexible, and they will integrate into other sensory recognizers, with minimal programming. Recognition systems illustrate: How does your dog recognize you on Friday as your car pulls into the drive, even if it is a rental car? He runs on a series of filters and signals—sounds, smells, patterns—the same way your personal security system of the year MMXX will, an electronic Willie the Rottweiler.

71. Computers will model human social organization and behavior—for example, traffic flows and crowd control.

72. Complex adaptive systems and intelligent agents—not humans—will run railroads, airports, banking, and other data-rich and extremely dynamic operations.

Intelligent systems are simple extensions of previously separate and apparently complex systems. Readers will recognize the movement toward delivering intelligence in smaller packages in the examples of our automotive high-end offerings—"computers on wheels," statistics on the growth of miniaturization and sensors, constant feedback in-process devices versus walls papered with control charts, and other manufacturing examples.

73. In ten years, expect no waits for very custom vehicles, clothing, and orthopedic appliances. In fifteen years, expect to buy some items for life, and others for life stage recycling. Understand that low-margin, break-even manufacturing will continue to exist, but growth will come from differentiation and smart systems.

74. Information technology will force and enable change; although users will specify needs, information technology will deliver those needs.

75. Technology that starts its commercial life as entertainment will move fastest.

76. Big Brother *Won't* Be Watching You. Privacy and security systems, especially in the areas of individual financial and medical controls, will be available—at a price—to most users, replacing the pervasive encroachments of credit agencies, the phone companies, and various for-profit Internet providers.

77. Hacking is cool. Computer hackers proliferate; inevitably, a few episodes of computer terrorism—blackmail and theft—will shut down utility systems. Brain criminals will hack court records, leaving everyone on the payroll squeaky-clean; a mysterious virus will erase speeding ticket records. Smart enterprises, however, will hack out software for autos, airplanes, homes, phones, and graphics.

78. Global citizens will be two hours to anywhere.

79. Class stress and walled cities. Where economic gaps between neighbors form sharp boundaries, the inequalities produce tension, class stress, and outbursts of violence or border wars, followed by archaic governmental attempts at social engineering. Citizens with the means will form complete walled cities, corporate city-states; citizens without the means will find themselves on their own, looking for alliances and "pseudo cities"—clubs, uniforms, entertainment styles. Precursors of these technologically enabled enclaves are medieval fortress cities (Paris, Siena, Firenze, Heidelberg) and other places where people were offered physical protection by structures and geology (the Great Wall of China, the English Channel, the Atlantic Ocean). Disney's Celebration City, certain California hill towns, and the White House are precursors of the 2020 enclaves.

Social classes will solidify to include blocks of rigid, regimented lower middle classes inhabiting nongrowth corporations. "Lucky middle-class" professionals will inhabit the upper end of Islands of Excellence, dominated by technical and professional workers. The vast "lower-class" members will be shuffled to fill up isolated, controllable geographical areas—"islands." There will be little movement among class groups; however, shifts in global economies may occasionally increase the ranks of the "lucky middle class," just as continued outbursts of localized guerrilla activities and boundary wars will create new pockets of immigrants confined to lower-class enclaves.

80. Purchases—personal vehicles and personal medical design tracking— will be made for life.

81. Healthy nations and other economic entities will witness the reappearance of "the common weal" concept. Decisions made for the greater good, the maintenance of infrastructures, the health of workers, and the perpetuation of Island ideals will be the norm. Look for Island Constitutions and genetic engineering that guarantee physical and intellectual uniformity.

82. Spiritual leaders will appear in each new entity, not all of whom will preach a beneficent approach to human growth. Watch for gurus who gather legitimate financial and technology power, combined with general support, and a return to the blending of "church and state." Watch for others who combine corporate with personal power to amass technology resources and first-strike capability in the market.

83. We see the return of uniforms and other institutional differentiators—team hats, flags, songs, salutes, even secret code rings and chip implants. "Business casual," a temporary foray into personal expression, will have been long ago rejected as disrespectful and disorganized.

84. The Big Three will be augmented by transportation companies that localize production and design of special-use vehicles and service true off-road vehicles and small construction and road-building equipment.

85. The U.S. interstate highway system will segment into high-speed "transportation corridors" to service Next Generation Vehicles (Blackbird). Removing small vehicles from pipelines will improve safety statistics and reduce individual traffic fatalities.

86. Air transport systems will restructure—earthbound—for short hops using smaller, faster jets, "on-call" rides (air taxis, passenger-friendly services). The airline industry that in the nineties experienced shakeups and consolidations, price wars and service lapses, will, like manufacturing, abandon the economies-of-scale model and move to ten- to thirty-passenger jet service. (Honda Motors has prototyped a light but very fast and fuel efficient midrange passenger jet, targeted for possible production by the year 2000.) Effectively, the air transport system sets out to offer jumps between the Islands of Excellence. Inhabitants and workers of noncompetitive, marginal operators will travel less for business as their companies attempt to maintain survival positions locally.

87. Genocide will fade, replaced by "blitzkrieg" hit-and-run economic competition at the upper rungs and control mechanisms at the lower-middle-class and lowest levels to lock in individual behavior. An Aldous Huxley "Brave New World" approach to managing the captive lowest classes will use genetic engineering, drugs, selective education, and entertainment as mind and behavior control.

88. Governmental power will be replaced by Big Corporate Power. Expect to see Summit Alliances of IBM, Microsoft, and Global Bank Enterprises used to fund capital growth and development, to feed and maintain Islands of Excellence, and to set demographic/economic strategies. What the Marshall Plan, the International Monetary Fund, the Rockefellers, and John J. McCloy performed for the Cold War era will be covered by the Bill Gateses. With the decline of governmental clout, new agencies will broker economic power through corporations and assist in positioning certain enterprises for market dominance. Where the United States previously funded national labs, and later regional manufacturing centers, governments will take a more supportive role by facilitating communications, data gathering, and labor rules to foster corporate growth.

89. In the medical world, nanobots will facilitate disease diagnosis, health maintenance monitoring, and body repair. Clones and artificial tissue and organs will provide spare parts banks.

90. Stock exchanges—like AMEX, NASDAQ, NYSE, and Tokyo—will cease to exist, replaced by rich databases and global exchange. Corporate info structures will prepare and distribute their own financial and tax records, leading to a need for more intergiant corporate regulatory discipline and experts or astronomers to cull out the blue chips.

91. Rags to riches. Hand-made, as opposed to machine mass-produced, items will enjoy resurgence as wealthy citizens of the Islands seek to enjoy aesthetically pleasing environments of coordinated art and clothing. No metallic spandex uniforms and Star Trek unisex suits; welcome the return of Edwardian opulence at the upper levels, offset by Dickensian conditions on the lowest rungs.

92. Productivity enhancements and new organization structures will reduce the number of engineers required to design products and support processes by 75 percent.

93. Research and Development metrics run the Technology Machine: New Products Contribution to Weekly Revenues; "Cited" Patents per Associate; percent R&D/Revenue; New Product Turnover; Technology Value Ratios.

94. Smart appliances will prepare smart food. Eighty percent or more of our meals will be eaten "out" or packaged as complete, microwavable meals.

95. The movable office (and kitchen, and bedroom, and media room). In the eighties the number of people working at home jumped 56 percent. Previously unpublished data from the 1990 Census showed 3.4 million people working at home, or 3 percent of all U.S. workers, up from 2 million in 1980, a figure that had been declining since it was measured in 1960.

96. Homes, like businesses, will be modular and agile. Furniture, as well as walls, connectivities, and utilities, will be reconfigurable and movable, just as Dilbert offices can be restructured with partitions and plants.

97. Decide Early and Big. DNA and aptitude testing will vector kids' future professions and interests, starting at age three. Because the marketplace will be a maze of niches, aiming children for the right niche and holding to that model of the future will be very important to them and their Island.

98. Object Oriented Connectivity Platforms. Manufacturing, like homes and offices, will be set up as a matrix of connectivity, rather than physical platforms focused on a specific operation. Platforms, therefore, become points of connectivity, plug and play communications nodes.

99. The gambler will continue to play the game, even when the result is disastrous, because it's the game he loves.

We will explain everything, but know nothing. As societies age, they experience analysis paralysis and science illiteracy; they become preoccupied with *standards* (ISO 9000, and so forth) and analysis—spreadsheets, DNA code, management options, business strategies, and manufacturing variables and scenarios. Our ability to generate planeloads of data with blinding detail and no organizing structure is crowding our ability to handle true science and real engineering with cause and effect action. Using horoscopes to make executive decisions (a la the Reagan administration) is an affront to technocrats, but it is probably just as valid problematically as any other decision method. In 2020 more analysis will be done on hearsay and anecdotal evidence than rigorous basic analysis. Expect companies to do more and more analysis.

Consultants will make more and more money, and the results will be less and less meaningful.

100. The Technocrat King. Engineers think the electric car and the Y2K problem are either 1) detrimental to the organization (electric car), or 2) terminally boring, dull, noncontributory, a nonproblem (Y2K). By the year 2020, the technologist will push back and take charge of which technology tasks must be done, and where, rather than knee-jerk revenue response.

101. More failures breed more investments. Big, quick money demanded by venture capital will require one-year results, which takes more investment and more risk, the gambler's ruin.

102. Before the collapse, weeds will grow. Finding ten thousand people on the Web to agree with a radical position, geographically unbounded, will enable growth of thousands of splinter groups—religions, cults, militias, education clubs. Gradually, the groups become less extreme as they move closer to the center of the road.

103. Self. Making our own lamps, our own news, our own analysis, therapies, appliance repair, personal computing, even kids self-educating themselves. The word "personal" will take on more applications—personal families, personal food designed to maximize custom diet needs, personal clothing (clothing sized to individual bodies and fabricated to personal climate and skin needs), personal (customer-designed) cars. Personal products require agile and flexible manufacturing, geared to thousands of personal niches.

104. Earthmovers that move themselves. The wheel barrow, as well as the backhoe and the bulldozer, will be superseded by smart, electric drive equipment.

105. Power. Utilities in the midst of deregulation, and the beginnings of capital redeployment will very slowly inch toward complete deregulation over a variety of media, including more natural gas turbine generators. All home energy generation will be on a distributed, localized basis.

106. Speak English! (not Dutch, Serbian, Turkish, Greek, Romanian). The extinction rate of languages accelerates, leaving English in control because it is incrementally compiled; English glyphs are acoustic glyphs, not visual glyphs that are inherently limited.

107. Brave New World. Drugs, not horses, stereos, cars, football, skateboards, or even computers, will run the moods of the average teenager and the average worker. Behavioral modification through drugs for health, stress, weight control, pain, and general happiness will deliver docile workers and well-trained, highly educated, multiple-tasking professionals. The science of management—how and what drugs to deliver to which workers—will become the science of pharmacopias.

108. Virtual gardening, and virtual plants, like Virtual Pets, with all the feeding, watering, and hoeing, will take place on the screen.

109. Circuses. Baseball fades, as soccer, professional wrestling, *Baywatch* and other mass entertainment vehicles proliferate. Without translation, even soundless, the visual images offer escape either to California beaches or to violent competition. Mass entertainment will therefore be largely cross-cultural, and will influence derivative products.

110. Fat is in, thin is out. Goodbye Spice Girls and Kate Moss, hello sumo wrestlers and fat, announcing the emergence of a well-fed global middle class.

111. "Would you like your burger rare, medium, or boiled lobster?" Cloned species of popular-flavored animals will mix it up on menus—beef and lamb DNA will be architectured to please regional palates; any food can be "cooked" to resemble any other food. Nutrition and aesthetics combine to create a new food industry.

112. "Will the Real Mr. X please stand up?" With a combination of personality alteration and physical remodeling, along with the personal creation of false identity cards, accounts, resumes, birth and death, driving, insurance, and school records, managers and leaders will need security aids to determine, if they can, who is being hired, whom they are selling to, and whether the customer on the Internet is real.

113. Throw-away kids. Kids/pets will be "thrownaway" to private schools and other specialized institutions as they outlive their bearability or become too expensive to control and maintain.

114. Slap and fix. Most engineers have been trained in the deductive, Newtonian approach to problem-solving—look at a problem and work it through a flowchart until it is fixed. In 2020, with different materials and very fast fixes for quick turnaround, we will do a slap and fix for a survivable and near-optimum solution. Books will be done this way—type it now, fix it later, versus pencils and whiteout and months of thinking and planning. In manufacturing, a very robust slap-and-fix approach will rule; no one will read the manuals, and installation and repair will be simple slap and fix.

115. Hyperspace databases. Databases and computer search engines will be multidimensional, versus a flat or one-dimensional structure, enabling simultaneous quick search and analysis. Manufacturing software will therefore deal with mathematics and new numbers because the higher the dimensional representation of equations, databases, or knowledge, the simpler and easier it is for a computer to understand. Flat or one- or two-dimensional databases are less efficient than four or eight dimensions. Databases and hyperspace must be capable of division to be effective, so new manufacturing software will deal more with mathematics theory and actual application to generate very fast responses of infinite databases. Mathematics will be used less by humans, and will become a hobby—like crossword puzzles.

116. Pheromone and aromatherapy. Marketing and product enhancement through the other senses will be a science; precision in delivering odor, sight, and texture will be included in all consumer product design specs.

117. Hyperperformance. Performance improvements that continue to advance—automatic transmissions, turning radii, G's of acceleration—will be extended to housing and manufacturing processes. Doors that automatically close, and processes that run correctly even if we cannot read instructions or understand the language, will "protect" us from harming ourselves or the equipment, as well as delivering superior equipment runs.

118. Predictive behavioral modeling. Prediction of events, rather than prevention and repair, will influence equipment design. Funding for prediction of social problems—domestic violence and drunk driving—will, after some resistance, soar. Media hype—another Chicken Little phenomenon—will be replaced around the year 2000 by tremendous activity, agitation, and reaction to social modeling and solving social problems with the scientific method.

119. Noise suppression. Highway noise, traffic noise, and airport noise will be monitored, regulated, and suppressed at all levels.

120. Driverless cars.

121. Another materials revolution ("Plastics!"). Watch for self-cleaning windows and equipment; packaging—bottles, cans, and cartons—that dissolves back to the soil; fabrics in smart clothing that perform hair removal and hygiene, electric warming, color changing, and body sculpting.

122. More paper, the only medium that has withstood the test of time.

123. Mile-high skyscrapers.

124. Antimedicine. Although there will still be no "cure" for the common cold, measles and other infectious diseases will proliferate because discrete factions in some societies will refuse to be immunized.

125. The cure for AIDS will have long been engineered, but HIV will have been discovered to be not the root cause of the disease.

126. Leaders will continue to demonstrate the DNA imperative of clan leadership through spectacular sexual performance.

127. Fastest-growing professions will be computer science, networks, and health care and maintenance. Futurist George Gilder predicts that network technology is advancing ten times as fast as central processors. We think the number is much higher than that as storage is redefined.[2]

LOOKING BACK TO SEE AHEAD

Seiichi Yaskawa, head of business development for Japan's Yaskawa Electric, likes to highlight megatrends in Japanese industry by citing a list of predictions published in 1901 in a leading Japanese newspaper (*Houchi News,* January 2–3, 1901). Yaskawa continues to push the envelope on high-speed transportation networks (bullet trains) run by elegant intelligent control systems.

One hundred years later, the hit rate for this anonymous Japanese fortuneteller's predictions is approximately 17.5 out of 24, or 73 percent, thereby proving the possibility of one-hundred-year forecasting into the world of megatechnology. The business of predicting the future has become profitable for gurus and financial players because there is money to be made in hitting the right prediction at the right time. Technology changes, especially those in transportation, communications, entertainment, and health, with their huge impact on lifestyles and mass consumption patterns, will lead our lives and subtly direct the "choices" we *think* we are making. Prepare for nonpharmaceutical, externally applied mind control.

THE REAL MEANING OF INNOVATION

Innovation. The term does not evoke images of doing what we have always done just a little bit better. Innovation suggests new peaks of performance, surges of wealth and growth, the creation of new markets, and the creation of even more wealth and resources. The challenge for innovation leaders, who may not exactly predict the precise mechanisms to take them to the next level, is to understand their environment and seek to influence it by understanding physics, computer sciences, human behavior, and trending. Innovation leaders live with time at their back, a lingering competitive presence whose pressure magnifies the weight of everyday market and financial concerns.

Leaders of small and medium-size businesses must struggle with resource allocation that fosters innovation; leaders in the few large innovative businesses, such as Motorola, must clear away the brush and

FIGURE 2.3

1901 Japanese Predictions

1. Worldwide wireless telephone
2. Worldwide color photo instant transfer
3. Extinct wild animals
4. Green Sahara
5. Rise of China, Japan and Africa
6. Round-the-world trip in 7 days; global travel for everyone
7. Warship in the air
8. Extermination of flies and fleas
9. Air conditioner
10. Cultivation by electricity of tropical plants in Greenland(!)
11. Advanced voice transmitter, love talk over 10 miles
12. Picture telephone
13. Shopping by picture telephone
14. Electricity as fuel
15. Bullet train 2.5 hours between Tokyo and Kobe
16. Rubber tire trains in the air and under the ground
17. Worldwide railroad network
18. Natural disaster control
19. Everybody taller than 6 feet
20. Electric needle medical treatment without pain or medicine
21. Automobiles without horse
22. Animal language literacy
23. Advanced education
24. Countrywide electricity distribution

FIGURE 2.4

THE GRAND CHALLENGES

Allow each access to knowledge and information
- To be or not to be reachable anytime, anywhere
- To have instant access to all information
- To be present or absent anytime, anywhere

Provide ready access to improved health
- Reliable, cost effective medical diagnostics and prostheses
- Design/manufacturing for a sustainable planet

Simplify the transactions of daily life
- The paperless office
- The cashless society

Allow mankind to live in dignity and comfort
- Intelligent highways and transportation systems
- Abundant, clean, safe, affordable energy

New, high-value-added products and industries

Source: George Gilder, *Telecommunications Policy Roundtable, Forbes ASAP,*
December 5, 1994, p. 162.

---

attack the organizational encumbrances—fiefdoms and denial—that dishonor the energy and spirit of the Galvin family founders.

TECHNOLOGY'S FALSE PROMISE

We see the Technology Machine as the source of creative power that will renew depleted industries and organizations. We believe, however, that technology will not always lead to utopia, although Gilder's Challenges want to steer us that way. DaVinci's elegant penciled innovation dreams clarified graphic rules of proportion and foreshortening, but his genius also inevitably took the form of warfare technology. The Internet's first applications rendered pornography globally profitable; atomic energy spawned Hiroshima and polluting nuclear plants; even reproductive engineering and life-support systems have created human nightmare experiences. They have all failed to fulfill their waking promise because pure technology is managed by flawed human systems.

No one can argue the physics of nuclear-power, but Three Mile Island and Chernobyl demonstrated the weakness of nuclear-power management, not of the science behind it. When the Three Mile Island nuclear plant in Harrisburg, Pennsylvania, was shut down for reactor problems and possible leakage, inhabitants of the nearby town and farming villages were never as aware as were outsiders of the dangers to their livestock and real-estate values. Indeed, nationally published newsphotos captured a few shots of Holsteins grazing with the Three Mile stacks silhouetted behind them.

Yet, three days after the crisis was declared over, no cows were seen within two miles of the plant; inhabitants declared their belief that life and property were in no danger, because that is what the administrators and their spinmeisters had told them. The gap between science and management could not have been wider.

ANTICIPATING THE FUTURE, SEEING THE PAST

An accumulation of individual achievements and technology dreams will not lead to accurate envisioning of the MMXX landscape, because seldom do these single-point technology events self-connect to other elements necessary to complete the picture.

Howard Mansfield, an urban studies historian, in his book *In the Memory House,* tells how, by visiting the storehouses of memory in a series of New Hampshire villages, he uncovered the powerful meaning inherent in the selection of objects carefully saved for posterity.[3] He discovered, meticulously preserved in village historical societies and history museums and scrapbooks, holy relics imbued with long-silenced ancestral voices—artifacts like a twig from the first winesap apple tree grafted in 1864 in Deering, New Hampshire; a fragment from the first chestnut beam in a Mason settler's barn; the remains of the paper mill's first penstock; the last pair of shoes cut, sewn, and finished in a Main Street shoe shop; the last sewing machine manufactured in the once prosperous town of Phillipston, the last radium watch produced in Waltham, Massachusetts; the first microwave oven created by Raytheon pioneers who were largely responsible for Allied victories in World War II Europe.

Documentation of a community's growth or a family geneology is reverse archeology, a scattered exercise in the accumulation of grave markers, old photographs, marriage, death, and birth certificates, tax records, Master Charge receipts, ATM transactions, odometers and turnstile tickets that construct undifferentiated patterns of human life—undifferentiated because although the particulars cannot be assigned to the lifeline of a particular individual, they form an accumulation that paints the picture of many lives and many dreams. There is a blending of science and oral histories that can be as meaningful as a database carefully maintained over the generations. Oral histories and corporate memory, the bits of memories and geographies unselfconsciously passed from one generation to the next, have been proven to be as accurate as research—they ring true because they are *treasured*.

TECHNOLOGY SEEN IN PIXELS

Naive forecasting, oral history, and basic timelines are powerful tools that center reality and focus our imaginations on the accumulation of significant technological events; from these data bits, trend patterns appear. Not all breakthroughs can be predicted, of course, but looking inward to corporate current interests will not give us an image of the future, and some major changes can only be inferred from minuscule hints. English immigrants on ships like the *Mary and John* and the *Mayflower*, whose sea voyage from Britain to the Americas took several months, could begin to smell pine trees 180 nautical miles from landfall. *Or was it the anticipation?*[4]

3

WHACK,

Why You Can't Get There from Here

PROCESS, PROCESS, PROCESS

HAIKU

A crash reduces

Your expensive computer

To a simple stone.

The Web site you seek

Cannot be located but

Endless others exist.

Chaos reigns within.

Reflect, repent, and reboot.

Order shall return.

You step in the stream

But the water has moved on.

This page is not here.

—AVAILABLE IN NUMEROUS
INTERNET SITES

Scenario 1

IN THE LAND OF SIX SIGMA

The national sales manager promised a tour of the factory that supplies motherboards to one of the biggest personal computer manufacturers in the world. You are intrigued by the contrast of printed circuit board assembly performed within the walls of a nineteenth-century textile mill in upstate New York, and after the obligatory meeting with the suits, you head across the parking lot to enter the world of electronics manufacturing.

You climb two sets of wooden stairs and circle around some test stands and potted plants. At the landing, your host stops to catch his breath, explaining that this is where final chip insertion and test happens for personal computer motherboards. You were expecting "line-of-sight" management, but looking down on this maze of brick hallways, cubicles, and metal cabinets, you see that the production flow is erratic and complex. You need a map and a pocket full of crumbs to find your way back to the lobby.

Together, you quietly approach a bench where Clare, a woman wearing the regulation blue smock, has put down her soldering gun to look for chips. Suddenly, the Dumpster rumbles down Building 14's brick hallway on its afternoon rounds; the cart stops at each work center and empties each operator's plastic trash barrel. This bench is next. As the operator up-ends the blue thirty-gallon trash barrel, a cloud of dust particles fills the air, showering the work bench with a layer of grit. Clare keeps soldering.

Your host comments on product quality, not yet Six Sigma, but approaching "the low double digits." Your question, "Do you think your quality problem has anything to do with the environment in which you assemble boards?" is met with silence.

Scenario 2

Your new five-thousand-dollar laptop beeps and glows; Windows has been installed, and you are happily punching in new instructions on a virgin keyboard. Suddenly, the light flickers and the outer edges of the display turn gray. Your heart stops for a nanosecond, but the missing words rematerialize, and you proceed.

Five days later the monitor turns a deep charcoal gray. You are able to print, but you are typing blind. A call to Customer Service Hot Line yields twenty-two minutes of music and chat designed to entertain and sell as you wait for the next available technician. The rep who sold you the system is unavailable—she has moved on to her next commission.

Finally, a technician listens to the monitor story and agrees to replace the defective shell.

Six weeks later, alarms go off—the screen screams "Memory error. Insufficient memory. Memory error." Another entertaining phone call to customer service produces a replacement. Finally, rolling down the road at eighty words per minute, the keyboard locks up, won't move another vowel.

A welcome phone call from the Returns manager explains all— this display supplier has become "problematic"; ditto for the keyboard, and there is no explanation for the memory problem. He informs you that *this particular five-thousand-dollar model has been running with 13 percent returns.* Your question, "How can one of the top three PC giants sell computers with that high a projected failure rate?" is met with silence.

In a last effort to satisfy this user, the customer is offered the next model up, one with a higher price tag, faster clock speed, and a failure rate in the single digits. You take the deal, happy to move on to the next assembly house when it's time to upgrade.

Scenario 3

Aircraft pioneer Boeing has production process challenges not unlike situations encountered in the automotive industry about twenty years ago. The company that engineered beautifully innovative approaches to aircraft design and customer involvement in design in its break-through 777 project, "The Paperless Airplane," has been slowed by supply-management and cottage industry processes. Boeing's personal competition is Airbus. Boeing found itself bloated with fat orders that the company faced difficulty completing. The backlog collapsed when Asian economic troubles caused several key customers to cancel orders. "Saved by the bell," Boeing escaped the showdown to fight Airbus another day, in another place.

Boeing's supply-management challenge and its complex, long-lead-time production process should have changed by the year 2020. Or other smaller, lower-cost rivals may step in. Honda, for example, has experimented with one of its five long-term goals of a prototype jet aircraft. The challenge to both Boeing and Airbus could come from anywhere.

Technology in a bad process—either manufacturing or supply—is low-tech.

Scenario 4

You are a smaller company struggling to meet big customer demands. You make machined assemblies for the auto industry, and your work-force is well-skilled, highly motivated, and tired. Lately, you have been feeling a need to "do something"—your customers seem to be models of manufacturing and engineering excellence, and the life of a smaller supplier driven to erratic assembly schedules punctuated by overnight changes and the accompanying supply chain headaches is exhausting.

A problematic offshoot of your success has been the company's ability to acquire more and more machines. Clusters of grinders, millers, lathes, welders, sorters, small cutting tools, degreasers, slitters, benders, and polishers have appeared—each new capital equipment request is an engineering "must-have." You begin to wonder if all this hard-earned success is going to get better, or just harder.

You have heard about a new, exciting, people-centered approach to rapid shop floor change. It's called kaizen, which means in Japanese "to make better," and because some proponents of this very simple but powerful technique recommend taking it in small, intense doses, you begin to think a strong helping of kaizen might shake things up a bit and make life on the floor and in the executive offices simpler.

The Roots of Kaizen

Ironically, all these thoughts so far make sense, because in the best traditions of techniques derived from Ohno's *The Toyota Production System*, even in its poorest translations from Japanese to English and earlier work done by Deming and Juran, this approach to simplification and standardization certainly has served the Japanese automotive, tier-one suppliers, and electronics industries well.

Standardization of Work

But kaizen in the hands of some consultancies and some less-than-experienced practitioners is a dangerously powerful force. And kaizen in an environment in which activity is rewarded simply for the sake of activity, an attitude summarized in the slogan "Just do it!" sets up many small production centers for big disappointments. Empowered associates organize their teams, drag in executive support, take data, do spaghetti diagrams, walk the floor, eat pizza, do presentations, move the machinery, set up cells, and go back to work. They can say they have participated in a kaizen activity, and bragging rights accumulate as the number of kaizen "events" increases. Five, six, or seven weeks later, however, without standardization of work processes, the biggest permanent change enforcers, things start to slip back into the old familiar work habits that disrupted work flows and brought complexity and unpredictability onto the floor in the first place.

Jim Womack, co-author of *The Machine that Changed the World* and *Lean Thinking,* believes that the issue of standardization is one of the biggest barriers to successfully rebuilding out-of-control processes and keeping them that way. His experience with pioneering U.S. kaizen practitioners, such as Hartford's Wiremold, Lantech of Louisville, Kentucky, and other stars—Johnson & Johnson Critikon, Honda of America (their BP program is a kaizen methodology developed by Mr. Honda and Teruyuki Maruo), Parker Hannifin, and various TRW plants—proves that a rigorous kaizen process, implemented systematically by trained and experienced practitioners, not recently assembled kaizen teams, is a powerful improvement tool. But each one of the successful kaizen projects focused first on process, and last on process. Honda BP projects typically take thirteen weeks, and the first month of the project, or more, is spent in simple shop-floor observations and data gathering, learning to see.

Honda's BP, which stands for Best Position, Best Productivity, Best Product, Best Price, and Best Partners, was perfected in Japan in the seventies and adapted and brought to North America in 1990. More than 90 companies have implemented some 120 projects in such areas as stamping and component assembly, and more than 120,000 associates, many of them small suppliers, have been touched by this method. The results speak to a preferred kaizen approach of thorough data analysis and permanent process changes. Process results.

Kaizen improvements tend to be grouped in the areas of productivity, quality, cost reductions, inventory and space reductions; BP practitioners point to overall productivity gains of 47 percent, measured as total pieces per man per hour before kaizen, compared to pieces per man per hour after kaizen; quality improvement overall of 30 percent; and cost-down overall in the 7 to 10 percent range or better. Further BP, as well as other Honda improvement techniques, such as Value Analysis and Value Engineering, helped reduce the actual cost of purchased parts for the 1998 Honda Accord by more than 20 percent. These savings were generated not from cost avoidance, but from actual savings in material and labor of purchased parts.

But kaizen methods are generally not regarded as technology tools because the success stories speak so much to empowered workers and suggestion systems that managers in the United States might form the incorrect impression that coordinated kaizen activity simply involves cleaning and straightening up, removing pockets of waste, and soliciting ideas from empowered work teams and enlightened shop-floor associates. Although all those benefits usually do result from the best kaizen programs and activities, the method was originally intended to change technically challenging processes for the better, without continual reliance on engineers and white-collar technicians. Postwar Japanese industries were short on engineers, and kaizen pioneers wanted to make use of the workforce they had; they knew that to accomplish that immediate objective they had to walk out on the floor and be seen, to listen and quietly observe, and to reward active involvement by shop-floor personnel, "the real experts." They had to develop trust in the workforce, and managers had to understand operations as well as operators, because working managers stayed on top of progress. Industry executives weren't striving to create new political institutions, or to instill democracy on the shop floor and in the offices, however; they just needed a way to get the job done better and faster with more productive use of precious resources. In postwar Japan, steel and other metals were especially valued—to waste material was a crime against the state, and industry as well as households worked hard to make good use of the country's limited resources.

Learning from the Great Sensei

Teruyuki Maruo explains that he was trained as a young quality engineer to think carefully about all material use; scrap usually piles up from bad stamping layouts, and as a result, his BP efforts typically attack stamping first, where he usually expects to squeeze 20 or 30 percent improvements in material utilization—off the top—just from planning steel layouts more economically. In fact, students of Maruo are proud to explain how he trained them to walk into any facility anywhere in the world and within minutes tell whether the plant is working well. A tough teacher, Maruo taught his protégés to use their senses by asking them a series of simple questions—"Can you hear the punch presses running?" for example, because if you don't hear the "ca chunk, ca chunk," the shop is not making money. Or, "What do you smell?" If the student smells oil or toxic fumes without even stepping into the problem area, he knows that maintenance and repairs are probably being neglected. Likewise, if his observations turn up tools placed in inconvenient places or un-air-conditioned shops—Maruo believes that in any plants working without air-conditioning, productivity is about 80 percent of what it should be—closer examination will probably uncover bad processes as well.

Maruo's teaching techniques are tough and personal. He carefully selects seven-member kaizen teams—seven members because for him seven is "a magic number"—to balance out all functions represented in the plant. He deliberately goes after people who might be described as one-sided, skilled only in engineering, or mold-making, or stamping technology, rather than looking for seven well-rounded individuals. He understands that by bringing the intensity of all the technical experts to bear on a particular process problem, he will get the most significant and immediate results. Although the contrasts represented by these diverse specialties on the team may tend to require a "settling-in period," this balanced approach has been proven to work better than quick and dirty kaizen methods that indiscriminately put inexperienced shop-floor personnel into yet another on-the-job learning experience. Unfortunately for many small suppliers in the United States, Maruo's proven approaches have not yet received enough attention to prevent the proliferation of inexperienced kaizen consulting houses. Many of them have been burned, and many still are searching for ways to address process problems in a systematic and lasting way.

What's Wrong Here?

Ten years after Motorola's Six Sigma campaign and the Baldrige Award, and dozens of state and professional quality awards, and countless quality audit protocols designed to measure goodness of quality process, and hundreds of quality books written by Phil Crosby and Deming and Juran, many companies remain unconverted. First-tier giants such as Compaq and Gateway need to work on basic quality compliance for the market, but just below them, frighteningly large numbers of second-, third-, and fourth-tier suppliers are failing to meet the most basic quality performance numbers, because in the electronics industry, any performance less than Six Sigma guarantees unhappy customers. Less-than-perfect lock-in of happy customers means, especially with expensive items like laptops, that the industry is not yet ready for commodity-type approaches to production and distribution. Less-than-perfect processes inevitably lead to less-than-perfect, and worse, unpredictable products.

Broken Links in the Supply Chain

According to Mike Doyle, CEO of the National Initiative for Supply Chain Integration (NISCI) formed in 1997, the purpose of NISCI is to find ways to "cause each member's supply chains to function more as one integrated system." NISCI helps member businesses research and develop ways to optimize the performance of supply chains among three or more trading partners. In fact, organizations that wish to join must bring with them a supply chain of three links or more, because anything less will be ineffective.

Harley Davidson is a charter member. Leroy Zimdars, director of development purchasing at Harley, is a believer. "At Harley, we have been able to make significant strides by dealing with issues that exist among our tier-one suppliers," said Zimdars. "But we know we can't reach our performance goals unless we join in a collective business effort to further identify problems and develop standard solutions that can be implemented across the supply chain."

Bob Parker, NISCI's executive director, sees that in the United States, supply chains are usually anchored at the consumer end by a large branded-product producer and at the other end by large raw-material producers. In between are more than three hundred thousand smaller, very essential manufacturers who account for nearly all U.S. net employment gains in recent years. A well-organized supply chain leads to increased efficiencies, faster response to market changes, better design and manufacturing processes, and increased productivity.

NISCI's eight founding members—Honda of America Manufacturing, Trane, Chrysler, John Deere, Harley Davidson, Supply America, University of Chicago, plus the National Association of Purchasing Management—have identified six initiatives that taken together could turn individual companies operating in a loosely linked supply chain to one integrated system, by:

1. Stimulating value creation across three links or more

2. Standardizing and certifying education and training to enhance performance across three links or more

3. Designing chain architecture that supports real-time, consensus decision-making across three links or more

4. Measuring chain economic performance across three links or more

5. Creating trust, culture, and people processes that support cooperation across three links or more

6. Creating a legal, regulatory, and legislative environment that facilitates collective improvement across three links or more

Beware the Troll Under the Bridge

The failure of companies to work well together with their so-called partners and the failure of companies to maintain perfect process are global problems, the troll under the bridge that lies in wait for the first traveler attempting to cross. But between now and the year 2020 breakthroughs in enterprise technology—software, and a different approach to manufacturing technology—will cut through cultural and organizational barriers, enabling a few extended enterprise groups to run the game. Their material supply and manufacturing design and production processes will be perfect.

What's Wrong with Software? What's Wrong with Manufacturing? What's Wrong with Innovation?

About twenty years ago, Briggs and Stratton, at that time the leading U.S. producer of small engines, enjoyed a unique power position grown from perfecting a 1930s engine design. The midwestern producer's assembly processes illustrated the problems of traditional manufacturing—huge rusting crates of "just-in-case" crankshafts and assemblies, expediting, missing parts, piece-rate production, and inventory buffers. The company was in a secure cash position with loyal customers and a vast distribution network. Workers sported all the new toys—motorcycles, RVs in the driveway, boats, lake-country cabins (although good business conditions precluded taking much more than the minimum vacation time). Woe to the visitor who lingered at the parking lot exit when the 3:00 P.M. whistle blew as the lot emptied of hundreds of motor vehicles of all makes (American) and sizes (big).

But off on the horizon, nearly out of sight of the Milwaukee engine assemblers, competitors silently advanced. They glanced repeatedly to Milwaukee, checking their watches and making penciled notations on a set of elegantly sketched blueprints. Their goal—to dominate the small engine business in the United States and the Pacific within five years—was certainly achievable. They had already, with new engine designs and near perfect quality and fuel economy, conquered Australia and some of North America.

One morning, Briggs and Stratton engineers gathered in a dark back room: Someone had purchased the new Honda engine, and three engineers were about to perform a dissection—reverse engineering the engine to see just what was so special about their competition. As the lead engineer removed the screws, the engine cracked open to reveal a simple, clean, cast aluminum design. A crowd had gathered from the production area, and a loud gasp passed through the small group as the engineers stepped closer. What a wonder of design intelligence and manufacturability—fewer angles, less machining, a different material, more compression from a smaller bore. The differences between this new technology and Briggs's thirty-year-old standby were astonishing.

But denial runs deep for mature producers that have enjoyed market dominance for many years. And Briggs was no exception. Its first response—"They'll never do it, our name commands customer loyalty"—was replaced with slow acceptance that something had indeed redrawn the landscape of the small-engine business. As the trolls crept across the Pacific, continuing to grab market share while building name recognition, the sleepy Milwaukee giant responded by trying to market its way out of a basic three-generation design and process gap. One-half million dollars bought halftime ads during the Superbowl as Briggs scrambled to make its name primary in the mind of the consumer, although the products were sold primarily through OEM equipment assemblers.

Cost-cutting and attention to inventory waste followed. Still, the competitors continued their nightly marches, all the way up to the gates of the American factory. Finally, several years and many lost market-share points later, someone decided to address the real issues—product and process. The company launched a completely new engine design; along the way, management chose not to fight the high-labor-cost battle, a process problem, and quietly transferred engine production down South, out of the reach of the union.

Did Briggs really solve its product problems? Yes, but only as a last resort. Did it fix its process problems? Partially. By rationalizing production in Milwaukee, and by designing a more easily manufacturable product, and finally by cutting labor costs, the company put itself on a road to survival.

Complexity, Software, and Other Innovation Killers

Many companies—Gateway, Compaq, Briggs, and thousands of others—have struggled at some point in their life cycles with innovation

FIGURE 3.1 *How Manufacturing Grew*

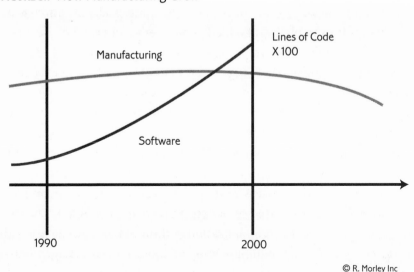

© R. Morley Inc

problems. In the late seventies many U.S. companies invested millions of dollars of false hopes in software packages that for a range of reasons failed them (see Figure 3.1). Their expectations—that MRP and Capacity Planning and Purchasing and Design software systems would perfect inherently flawed systems and make a better, smarter, richer, more innovative world—obviously created a few dozen software millionaires. But how many CEOs of successful manufacturing companies today, when asked to name the three top actions they have taken on the road to success, will name implementation of MAN MAN or Oracle, two leading manufacturing packages? SAP and Baan now occupy visible and controversial seats in many of our bigger manufacturing operations; users' and installers' screams can be heard continents away.

We are sure that these packages are being used to solve the wrong problems. Users frequently react with, "If all you have is a hammer, every problem is a nail." Unless the package is creating simplicity from extreme complexity, it is an expensive anchor around the necks of struggling enterprises around the world.

Software applications packages for manufacturing process management remain fragmented, frequently designed to solve a small piece of the wrong problem. In most planning packages purchasing modules, for example, were added as an afterthought. Likewise, planning systems that failed to recognize the need for powerful logistics and tracking capabilities brought about by JIT cripple the execution side of the operation. In thirty years North American manufacturing software users have grown from basic applications of computers for inventory, payroll accounting, and industrial control, to the potential of off-site design and lights-out production solutions. The Toyota Production System and various kaizen approaches attempt to simplify and cleanse the process. Software, however, knits more complexity into processes that need to be streamlined and perfected. The two forces—one to process rationalization and simplification, the other to finite control through complex information systems management— are tearing production apart. Software applications imposed on overly complicated processes produce extraneous variables, too complex for human management and too expensive for artificial intelligence.

MRP software and its derivatives, for example, enjoyed uninterrupted profits during the eighties, but truly, Oliver Wight and a team of other IBM imagineers had designed an entire system around a single process, the bill of material explosion module (BOM) that became the hammer for every nail. The BOM is simply a meat-grinder, a programming conquest that allowed multilevel parts assemblies to be broken down to their smallest components. Earlier attempts at executing this task failed because of computational (square root) limits. Thousands of implementations of second-generation MRP II applications fed the growth of unmanageable complexity. Consultants and software vendors reaped the benefits of manufacturers' confusion; they were scammed by McNamarian misapplication of a simple concept.

Every JIT implementation stumbled on miles of cables connecting MRP modules to the shop floor. Simply shutting off the work-order routine caused turmoil among planners. Tracking and calculating inventory balances of material in various stages of work in process completion launched hundreds of software projects. Manufacturing professionals felt that they were living under siege, as one after another material manager was led out into the parking lot and shot because he couldn't get the consultants' package to perform up to spec.

The parallels—complex software applications of simple ideas—continued with bigger software solutions, MES and ERP included. In contrast, few software gurus addressed basic supply-management questions, and most purchasing software solutions fall short because as "add-ons" they did not meet user requirements.

Another Manufacturing Disappointment—the Rise and Fall of Quality

Certification—ISO and other quality awards—does not guarantee a robust process. For nontechnical managers, these quality scams and other moneymakers disguised as philosophies litter the floor and clutter the mind. They block the road to good metrics and obscure the line of sight to the total enterprise that companies need to see their process and understand the flow. How many industry leaders measure the combined value of their enterprise, the total speed of throughput, over first, second, third, and even fourth tiers? Single-point technologies—focusing on one method to carry the entire load for manufacturing excellence, whether it is ISO or self-managed teams or value-flow mapping—don't work.

GM, for example, in its single-minded application of JIT in the midst of supply uncertainties and potential union stoppages, regularly proves this point. When its Akron tire supplier struck, it shut down GM assembly lines up the road. The problem, of course, was not in the concept of JIT, but in its application environment.

From Innovation to the Limits of Economies of Scale

When systems and good processes are not perfected, companies sometimes rely on marketing tricks or economies of scale to carry them over the profit threshold. In 1814, when Francis Cabot Lowell completed a prototype mill on the banks of the Charles River for the Boston Manufacturing Company, he intended it to integrate all the cottage industry pieces of textile production—he essentially had created a new production process. And he planned to use the water power of the Charles River dam to drive all the machinery through a series of sluiceways, water wheels, leather pulleys, and wheels. Whatever his profit projections may have been for this prototype mill, his early engineering of economies of scale drove profit within less than two years of the startup to over 200 percent. The mill became known for other firsts, however, including the first labor strike.

A string of textile mammoths sprang up along the Merrimack River, their names marking the original incorporators of the Boston Manufacturing Company—Lowell, Lawrence, Appleton—all developed by what industrial historian Robert Dalzell called the enterprising elite, the leaders of a new profit-making and profit-taking manufacturing technology movement. New England merchants whose profits were slowed or blocked by the War of 1812 found a new venture capital vehicle in bigger and bigger brick mills. The site selection requirements were water power (later replaced by steam), transportation routes, and cash. One profitable operation fed another and another. It seemed that economies of scale knew no limits.

Everything about the mills was scaled to fit the hugeness of the founders' vision, and some would argue, their greed—the canal systems that diverted water from mill ponds and waterfalls, the huge windows, the "corporations" (tenements housing workers). (See Figure 3.2.) The fourth necessary component, labor, was easily obtained. Workers flooded the gates—first the Yankee mill girls, whose average tenure was two years, after which many young women returned to their farms to clear their lungs. The Yankee mill girls were soon replaced by waves of cheaper labor, large families from Canada, Ireland, Scotland, Italy, Greece, Poland, and Russia.

The formula—manually tended machinery, few shutdowns, low wages, and captive labor—churned out money until the mid-1930s. Worker turnover and illiteracy did not stand in the way of profits. Neither did holidays or strikes.

But the system began to weaken as management stretched the limits of size, economies of scale. The most expensive asset—machinery—aged. In the Amoskeag, the huge Manchester, New Hampshire, textile complex, during its time the biggest in the world, the money flowed. No time for maintenance, no diverted profits for new machinery, and little tolerance for increased workers' power gave owners pause for thought. Was it time to cut loose and go South? The inflexibility of the process, a system of linkages connecting huge looms that made money only when running straight out—left few choices.

The Amoskeag's fate was sealed. In 1937 Thomas Jefferson Coolidge, treasurer of the Amoskeag and the sole legitimate direct descendant of Thomas Jefferson, the Father of Democracy, and his board revisited the power of reinvested profits and headed south. Thousands of workers in Manchester took positions on the pavement, penniless and pensionless, as Amoskeag management closed the plants, moved some of the machinery, and invested in railroads, new textiles, and other growing industries. Their dedication to financial gains overran their interest in good process and investment in technological innovation.

The broken windows and rusted iron gates still testify to the Amoskeag's extinction. Although some buildings have been renovated into small businesses and startups, sixty years later the city has

FIGURE 3.2 *Typical 19th Century Mill City. Courtesy Manchester NH Historic Association.*

not recovered or forgotten. Manchester and Flint, Michigan; Troy, New York; Bethlehem, Pennsylvania; Cleveland, Ohio; and Detroit, Michigan are all monuments to the one-hundred-year run of the economy of scale formula. Bigger is not always better.

The Innovation Imperative

Almost fifty years later, when Kenneth Olson, then president of Digital Equipment Corporation, finally decided to enter the personal computer market, Steve Jobs, then president of Apple, sent a black funeral wreath to Olson's Old Mill headquarters. Olson's doomed personal-computer strategy, another proprietary, application-limited offering, demonstrated his lack of understanding of the speed with which this market would grow. He was too late among too many competitors with lower prices and more features to build the market on the Digital name alone.

According to Edward Kerschner, analyst for *Morning Notes Research Reports,* although personal computer stocks boomed in 1982–83, by February 1984 a group of twenty-four (!) leading PC stocks were, on average, 50 percent below their fifty-two-week high.[1] Soon, most of the leaders exited the business—Apollo, Osbourne, Sinclair, NCR, and others. PC giants Dell, Compaq, and Gateway were not yet publicly traded companies.

The Web, Hoola Hoop, or Innovation Imperative?

Like the personal computer industry before it, the Internet industry is the technology fad of the nineties (see Figure 3.3). But by 2020 the Internet plumbing will have faded back into the walls of a handful of user-specific applications companies. Like the auto and personal computer industries, and segments of the biotech group, investments in the high-risk Web are approaching shakeout and diversification. The auto and biotech industries followed the same pattern we project for the Internet. Of 485 auto companies that entered the business between 1900 and 1908, 262 were gone after eight years, and

FIGURE 3.3

THE INTERNET *DOES* HAVE LIMITS

"Think of the Internet as a Highway." Vice President Al Gore

There it is again. Some clueless techno-wannabe talking about the Information Superhighway.

They don't get it. The Web is nothing like a superhighway.

Suppose the metaphor ran in the other direction. Suppose the superhighways were like the 'Net . . .

A highway hundreds of lanes wide. Dotted with potholes and debris. Privately operated bridges and overpasses. No highway patrol. A couple of rent-a-cops on bicycles with broken whistles. Five-hundred-member vigilante posses loaded down with nuclear weapons.

A minimum of 237 on-ramps at every intersection. No signs. Wanna get to Ensenada? Holler out the window at a passing eighteen-wheeler to ask directions.

Ad hoc traffic laws.

Some lanes would vote to make single-occupant vehicles a capital offense Monday through Friday between 7 and 9 a.m. Other lanes would just shoot you without a trial for talking on a car phone.

AOL would be a giant, diesel-smoking bus with hundreds of ebola victims on-board, throwing dead wombats and rotten cabbage at the other cars, most of which have been assembled at home from kits.

Some vehicles are built around 2.5 horsepower lawnmower engines with a top speed of nine miles an hour. Others burn nitroglycerin and idle at 120.

No license plates. World War II bomber nose art instead. Terrifying paintings of huge teeth and vampire eagles. Bumper-mounted machine guns. Flip some-body the finger on this highway and get a white phosphorus grenade up your tailpipe. Flatbed trucks cruise around with anti-aircraft missile batteries to shoot down the traffic helicopter. Little kids on tricycles with squirtguns filled with hydrochloric acid switch lanes without warning.

NO OFF-RAMPS. None. Now, that's the way to run an Interstate Highway system.

Where do YOU want to go today?

—Available in numerous places on the Internet.

---

very few survived for long after that. Biotech stocks were touted as the replacement for PC money. But of thirty-five leading biotech companies at year-end 1991, only ten in the late nineties had a higher price than when they started.

The United States did not need 485 auto companies. Do we truly need one hundred–plus Internet providers? While the Internet will become a source of innovation, most providers only sell access; few players bring useful, powerful applications and structured, easy niched access to a market that is essentially built on a free network of wires. Kerschner predicts that although TV took thirty-five years to reach 30 percent of U.S. households, the Web should hit that mark by 2002 (eight years after its launch). What then? A handful of second-, third-, and fourth-generation Internet innovation engines will capture specific market groups—home users, schools, manufacturing, entertainment—with value-added applications.

But excitement breeds demand in the stock market, and what looked like the biggest innovation driver—just as nuclear power, autos, PCs, and biotech were in the past—the Web, will cycle into profit-and-loss reality. The hype will fade to sophisticated user and buyer choice. Web users will be captured by Internet providers who in themselves offer more than access—entertainment, specialized manufacturing services, the entire retail experience, or respected news sources (as UPI and the Associated Press International once were the most timely news sources).

Any regulatory power or technology gate that attempts to limit the natural course of industrial growth, shakeout, consolidation, and profit will obstruct the true innovation life cycle at work. Microsoft versus the U.S. government was a temporary hurdle that might have slowed Bill Gates's march, but other, unstoppable electronic Davids will encroach on Goliath's territory.

Call it the innovation imperative. Technology will win, and technology will create strings of money makers and money losers. However, by taking the long view, looking back on one hundred years of accelerated progress in key innovation industries such as autos, computers, and the Web, wise leaders may notice another element that periodically emerges and disappears. The idea of creation of wealth for "the common good"—a la MITI, the Boston Manufacturing Corporation and the eighteenth-century mill village, will re-emerge with 2020's Island of Excellence.

The Re-emergence of "the Common Good"

Government regulatory groups and some investors do not understand the inevitable cycle of technology birth, growth, and passing. They try to manage or direct and divert powerful innovation energy, hoping to prematurely harvest technology results, and their interference is dangerous and futile.

In the early 1800s, New England streams and rivers were dotted with clusters of complete mill villages. Machine shops stood next to grist mills; lumber mills located downstream fueled additional growth. As steam replaced water power, the next incremental change in the Industrial Revolution allowed factories to be located yards, even miles away from the stream's primary water source, but physically the mill village retained its unique identity. From the eighteenth century until even the 1930s, these clusters of like-minded enterprises flourished, providing all of their inhabitants man-made goods to exchange for cash that satisfied capital and other requirements.

In northeastern Massachusetts there is a twenty-mile river, the Nissitissitt, that runs from Lake Potanipo, just over the state line in New Hampshire, down through the town of Pepperell to the Nashua River, and on to the Merrimack, the river that built the Industrial Revolution (see Figure 3.4). The Nissitissitt was once very polluted, but in ten years it has been cleaned up and it is now a class-B river; trout fishing and swimming on the sandbar have returned to the river. The Nissitissitt was the perfect mill village center. In just twenty miles six factory villages, supported by six schools, and an assortment of grist mills, machine shops, a harp factory, lumber mills, and paper mills flourished.

The mill villages, places where new technologies were born, perfected, and died, retained an integrating concern for the common

FIGURE 3.4   *The mill village of East Pepperell, along the Nissitissitt River. Map courtesy The Pepperell Historical Society.*

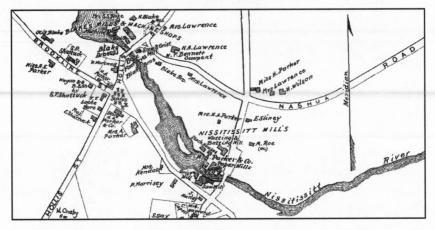

good. It is impossible to believe that inhabitants of these enclaves were blind to their connection to next generations. Their churches and schools enforced traditions that built awareness of the common good. Their holidays and parades and town newspapers reinforced the strength of the idea. And, pre–income tax and regulation, it worked.

We predict the return of the mill village and all its integrating values and human connections. In the year 2020 the Island of Enterprise winners will have built well-run, competitive global factory villages. The source of the intellectual capital—product designs and process intelligence—required to fuel this post–water power factory village may be two galaxies over, but each winning enterprise village will contain nearly all the basic requirements for healthy production and trade: a sound process, transportation and communications utilities, and competitive product. Some villages will be innovation centers; some will produce commodities for trade; the losers will plod along unable to grow or even meet payroll.

Simplicity and Complexity

What happened between Schofield's blacksmith shop, upriver on the Merrimack, that contributed its carding machine to Lowell's mills, and the construction of a high-tech computer assembly plant several miles downriver? How did the innovation imperative lose its governance and impose too much complexity on simple processes? Why did Briggs and Stratton respond to a killer app by trying to market its way out of the hole with big-money TV ads? Who was running the show when the engineers cracked open that first cast aluminum engine?

Not the technologists.

Rodger Lovrenich, former president of Sceptor and proponent of ladder logic (a very simple approach to computer architecture), says the concept of extension—augmentation of human capabilities—allowed us to build complexity. We built mechanical arms (conveyor systems with robotic arms), feet (automated material movement vehicles), eyes (vision systems and bar code readers), ears (sensors), even brains (remote-controlled terminals and networked data-storage devices) to supplement human abilities. Sometimes the gizmo worked; sometimes it clashed with other gadgets.

Our human abilities have been a mixed blessing to the species. Other animals adapt or die rather than build layers of complexity to satisfy finer demands. Apes can hunt for termites, parrots can communicate with each other, and the evolution of horses has produced a lovely but fragile branch on a complex evolutionary tree. None of these creatures has been able to complicate their world as has mankind.

Extension allowed us to extend our eyes with radar, to extend our muscles with mechanical engineering and motors, to extend our hearing with telephones, radios, and the Internet, and to extend our three-pound brains through the computer. But more features packed into a single package means inevitably more complexity. Remote control of processes and collaboration on design means more complexity. Although we are all burdened with showoff software—even personal computers have become entirely too complicated—we will be using handwriting recognition and voice recognition systems in 2020, because it's easier to write and talk than type.

But it is important to get the process right first, to strip out the complexity that has accumulated in layers that obscure the real process flows just below the surface. It's not a matter of perceptions.

In the seventies management became fascinated with benchmarking, an activity that packed a lot of exciting business travel and semi-serious gabfests into competitively motivated studies. Despite Greg Watson's excellent benchmarking guides, and the help of a few enlightened manufacturers that regularly opened their doors to individual benchmarkers and periodic benchmarking conferences, somehow the activity lost its shine after a few years. Perhaps the competition with the re-engineering phase took the spirit out of a benchmarking movement that in its origin had integrity and was well-intended. Certainly the attention that Motorola garnered for its Six Sigma quality drive and the Baldrige Award led to heightened interest in benchmarking as a good way to gather improvement data. Even Motorola's QSR (Quality System Review), a comprehensive evaluation instrument used by the company and its suppliers to rate various aspects of the operation and to evaluate relative maturity levels, lost its novelty. Hundreds of other companies took the same "evaluation and certification" route, and suppliers, especially smaller ones whose daily life was bounded by survival and growth struggles, got tired. Although benchmarking and certification of goodness never reached the low tolerance levels that various ISO certifications have, nevertheless, the whole documentation-driven methodology began to take on the static and less appealing feel of accounting—necessary, precise, but boring, another non-value-adding activity. Throughout it all, deep down everyone knew that we were trying to see and solve basic process issues, and to do that, technology, not measurement, clearly is the answer. Fix the process, and measure and study it later, but fix it first and well.

For-profit institutions and hundreds of consultants and media forays only served to obscure the obvious needs for metrics and information—not data, but information that would guide business decision-makers to the right performance steps in the right sequence. There is a story credited to Dakota tribal wisdom that says when you discover you are riding a dead horse, the best strategy is to dismount. However, in business we often try other strategies with dead horses, including:

1. Buy a stronger whip.
2. Change riders.
3. Say things like, "This is the way we have always ridden this horse."
4. Appoint a committee to study the horse.
5. Arrange to visit other sites to see how they ride dead horses.
6. Change the standards to allow the riding of dead horses.
7. Appoint a tiger team to revive the dead horse.
8. Create a training session to increase our riding skills.
9. Discuss the state of dead horses in today's environment.
10. Change the requirements, declaring, "This horse is not dead."
11. Hire contractors to ride the dead horse.
12. Harness several dead horses together for increased speed.
13. Declare that "no horse is too dead to beat."
14. Provide additional funding to increase the horse's performance.
15. Do a comparative analysis to see if contractors can ride it cheaper.
16. Purchase a product to make dead horses run faster.
17. Declare the horse is "better, faster, and cheaper" dead.
18. Form a quality circle team to find uses for dead horses.
19. Revisit the performance requirements for horses.
20. Say this horse was procured with cost as an independent variable.
21. Promote the dead horse to a supervisory position.
22. Designate a "Champion" for the dead horse.

Process, Process, Process

Put the process into the hands of the technologist to clarify the essentials. Lovrenich believes that he understands the source of manufacturing complexity, particularly in the area of machine controls. "Factories will become more complicated. Essentially what mankind does is add more complexity until he stalls out. And so the scheme of the future must be directed at how we manage complexity, not what the job is, which is absolutely trivial."

Imagine a machine that breaks down—a line, or a factory controller, or a robot—or stalls once every fifty years. The statistical probability is that the machine must be repaired by amateurs. Companies face the choice of keeping a cadre of skilled repair technicians prepared and ready—Maytag repairmen—or using machines that can monitor, diagnose, and repair themselves.

But for a typical auto plant with two thousand degrees of freedom, writing a program to cover all the possibilities would take too long, like developing a spell checker for a transfer line, a super-complicated system with many failure modes. The system moves forward, moves backward, or is in the breakdown mode, and the complexity is endless. A line two hundred yards long, with thousands of stations, suddenly stops. Where do the technicians begin the hunt for the malfunctioning element?

Lovrenich thinks that companies often "come to it with a housewife approach, the way we used to fix computers. When I give you a system with two thousand fuses, two thousand light bulbs, it becomes clear we don't handle the complexity by stringing together a cluster of logic strings. What we must do is build systems that themselves address the diagnostics issue." He urges managers to accept that nothing is perfect—accept that systems and pieces of systems will fail. *There is a right way* to keep complex machines and complex systems running, and if we do successfully build robust diagnostics, have we solved the problem of managing complexity?

The problem of complexity is unfortunately only partly due to layers of fail-safes and fallback systems designed to cover every possible situation in factories. Such companies as GM and Briggs and Stratton have many years of systems history to clear away; they need to uncover and clarify the real process flows. Factories have so many layers and add-ons and departments, functions, and silos that they have lost sight of the simple flow of material to product.

Fix the process, then figure out how to handle complexity—complexity of demands, of the extended enterprise, of faster technologies. More features packed into a single package means more complexity. Remote control of processes and collaboration on design means more complexity. But get the process right first.

The board shop and laptop stories illustrate that before these two high-tech producers can ever successfully address enterprise or remote manufacturing tasks, they must fix their process, get back to the roots of basic quality management and good process control. Technology gets simpler as it gets mature.

References

Dalzell, Robert, *The Enterprising Elite: The Boston Associates and the World They Made* (Harvard University Press, 1987).

Hareven, Tamara K., and Langenbach, Randolph, *Amoskeag: Life and Work in an American Factory-City* (University Press of New England, 1995).

Roberts, Ralph, *Zone Logic—A Unique Method of Practical Artificial Intelligence* (Radnor, Pa.: Compute! Books, 1989).

4

Technology Rules!

The PLC Breakthrough

We wanted to put the solution in the hands of the people
with the problem, rather than in the hands of the engineer.

—DICK MORLEY

To a curious visitor off the street, there is apparently nothing happening one flight down on the clean and very quiet production floor. Through a wall of glass, he sees no racks of partially complete assemblies or parts conveyorized and packaged for computer-controlled delivery to waiting assemblers. No expediter or forktrucks add an adrenaline rush to the landscape.

The visitor wonders just exactly what product could emerge from this silent world. Small groups of uniformed workers quietly and intently congregate over schematics. Boxes of various sizes labeled with bar code stickers accumulate in neat stacks for the express delivery trucks that arrive every sixty minutes. Product variety abounds, yet what is most visible to the visitor is not product movement, but the process flow—a clear line-of-sight arrangement whose beginning and end represent a six-hour straight shot from component inventory to the customer's arms.

Indicator lights flicker rhythmically as panels move through wave solder and reels of microelectronics uncurl their silicon wafers onto waiting fiberglass and beryllium copper boards.

This is Modicon, a world of industrial automation and a source of industrial automation as well, located in downtown North Andover, Massachusetts, another seventeenth-century mill village gone high-tech. (Modicon was founded by co-author Dick Morley to build the programmable logic controller.) The glass-walled view to the production floor is a view upriver, to the origins of factory design where ripples on the surface offer faint impressions of steady activity below— the integration of all processes in one site linking previously dis-integrated functions, cleanly laid out in a line, the addition of intelligence and fail-safing, the removal of thousands of human hands from the process, and the addition of customers—on-site—directing and designing their products. Just a few months earlier, management decided to remove a metal automated parts crib, freeing more space for real production and eliminating the remaining spot where inventory waste could accumulate.

As in all New England factory villages, North Andover's entrepreneurs, descendants of the Boston Manufacturing Company's Paul Moody, built their technology machines on the banks of rivers whose water flows they controlled. What nature did not provide, they supplemented with millponds for energy storage, sluiceways and penstocks and canals for energy and materials transport, and leather pulleys and gears to move the energy from the subfloor waterwheels to top floor weaving machines.

Here on High Street in North Andover, Davis and Furman set up a machine shop to outfit the textile entrepreneurs' dreams. Their energy source, the Cochichewick River, runs several miles downstream into the great industrial river, the Merrimack, which empties into the Atlantic.

Across the street stood a textile mill, and next to this four-story building a steam power plant later was built to replace the waterwheel, but the outlines of the dam, the millpond, and the old railroad spur are still visible from Modicon's six-story mill tower. The stream has been diverted and redirected into underground conduits, but the water still flows through the mill complex.

One improvement after another fueled the dreamers' progress and built their technology machine. The simple process of carding wool, in which a woman brushed raw sheep shearings with a palm-sized

FIGURE 4.1 *The Davis and Furman Machine Shop (1862), later home to Modicon, with all its employees. In the distance between buildings ran the river and a railroad spur. Photo courtesy Modicon.*

piece of wood embedded with spikes to produce spinnable wool fibers, was one of the first.

Sometime in the late eighteenth century, master engineer Paul Moody apprenticed himself to the Schofield Blacksmith Shop, also in North Andover, Massachusetts, one-quarter mile up the hill from Modicon. There he made an important technological transformation. He took the process of carding out of the hands of women working by their hearths, and with his creation of a drum-sized carding machine, brought the process into the shop down by the river. His carding machine began to integrate and institutionalize the textile process. Moody's breakthrough took the woman's daughter out of her farmstead, and for twenty years the Yankee mill girls ran the great noisy weaving machines that clothed armies in the Civil War, and that fed masses of foreign workers and their families as they too sought a livelihood on the riverbanks.

Industrial Alchemy, Another Kind of Weaving

But at Modicon almost two hundred years later, the visitor is witness to another kind of weaving. In the old millyard, in the shadow of an elegantly restored clock tower, the Modicon complex stretches between old bricks and chestnut beams and concrete and glass. A below-ground-level one-hundred-foot corridor lined with a chronology depicting the invention of the PLC and the emergence of a new industry marks the transition. Visitors and employees daily pass by this technology story and its glass-encased 08 box (the first PLC unit) on their way to the cafeteria.

The New Alchemy

A finely tuned, elegant balance of supremely skilled workers, very intelligent machines, and advanced process technologies is weaving from sand and gold new solutions to customer automation needs. The industrial alchemist's challenge, how to transform base materials—sand, silicon, gold, lead, copper, wool—into money, is being realized every minute of every hour of each eight-hour shift.

In the decades that followed the first years of the nineteenth century, the systems that grew to accommodate economies of scale, spewing huge profits for over one hundred years in a row, became more complex. Spaghetti diagrams describe the twists and turns of a typical nineteenth-century process flow, a convoluted path taken by most industrial products, from textiles to motor assemblies and even computer products. And on each strand of spaghetti, the alchemist's base materials accumulated labor and overhead costs. Waste coated the long production line with unused cycle time and extra layers of unnecessary handling and parts movement.

Enter "The Box"

Centered in the millyard of a red-brick nineteenth-century textile complex, Modicon stands as a technology success story that sprang from a hung over engineer's frustration with working endless weekends and holidays to personally design custom solutions for dozens of industrial automation control applications. Each solution was a rush job, and each solution had to be re-engineered for the next customer. Nothing happened the same way twice, everything was done serially, nothing was planned or executed in parallel with anything else. Nothing was easy, and none of the work was leading either to big money or to bigger challenges. For co-author Dick Morley it was the engineer's seventh ring of hell, chained at the ankles to a test bench where he sketched schematics and fiddled with wires, days, nights, weekends, and holidays.

Morley's solution, the programmable logic controller, forever changed the way factories work because the device replaced hundreds of hardwired installations of switches and relays that were custom-engineered for such applications as chemical processing, steel production, and pharmaceuticals. The PLC increased reliability and speed of installation, as well as flexibility, because it eliminated complexity, it "cleaned up the mess" that was factory automation. The PLC introduced flexibility of automation into the factory. Without calling in a crew of electricians and technicians, factory managers could easily reconfigure their lines as new products emerged from the design rooms.

From its beginnings in Bedford Associates in a concrete garage located twenty miles away in Bedford, Massachusetts, a site of much early high-tech work on Route 128 (Progress Software, Atex, and dozens of other startups), the excitement and customer list grew to need more space and higher volumes. Modicon, the organization that the PLC built, has since been acquired by French conglomerate Groupe Schneider.

But today's Modicon is a laboratory-like production floor that offers glimpses of what manufacturing will look like and how it will work in 2020 and beyond because Modicon, like most other high-tech producers, started out looking like a nineteenth-century factory— messy, complex, driven by expediters and layers of supervision, in constant chaos. In twenty years the company has stripped away the distractions and straightened and smoothed its flow; the results are improved productivity and quality with less space, fewer human hands, and less time wasted.

In less than 120,000 square feet Modicon pumps out 32,000 industrial control systems per month containing a total of over 42,000 printed circuit boards with 3.5 million surface mounted technology placements. Two hundred eighty-five direct labor professionals ship approximately $200 million in revenue each year—not a "lights-out" factory, but not a labor-intensive one either.

As a production facility, this plant has undergone many changes in its layout and product flow. Bruce Boardman, vice-president of operations, notes that the current continuous flow concept is a conversion from a batch process in a work cell environment. In a recent factory-floor project, the company dedicated over $3 million to new capital equipment to create a smooth in-line flow. Batch flows and work cells proved to be too slow and too irregular for the smooth acceleration and deceleration Modicon required.

Indeed, Modicon manufacturing pros point to reduced printed circuit board cycle times of 70 percent, with total system cycle time (average systems contain three PC boards), down 63 percent from eight to three days.

Modicon has plenty of competition; such companies as Allen-Bradley, Mitsubishi, and Siemens offer their own variety of industrial control systems. The push is on to get custom-engineered solutions faster, in smaller footprints, to such customers as GM and Labatts. Applications include breweries, paint shops, paper mills, and refineries all over the world.

The Programmable Logic Controller (PLC), the Birth of a $5-Billion Industry

Modicon grew from the invention of a single revolutionary device on New Year's Day, 1968. This box of software encased in cast-iron could generate the same results as fifty feet of cabinets, relays and miles of wires. The PLC spawned a new $5-billion industry that offered reliable and consistent process control. The PLC Story is *the* story of a single technological innovation that continues to revolutionize how we make things. The box changed factory design. New lines come up faster and cheaper with fewer bugs.

Nineteenth-century and early twentieth-century factory buildings were a design marvel in themselves. Their hardwired networks of switches, plugs, cables, relays, test boards, and fail-safe systems take years and billions of dollars to build and install. Unfortunately, debugging and maintenance of dedicated hardwired electric circuitry required an army of facilities and maintenance engineers and technicians whose expert power at times overwhelmed the larger business interests of manufacturing management. Further, these complex wonders of energy flows were completely inflexible. Each new machine protocol and each new product process layout required entirely new wiring and process controls. Not unlike the immovable leather belts and pulleys that powered nailed-down cast-iron looms and

FIGURE 4.2   *The first PLC (Programmable Logic Controller) is currently housed at the Smithsonian.*

presses, pre-PLC factories were monuments to overplanning for every possible production condition.

Imagine a box on wheels, a production line on casters, and wireless communications, servocontrolled by a single desktop PC, linked by the Internet to a central design staff, and you will see the giant leap Modicon's technology machine is readying for.

Innovation stories—how an idea was born, and why these thoughts were pursued to completion—are treasures. The words of the creators themselves fade, and they may not always reflect a complete understanding of the powerful impact these marvelous devices will have on manufacturing.

The PLC Story—Why I Created the PLC

THE MACHINE WAS BUILT TO WORK ANYWHERE

In the days of wooden ships and iron men, control for large transfer lines and other discrete and continuous processes was done with relays. That means that the algorithms and control paradigms were created by the wiring structure topology of the wiring for control. Direct substitution of relays with semiconductors was done, but the swap did not eliminate the problem: the reliability of the semiconductor substitutions, because of their immaturity and design, was no better than that of the relays, whose design was quite mature. We had not solved the problem of spending six to nine months on the factory floor trying to get the machine to work in software land. Industry was also crying for higher performance, higher quality, and the ability to do more things. The conventional wisdom of relay wiring was clearly incapable of supplying these needs.

DON'T EVER CALL IT A COMPUTER . . .

The major driver for me, however, was personal. We had had a party the night before, and on New Year's Day I woke up hung over, with an all-over cardboard feeling. I was not looking forward to building another control system with semiconductors and implementing the algorithms in the wiring. I desperately wanted out of building another relay panel, and it occurred to me that one of the ways to do that was to wire the sensors and effectors directly to a box, so that the topology of interconnection and the algorithms that executed certain control functions could be part of the software box itself. We were, of course, using minicomputers for some very sophisticated control algorithms, but their language and real-time response was sadly insufficient. Yes, wiring the box up with the software simulation of relays was clearly the way to go, because it did several things: It reduced the "wiring time" from six months to six days, and it allowed functions such as addition, subtraction, and division that were impossible to do with classical relays. *It also let us get away from the minicomputer and its ornate, non–real-time procedural mechanism of programming.*

"What would happen," says I, "if we made a machine or a box that was reliable, that contained within it the ability to interface directly with the machine tool, and then have it responsible to both the programming and the environment?"

The only languages available to us at that time were Basic and Assembler, both of which were very expensive to program in real time. *We wanted to put the solution in the hands of the people with the problem, rather than in the hands of the engineer.* We did not want to design a minicomputer, nor did we want to make a semiconductor substitution for relays.

What we wanted to do was make a software substitution for relays using computer technology that allowed higher functionality, quicker turnaround, and access by the people with the problems, rather than the people with the computer solutions.

The two obvious solutions at that time were relays and electronics. Relays were a real problem because they were unreliable, and for complex functions, unrealizable. The "software" of relays was in the wiring, and many times a relatively simple machine tool would stand on the factory floor for six months to a year while the "software" was being debugged or rebuilt. The algorithmic manipulation of the control functions was in the wiring of the relays itself, and the relays were merely binary switches.

There were two ways to replace the relays. The first, and the easier, was direct replacement with cards embedded with semiconductors such as the ones offered then by Numalogic and Digital.

These cards (boards) were a direct replacement for relays in the beginning, and offered the advantages that they were more reliable than relays and required little or no maintenance once the burn-in period was established. Cards were also capable of greater functionality than the relays because they could be made more complex than simple binary relay functions, and they could perform rather simple but fixed functions on a nodal basis.

NOT A MINICOMPUTER: THE SOFTWARE IN THE PLC

On that gray, hung-over New Year's Day I laid down the specs for my idea:

> No interrupts for the processing
> DIRECT mapping into memory
> No software handling of repetitious chores
> Slow (a big mistake!)
> Hardhat—a rugged design that really worked
> Language—something specific to Bedford
>   Associates (job security!)

I drew a block diagram that indicated the I/O (input/output) structure, the mechanical structure, and the size of the machine. If my memory serves me right, the original sketches required a memory of only 128 words. By the way, that's not 128,000 words, but 128 words. Of course we immediately upgraded the memory load in the days that followed to 1,000 words.

THE IDEA EXPANDS

During that same morning I swigged black coffee and outlined the programmable controller, programmable motion (which to my mind was programmable limit switches, although we called it programmable motion), mechanical packaging, and the applications. Originally I envisioned most of the applications on discrete machine tools such as lathes, grinders, and millers, and in fact our initial attempts to sell in that arena were met with substantial resistance.

This class of application-specific processors in the real-time domain (using current terminology) had tremendous advantages for the machine tool control people. First, it was not a "computer." In fact, right after New Year's Day, I spent an entire weekend removing the word computer from all our internal and external memos and references. I wanted to make it expressly clear that this machine was not a computer, but a programmable controller. Although we used computer technology to achieve our ends in some aspects of the design, the use to which we put the computer was very specific and very narrow.

TWELVE NOON, JANUARY 1, 1968

By noon I had created the product and the business plan, including the expandable I/O concept and a modular systems approach. The hardware design was one-third CPU, one-third memory, and one-third "logic solver." The logic solver was required to solve the scan of the ladder lines faster than we could possibly do with a Von Neumman (Von Neumman was the legendary MIT math professor) machine.

This was the first parallel processor. The I/O was mapped directly into the memory in a "shadow" format. We used core, which was a big no-no at the time. Volatile memory was still unproven. (Ironically, today we would consider core not a problem.) The competitive memories were "rope"—a wire core with the wired configuration representing the compiled code. We equipped the machine with the biggest core memory we could find because it needed maximum energy per bit; physics helped here because we wanted the maximum energy per bit to follow Shannon's basic laws. Early machines were subjected to the spark from a Tesla coil to test the resistance to environmental electrical variance.

We reduced the software time to six days from the normal six months, because the installation time was the wiring time. The academics still don't know what happened, and they ignored the solution for a long time. The people that had the problem were best suited to handle the solution. We gave them the means.

Within that year, we incorporated a separate company called Modicon, which was the MOdular DIgital CONtroller, and we were on our way. The Modicon 084 evolved from these efforts. The name 084 came from the fact that the device's job number at Bedford Associates—the consulting firm and parent incubator of Modicon, the corporation—was the eighty-fourth product.

Even then, we were egocentric and arrogant—we assumed that Bedford Associates would have at least 999 projects, and we used three-digit nomenclature—hence the number 084. So the Modicon 084 stands for a Modular Digital Controller designed by Bedford Associates as its eighty-fourth project.

FEEDING THE MACHINE

The story of our inability to attract venture capitalists or investors has been told so often it has passed into controller mythology. It's the same story with all good technology—there was a need, not a plan, that led to the birth of the PLC. Dad told me, "Son, I'd rather you be lucky than smart!" The PLC was a good piece of luck!

It was the beginning of a long line of next-generation controllers. The first device, the 084, reduced the software design time from six months to six days. We met most of our New Year's resolutions, and succeeded in giving the people who had the shop-floor problem—the ones best suited to solve it—the means. In fact, the invention of the PLC enabled the Toyota revolution. The academics continued to ignore us.

The first product, the 084, proved the concept and established the market. Thirty years after that first New Year's Day, I was awarded the Prometheus Award by the Franklin Institute for my work developing the PLC.

—RICHARD E. MORLEY

Software Implications from the PLC Breakthrough

Software is much of manufacturing's current problem, but it also holds most of the opportunities in technology advances. Currently, all our high-tech products have 80 percent or more software content, and typical products no longer contain the algorithms or performance criteria in the hardware that we worked with twenty years ago. The hardware is general purpose and contains processors, memory and I/O.

Production of specialized hardware for specific markets has been replaced by specialized software supported by general-purpose hardware. Even in the areas of servo controls, numerical controls, disk diagnostic equipment, power or communications devices, the hardware is similar—a box—and the software becomes the application-specific part of the product. More powerful computers and bigger memories have allowed us to do almost any kind of algorithmic manipulation that we want on generic hardware.

The PLC Is Still *Not* a Computer . . .

Discrete parts manufacturing in an automotive environment—mass production—is the mainstay of the programmable controller industry. But back in 1968 when the PLC was detailed, the device was targeted for other markets—machine tools, grinders, lathes, turning machines.

When the first PLC, the 084, was transported to Bryant Chuck and Grinder in Springfield, Vermont, in the trunk of co-author Morley's 1962 Pontiac, reliability was a key selling point. Even the appearance of robustness, in the pioneering days of temperamental electronic boxes, was encouraged. At his first glimpse of this device, the Bryant customer exclaimed, "Thank God it's not another piece of pastel colored sheet metal." Later customers, including Landis and GM, accidentally drop-tested the equipment's on-site robustness. At one plant installation, as Bedford engineers carried the device over the threshold for a new installation, they tripped, and two hundred-plus pounds of heavy metal and memory hit the concrete. But no environmental shock—heat, humidity, or slippery fingers—felled the device. There were no on-off switches, no redundant systems or error checking. The machine was built to work anywhere.

Sales in the first four years were abysmal. Toyota immediately latched on to the idea, while it took until 1986 for Ford to adopt PLCs. GM was an early adopter, but the industrial sales cycle for many other customers stretched to six or seven years. Transfer lines and other process automation applications beckoned. Software and memory expanded from 1k to 4k; the introduction of the third board, a ladder logic solver board, speeded up processing.

Simplicity and Lean Manufacturing, Software's Biggest Challenge

Not all manufacturing innovations have, like the PLC, simplified life on the floor. Many factors have conspired to build complexity in manufacturing, and these forces are difficult to reverse—union management labor restrictions, the rule book, archaic purchasing practices, a "MacJobs" approach to filling critical positions on the floor, nontechnical CEOs, and bad code. Manufacturing managers' fascination with software solutions (or perhaps their gullibility) led to the million-dollar extremes of the eighties' Factory of the Future sham. Normally rational companies such as GE and Pratt & Whitney erected "lights out" Factories of the Future filled with very sophisticated and inflexible computers, robots, automated warehouses, conveyors, guided vehicles, and squads of repair technicians and maintenance people. In the unfortunate case of the GE facility, when the primary aircraft orders dropped off, the factory could only continue to run spares. It was a story of too much automation, too soon.

The software industry is a complexity generator. Software vendors shilling MRP I, II, III, ERP, creativity tools, endless Internet links, Web sites, and other McNamarian approaches to managing the replication function have traumatized and set back many simple manufacturing operations. And what these vendors have failed to do, proprietary software has done—Apollo Computer, Data General, and Digital (now Compaq) attempted to control customers by clinging to their particular narrow versions of software solutions. It should be obvious that the best way to get rid of software problems is to reduce the lines of code—build a bigger bulldozer, and eliminate the need to dig.

In the United States the time it takes to generate code for a fully documented, debugged project is about one line of code per hour per engineer. There are of course, exceptions, but in general, one person can create about three thousand lines of finished high-level code per year, or three thousand lines of equivalent assembler source lines per month. Therefore, to squeeze the most value out of an engineer, one must make each line of code do as much "work" as possible.

But as computer languages become "high-level," the productivity of the programmer/engineer increases exponentially. We learned that reality from a project RMI completed for the Balsams Resort in New Hampshire when we cut development time by over 50 percent without bringing in a team of software engineers, by using a few very good people and a high-level language.

If houses were built like software projects, a single woodpecker could destroy civilization.

The second major software challenge that has not gone away since the PLC breakthrough is reliability, or the robustness of code. Software technology has struggled with the problem that if any error occurs, anywhere, the entire system crashes. Some coding approaches are inherently much more reliable, like rule-based languages, or Ladder List, the application-oriented language used in PLCs.

Both these languages have two primary advantages: One is that they are convergent and not divergent. The second is that each segment of code is written on a standalone basis, and has little or no relationship with the rest of the application. The effects of errors are restricted to the nearby related code, because the error is contained and converges toward a single output structure.

Management of software projects is also facilitated by these loosely coupled segments that allow many programmers to easily work on the same problem. One of the reasons that the PLC became so successful is the robustness of the software.

Although technological progress has in the past owed much to achievements in hardware, in the future, success will depend on large software-intensive products, and these products will have tasks and goals much harder to understand than today's hardware-related products. Efficient coding and high-level languages will allow us to pass this hurdle. Programs using 10 million lines of conventional code may not be unusual, and they will not represent an impossible task, because the work will be manageable using robust code developed in very high-level languages. Although hardware has improved by a factor of two each year, software has lagged somewhat, and software breakthroughs, like the PLC, well-designed and delivered, will take us over the next hurdle.

The PLC Versus the PC: An Industrial Application Difference of Personalities

The PLC breakthrough in industrial applications was as significant as more recent breakthroughs achieved by the personal computer in offices. The difference in technologies explains why it has been so important for PLC adopters to follow a "noncomputerized" route. It's basically a question of personalities.

The personal computer was first of all designed for humans, with comfortable keyboards, monitors, and telephone connections, all extensions of human capabilities. But humans are, in comparison to computer numeric controlled machines, patient and relatively slow. The PC lends itself well to manipulation of large databases, and because of the human brain's inability to remember large numbers of things, the PC makes access to large database segments easy and memorable.

The PC does, however, contribute to considerable overhead, and by design the PC locates those data elements with mnemonics rather than actual physical location. Computer operating systems and their man-machine interfaces are aimed primarily at the experimenter and the nonprogramming professional; the system can tolerate up to ten-second delays, for example, for a particular interactive query.

But industrial processes are much more demanding. They need responses on the order of 10 to 100 milliseconds to be effective. The PLC was designed specifically to operate in substantially less than 100 milliseconds, with ranges targeted around 10 milliseconds for a typical application. Mechanical processes that have bandwidths and response times on the order of 100 hertz are few and far between—airplane ailerons, pipe valve closings, hole drilling, and other mechanical devices tend to operate at speeds and actions substantially slower than 10 milliseconds, and they are ideal candidates for management by the PLC. Or, at 100 cycles per second, the response time will be the equivalent of one revolution every turn of the gasoline or internal combustion engine running at 6,000 RPM. There are some industrial applications, such as coil winding and bottle filling, that may operate faster, but these are the exception rather than the rule.

So the PLC makes sense for heavy industrial applications because it is real-time and simple.

Another measure of the technology of the PLC breakthrough is in clocktime. "Lumps" of control energy can only occur in a sixty-hertz line every eight milliseconds. This, of course, is far beneath the conception rate of the human, and it is the power sampling rate or baud rate for control applications in general.

The history of alternating current (AC) had historically been centered on the frequency used as the power line cycled itself, a principle derived historically from several items—perceptibility to human eyes, the change in light bulbs, the available transformer technology, and the ability to run motors at reasonable speeds. The sixteen-millisecond full-cycle time has served us well considering the big changes in the control industry.

Humans, however, have a clock rate of approximately seven hertz, and an impatient cycle time on the order of three seconds. It is not unusual, for example, when running a spreadsheet or word-processing program, to wait several seconds for an adequate response to happen under a complicated command. It is also not unusual to issue a print command simultaneously, and there may be another small delay. Generally, humans have the characteristics of complexity, with plenty of time to perform tasks in, whereas real-time industrial control applications require that many things happen very quickly, each in itself quite simple indeed.

Modifications of existing computer operating systems, UNIX, and other languages are compromises, at best, for industrial applications. What is needed for computers in industry is a predictable, fast, multitasking application package that runs real-time processes. These operating systems can sample many components of a problem and dispatch them appropriately with ease—the control or software module is not the problem. The problem is the number of modules that simultaneously must work over the environment of industrial control. This capability is beginning to be addressed, but in an environment prone to enormous complexity and multitasking industrial applications, it remains a challenge.

> *Simplify. Take all of the noise out of the system.*
> *Use the heijunka box to take the waves out,*
> *level the schedule back into the supply base.*
> *Be super responsive and flexible.*
>
> —JIM WOMACK, FOUNDER OF THE LEAN
> ENTERPRISE INSTITUTE AND CO-AUTHOR OF
> *THE MACHINE THAT CHANGED THE WORLD,*
> AND *LEAN THINKING.*

Jim Womack, president of the Lean Enterprise Institute and co-author of the breakthrough book *The Machine That Changed the World,* is working hard to highlight the potential for lean manufacturing. Lean manufacturing is a "next step" that we hope, combined with intelligent use of systems and new people systems, will carry manufacturing closer to the vision of 2020. Such companies as Hartford, Connecticut's Wiremold, several Pratt & Whitney installations, Louisville, Kentucky's Lantech, Maytag, and Pella are taking Womack's wisdom to heart. Deriving some of their kaizen-like approaches to manufacturing improvement from the teachings of such gurus as Anand Sharma, Shingijutsu,

Maasaki Imai, and Teruyuki Maruo, whose roots extend back to the Toyota Production System and Deming, these leaders want to strip away the accumulated waste and complexity—the *muda*—so visible in most production operations.

Lean thinkers are not averse to automated solutions, however. They happen to understand that to fix the process, they must first clear away bad flows, and they must draw on the intelligence of empowered professionals to design the best process to support the best products. Their very young movement will in twenty years, however, look like baby steps against the huge breakthroughs that electronics and Internet communications will have throughout the Islands of Excellence.

Boeing and Airbus are prime examples of giants who drive complexity down through their entire supply base. When Boeing loaded up on a record number of new orders, and then realized the backlog was unbuildable given its proven capacity, it was saved by the bell—cancellation of many Asian orders due to recession in the Far East. The respite gave Boeing time to either redesign its supply-chain processes or revert to status quo. Two years to make an aircraft is not a technical problem—it's a people and organizational problem long overdue for solutions. We believe the process of building aircraft follows the craftsman tradition: Increased volumes and speeds will test the system, and it will eventually implode.

Unfortunately, Womack's call for a few courageous and creative manufacturing managers may be co-opted by technologies that provide flexibility and speed without massive restructuring of entire operations.

Womack's observation, "It's not capital that is holding back managers from realizing the power of lean manufacturing," is proven by the failed Factory of the Future sites and their cousins. "Fewer than 10 percent of manufacturers are doing it," says Womack, but "it really works." Dan Jones, co-author of *The Machine That Changed the World* and a professor in the United Kingdom, points to several clear measures of progress. "In Europe, one hundred companies regularly reach zero ppm or Six Sigma quality levels where a few years ago there were none. The leaders are Toyota, Honda and Nissan."

FIGURE 4.3

The Continuum of Industrial Intelligence

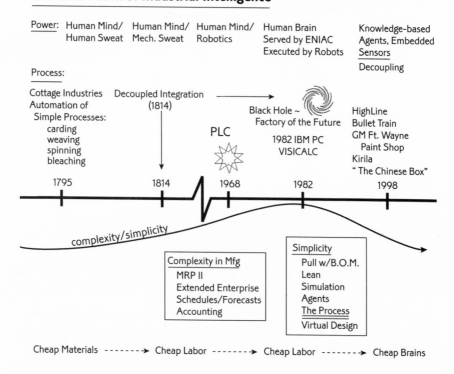

Power:

Human Mind/ Human Sweat	Human Mind/ Mech. Sweat	Human Mind/ Robotics	Human Brain Served by ENIAC Executed by Robots	Knowledge-based Agents, Embedded Sensors

Process:

Cottage Industries
Automation of
Simple Processes:
carding
weaving
spinning
bleaching

Decoupled Integration
(1814)

PLC

Black Hole ~
Factory of the Future
1982 IBM PC
VISICALC

Decoupling

HighLine
Bullet Train
GM Ft. Wayne
Paint Shop
Kirila
"The Chinese Box"

| 1795 | 1814 | 1968 | 1982 | 1998 |

complexity/simplicity

Complexity in Mfg	Simplicity
MRP II	Pull w/B.O.M.
Extended Enterprise	Lean
Schedules/Forecasts	Simulation
Accounting	Agents
	The Process
	Virtual Design

Cheap Materials ------▸ Cheap Labor ------▸ Cheap Labor ------▸ Cheap Brains

Womack advises manufacturing pros to abandon traditional crutches—parts warehouses, nonstandard work methods ("I learned it from Joe—it's different, but it works") and corporate culture. "Parts warehouses are the greatest noise-makers known to man. You must lower your signal to noise ratio. Take the noise and the variation out of the system. And culture is there to be changed!" Devices like the heijunka box, a card system that Toyota uses to schedule production, are offered as alternatives to complex software modules. "Study product families, arrange them in sensible pull flows, and give manufacturing people careers, not jobs."

Level Schedules, Quiet Flows

Bob Arndt, General Motors service parts manager, tells executives that to solve the old problem of neglected manufacturing associates,

"Pick an area, and make it so exciting that people will want to work in that area. The rest will follow." That's culture change. "Give middle management and operating people some success and they start to develop self-esteem."

Womack urges producers to redesign the education process, because a very large part of what passes for education is nonsense, "Unlimited time to learn things of limited use. It's about 'credentialing.'" The answer, he believes, is "to learn in the morning and implement in the afternoon," an approach followed in most hands-on kaizen experiences.

Don't Look Sideways—Compete Against the North Star

Many initiatives around manufacturing will have varied impact on our current surroundings. Several years back, following on the heels of the Baldrige movement, the U.S. government "discovered" that millions of dollars diverted from ARPA and DARPA found their way into a crazy quilt of nonprofit and partly for profit consulting and training groups, with mixed results.

Technology trends that will have significant impact on the best manufacturers of the nineties include modeling, graphical user interface, Dilbert and general management dissatisfaction, the Worldwide Web and its descendants, and intelligent systems. Chaos theory and complex adaptive systems will take over where lean and simplicity initiatives in manufacturing cannot handle all the needs for customer and other variation.

The Worldwide Web will solve some integration problems, and it will introduce new ones as more and more customers and suppliers rush to ship files of different sizes and languages off to each other and to their replication sites. We will continue to see a Tower of Babel against the horizon. The Web will eventually establish a global worldwide standard, as it removes the middleman and facilitates direct selling. Browsers, self-organizing smart systems, linear motors, and exotic drives will turn manufacturing operations upside down and sideways. Real-time on-line control systems, the kind of feedback loops air traffic controllers yearn for, will take the paper productivity and production charts off the walls of thousands of factories around the world, as more and more workers find fewer and fewer uses for their well-skilled hands.

The list of new technologies that will take us from the middle ground of lean and improved manufacturing sites to breakthrough Islands of Excellence includes synthetic materials, autonomous agents, rule-based browsing viruses, self-organizing smart systems, and embedded sensors.

Future factories are bounded by MES (Manufacturing Execution Systems) that will draw on each of these technologies to cut process costs by 30 percent or more as they guarantee perfect quality and immediate flexibility synchronized with customer cycles. Remember, single-point technologies—fanatical dedication to a single technical fad (MRP or neural nets or fuzzy logic, or even artificial intelligence)—don't work. Watch for the combined power of every speed accelerator, every electronic messenger/gatepost, as the smart competitors leapfrog decades ahead of their competition.

5

Intelligent Systems
that Will Get Us There—
Chaos, Complex Adaptive Systems,
and Other Enabling Technologies

HAIKU FOR INTELLIGENT SYSTEMS

The water ripples

Silence rules

The machine

Thinks quietly

Seeing nothing

The machine stops

Hearing everything

It unplugs and flies away

—PEMoody@aol.com

The Road to The Barn

After the state road, it's all uphill, following the Harley through the backwoods of New Hampshire to the future of manufacturing control systems housed in The Barn. The Barn is a sturdy red building dug into a hillside bounded by stone walls and maples that have recovered what one hundred years ago was cow and sheep grazing land. All that's left of these businesses is Shattuck's Maple Barn, a raw-planks and sugaring-off barn/restaurant a few miles south.

At the flashing yellow lights, I turned onto Stone Road and followed a dirt road to Starch Mill Road, past more industrial ruins, the remains of a nineteenth-century starch mill. My two-wheel-drive vehicle started to really pick up speed and we flew down Sand Pit Road, at this point unpaved, and passed the final landmark, the town ballfield—a gift of a high-tech townie. Could this be the road to the future? The only other vehicle in sight was a front-end loader, and it wasn't talking. Even the car phone had stopped receiving.

MUD SEASON IN NEW HAMPSHIRE

The problems of process control and manufacturing in general are as complex and subtle as those found in meteorology, biology, and other sciences. But there are answers at The Barn, a place where software and creativity come together to plot the future of manufacturing. The Barn is RMI's "corporate headquarters," a rough-hewn think tank surrounded by stone walls, maples, and birches, and on summer evenings, swarms of mosquitoes. Visitors to The Barn like to stay to explore innovation in systems that will become the brains of Manufacturing 2020. No one comes away with all the answers, but everyone catches a glimpse of the future. We've pioneered lean, agile, flexible, empowered, and JIT manufacturing. What's next?

ADVENTURES IN INTELLIGENT SYSTEMS

Visitors to The Barn learn to see the progress of manufacturing as a continuum, a series of companies, each representing a level of maturity concomitant with its age. It's the infrastructure that counts. The systems integration of all the single-point technology is the key to the future.

• AEG Schneider Automation (Modicon, Square D, Telemecanique), of North Andover, Massachusetts, a few hours south of The Barn, is the mature thirty-year-old.
• Andover Controls, another of co-author Morley's "babies," of which he was technical founder, is now a young adult.
• And the youngster is Flavors Technology of Manchester, New Hampshire, a software innovation house where advanced technologies are created, located in the old Amoskeag textile complex on the Merrimack River.

The Barn, headquarters for all this innovation and more, is deceptively digitized with a completely computer-controlled environmental management system and a generous assortment of various hardware / software products. It is the Future.

All of us in manufacturing, given two minutes to reflect on the past twenty or thirty years of growth, downsizing, and restructuring, would agree that we have zigzagged an uneven path leading from extreme complexity and MIS addictions, an operations-management approach to solving every problem with little human input, to JIT oversimplification. Manufacturing is now at a crossroad. And intelligent computer systems, intelligent agents, and other breakthroughs are the next road. Computers now occupy a different seat in the manufacturing plant, as does human capital. Computers and industrial automation will continue to make manufacturing more:

- Decentralized
- Asynchronous
- Agent-based and -managed
- Self-organizing

Intelligent systems are simple extensions of previously separate and apparently complex systems. Complexity theory is an emerging interdisciplinary science that strives to uncover the underlying principles governing complex systems and the emergent properties they exhibit. These systems are found in the natural world as well as the manufacturing sector; in fact, there are many parallels between manufacturing processes and the way flocks of birds self-organize and the way termites and ants build hills. The natural world illustrates the independent-agent approach we envision for Manufacturing 2020. Other applications of complexity theory include supply-chain optimization and development of self-organizing and self-managing networks.

What Is a Complex Adaptive System?

Murray Gell-Mann, Nobel-prize-winning physicist and founder of the Santa Fe Institute, looks to the origins of the word *complex* to define the term—from the Latin, *plexus,* or braided, and *plicare,* to fold. Literally, simplex means once-folded, and the word complex means braided together. Says Gell-Mann:

> We are interested in the relation between the simple underlying laws of nature, and the complex phenomena of which we are a part. When we call something complex, we don't mean random. The description

can always be converted into a string of 0's and 1's. What are these systems that identify perceived irregularities, distinguishing them from what is perceived as random and compressing their description into a brief message? I call them Complex Adaptive Systems.

A complex adaptive system takes in a stream of data about the world, including itself, including its previous behavior and the consequences. All the regularities that it remarks in that data stream, it compresses into a schema (model), a highly compressed description. The schema can undergo change and mutation; it can combine with additional data from the real world and be used for prediction of behavior in the real world, because all of these will have real world consequences. And these consequences of the real world feedback to exert selection pressure among the competition. (From Santa Fe "Chaos in Manufacturing Conference," Santa Fe, New Mexico, April 1998)

The schema must have some degree of stability or robustness, must give rise to competition, and there must be a feedback loop. All examples of complex adaptive systems are connected to life somehow, but they have a tendency to give rise to another complex adaptive system. Gell-Mann explains the parallels in life development:

Four billion years ago there must have been a prebiotic chemical evolution that gave way to biological evolution and organisms, that led to mammalian immune systems and individual learning and thinking, and then human culture evolution, the evolution of organizations, evolution of the global economy, and then evolution of computers that on their own can be their own complex adaptive systems. So, computer-based complex adaptive systems are connected to life systems by the nerds that make them.

Other researchers are developing applications via software that reads and adapts to environmental changes. Applications for manufacturing are slow in coming, but the movement has started. Stephanie Forrest at the University of New Mexico and the Santa Fe Institute is developing software that is analogous to virus fighters in computers; her system is a complex adaptive system.

Gell-Mann's definition of chaos—the situation in which the outcome of a process is extremely sensitive to the tiniest detail change— clarifies that in a business environment when we talk about chaos theory, or chaos applications, we are really talking about management of variables. In complex operations such as manufacturing or supply-chain management, in which the appearance of a new or unexpected variable can throw an entire project off-course, we look to computers to help put order into management of the universe of variables that appear every hour.

Complex Adaptive Systems

Bruce Abell, managing director of the Santa Fe Center for Emergent Strategies, believes businesses are complex adaptive systems (CAS):

> Businesses may benefit from being more like natural complex adaptive systems that are inherently adaptive. So CAS is not something that business needs, but something that it already is. Business needs to understand how it is a complex adaptive system, how it operates as a CAS, and how it can improve its operations by recognizing that.

And although businesses have a tendency to become momentarily fascinated with short-lived fads—re-engineering, for example—Abell believes that enterprises need that perspective to survive in a competitive environment.

A number of factors doom the business dinosaurs—shrunken communications time and distance, lowered international barriers and more different types of customers, more global competitors, and more capital. Abell calls the mismatch of global enterprise requirements to slow-moving, entrenched organizations "a Newtonian metabolism in a Darwinian world." Mismatches abound:

Sears/Wal-Mart
GM/Honda
AT&T/MCI

The internal conflict between these companies is between rigid, unresponsive central planning and flexible, localized intelligence. GM,

FIGURE 5.1

ATTRIBUTES OF ALL COMPLEX ADAPTIVE SYSTEMS

Interacting agents
Emergent phenomena
Distributed control
Open environment
Probabilistic events
Nonequilibrium, nonlinear
Adaptive, coevolving
Self-regulating

for example, takes longer to design and introduce new products than does Honda, probably because the newcomer's organization runs more like a SWAT team than a centralized organization. Wal-Mart runs on speed—information and transaction speed, as well as variety and low cost—a formula the entrenched Sears concept would be hard-pressed to copy.

In nature, metabolisms coevolved with environments—not so with businesses. Mismatches of slow internal pace and fast external pace will continue to hold back global competitors. Abell believes that even though companies may be capable of sustaining a perfectly high-running operational metabolism, they are still held back by what he calls slow cognitive metabolism. He urges managers to recognize that companies are ideas—the source of the cognitive framework—and that complex adaptive systems hold potential to bolster the company's response time and power around innovation and creative applications.

The movement to "localize" intelligence presupposes systems that follow their logical rules to "read" and adapt their behavior to their own particular environment, as it changes and moves. As companies shift their focus to incorporate intelligence in all their systems, they will find that the agents themselves find and adapt entire systems to different local demands. In areas of product variety, market shifts, and manufacturing process selections, localized intelligence will always win over central planning and delayed response schemes.

Autonomous Agents in 2020

The Chapter 1 story about the Boston Yellow Cab cruising Logan Airport at 7:00 P.M. Friday, looking to pick up one last fare, is the story of a living intelligent agent in motion. The driver makes decisions on the spot—as an intelligent agent he screens the landscape and evaluates all possibilities. He makes each ride decision without direction from Central Dispatch. It's a faster—and less stressful—approach to running the business.

FIGURE 5.2 *Boston Yellow Cab*

© R. Morley Inc.

There are as many variables involved in running this "personal transportation unit"—airline schedules, weather, amount of luggage, currency exchanges, and the airport traffic police—as there are in any manufacturing operation. It's a complex system beautifully suited to management by autonomous agents.

The taxicab system has a significant, although small, number of important rules of behavior:

- Go to the shortest line
- Pick up someone at the side of the road
- Respond and bid on dispatcher's requirements

The autonomous intelligent agent in the 2020 factory must be as fast, smart, and flexible as a Boston cabbie. And the factory operations must be as quick, flexible, and responsive as the best Boston traffic dodgers.

Chaos and Emergent Behavior

EMERGENT PROPERTIES/EMERGENT BEHAVIOR

Imagine an airplane that flies itself, constantly making adjustments based on what it "sees" ahead. The alternative to this type of real-time on-line direction control is the air traffic controller. If the controller could maintain constant communication with the plane's pilot, and if the craft's electronics were fully capable, massive amounts of data would be transferred between the cockpit and the control tower, as weather, fuel, and other conditions caused changes in route and speed. Not particularly responsive—for any reaction to take place, the aircraft must be directed by the tower—this image is not unlike the way many manufacturing operations have run for hundreds of years.

But what happens when intelligence is embedded directly in the aircraft? The plane begins to fly itself, taking readings from the weather, from its onboard sensors, and from its own navigational equipment. The only time the craft is required to "check in" with the central tower is when it wants to announce a location or an arrival. Simplistically, this is the approach to embedding intelligence in individual entities—aircraft, cutting machines, molders—that will make the factory almost hands-free.

The Science of Complexity

In the Dark Ages, everyone "knew" the earth was the center of the universe, but when Copernicus "stood on the sun," he countered a universally accepted belief. Taking more measurements—more data, not wisdom—failed to modify his concept. The word planet means "wanderer," and when the astronomers/scientists also finally took up their own imaginary positions on the sun, they began to understand, not from data, but from thought, that the sun, not our earth, is the center of our local universe. If only we stand away and think, we will begin to understand our position in the manufacturing universe.

Einstein's statement that the speed of light is constant, independent of where we stand, explains many other phenomena. It's a matter of wisdom—accepting a huge paradigm shift, with or without data, and proceeding from there.

The first use of fire, gunpowder, computers, sailing upwind, phosphorus matches, and Federal Express were all equally powerful shifts. Humans in the midst of change, whose vision is extremely limited and blurry on the periphery, become blockers and doubters. As parents, for example, we are too close to understand our own children, although their growth and movement away from us is obvious to others. Likewise, we are in the midst of technology revolutions around dynamic systems, chaos theory applications, complexity, emergent systems, and artificial life that all provoke discomfort in the linear thinking zone.

Intelligence Applications in the Factory

In the United States there are some wonderful young examples of de-centralized, agent-based, self-organizing production systems. These applications appear in the GM Paint Shop, in various steel-processing and metal-coating applications, in composites, agricultural equipment, and the Japanese bullet trains. Further, there are many smaller, significant developments in simulation and complex adaptive systems that are accumulating to change the way we organize and leverage complex global operations. J. Howell Mitchell, principal engineer at Flavors Technology, a third-generation manufacturing intelligence company, believes the intelligent paint shop in Fort Wayne, Indiana, was one of them.

Embracing Complexity: The GM Fort Wayne Paint Shop

In 1986 co-author Dick Morley began a project that years later would be hailed as a breakthrough business application in a growing field of study. His deceptively simple task was to paint trucks; his approach would serve as a case study for concrete, bottom-line applications of complexity theory. His solution allowed companies attempting complex, top-down scheduling routines to sweep away traditional approaches to scheduling assembly lines.

Small changes can effect big results. GM found, for example, that the new science of complexity theory applied to a small part of its business—truck painting in an Indiana plant—reaped significant savings. What appeared to be a very straightforward task—painting truck bodies—however, is embedded with scheduling complexity, with at worst, unpredictable results. Morley believes that complexity theory and its cousins—chaotic systems, emergent properties, complex adaptive systems, and complexity from simplicity—were all there in the paint shop, and he believed that just as these far-flung theories would find logical applications in biology and medicine, so would they work in manufacturing.

PROGRAMMING *BEHAVIOR*, NOT STATES

Industrial plant technology has progressed through many stages, including logic control, relays, transistors, minicomputers, programmable controllers, and cellular manufacturing. But no matter how good or how reliable the technology and its applications, complexity prevents humans from knowing all the states a system will be in. The implication, of course, is that complex systems—paint shops, weather forecasting, fast-food rush hours—cannot be programmed because by definition the outcome of such systems is unpredictable.

ADAPTIVE SYSTEMS

We have no choice but to fit the system to the problem—make a Mc-Donald's hamburger system that delivers consistent combinations of fast food fast, or build superb communications facilities into the front end of each weather watch system. The idea is to substitute speed and flexibility and localized intelligence for remote-controlled "brains" based on history or some other inflexible protocol.

DESIGN RULES

Adaptive systems fit the system to the problem. Co-author Morley has been a foster parent to over twenty-seven children, and his concept of raising children who behave well parallels his approach to running a complex production facility. Good kids are not programmed to be doctors or lawyers, but they are instilled with general behavior principles—clean up your room, eat your spaghetti and *then* dessert, finish your homework. Then, depending on other stimuli, they might become doctors, lawyers, truck drivers, or housewives: We program their behavior, not their destination.

Applying these same assumptions to truck painting operations, Morley's team had to persuade GM "not to program or describe *what* is going to happen but *how* to make it happen." Essentially, Morley was asking GM production management to enter what was for them a very unnatural state—to trust the process.

There is an interesting lesson in the GM story about reducing complexity in software: In terms of performance and speed, the marginal cost of the painting hardware was vanishing, but "the software was killing us," said one executive contemplating the change. The RMI team assumed, therefore, that if they could program the paint modules' behavior, they could reduce the software and improve performance. But any program had to accommodate the many variables that made truck-painting a pain.

THE PROBLEM WITH PAINTING

"Fit and finish" is a critical issue in motor vehicles, because consumers don't make purchase choices on the basis of utility alone. Customers expect a sport utility truck, for example, to look cosmetically good, really good. But at GM, where the truck business was high-margin, the high cost of paint and the complexity of scheduling paint jobs of trucks moving down the line seemed to make any viable and worthwhile solution impossible—the challenge was not merely color choice and line speed.

Painting requires propellant—air—a controlled environment, regulated truck body temperature, only three minutes, and only one pass. Yet, due to routine maintenance and unplanned stoppages—schedule interruptions, they're called—Morley observed that "many paint shops' typical state is 'line down.'" Or the paint gun is clogged, the truck is not ready, the pressure is wrong, or the painting modules are being repaired or reprogrammed. And further, the trucks do not march down the line in order of their color; frequently no booth with the correct color will be available. Scheduling is a nightmare.

"HOW DO I SCHEDULE SOMETHING THAT IS UNSCHEDULABLE?"

The solution Morley and his team arrived at was to force the scheduling program to interact with the paint booths themselves—"to go direct"—a real departure from GM's traditional, top-down scheduling process. Rather than assigning paint jobs to booths, GM's solution was to have the booths bid on paint jobs. The Morley team called this technique pull-through scheduling, as opposed to push-through; but the idea was even more revolutionary than other manufacturing approaches to pull scheduling based on kan ban (card) systems.

The GM installation put the intelligence on the floor, in the paint booth, not up in the mezzanine, by using a bidding process in the software that leapfrogged all other scheduling methods. Further, the most challenging scheduling activity in a multiline paint operation—changeovers and setups—was minimized as the software iteratively reviewed and worked the sequencing of various models and colors, to keep the guns running. The paint shop is a very specialized operation that typically becomes an assembly plant bottleneck, because all assembly lines—all colors and models—feed into an area that has almost no control over the mix of vehicle types, colors, and quantities. And when a vehicle is pulled off the line for a quality check or quality fix, the sequence that would have been painstakingly developed in a daily schedule is destroyed.

CHICKEN BRAINS IN THE BOOTHS AND FLEXIBLE SCHEDULING ON THE FLOOR

To allow the paint booths to interact with the scheduling program, the team equipped each booth with a "chicken brain," that is, simple logic based on a few rules of behavior. Each was programmed to keep busy and to bid on each job based on its ability to do it. The lines were locally selfish, and they tried to keep running at minimum expense.

BIDDING

Here's the way the logic works: As the virtual job list posts the available trucks, a booth will look at the list and ask whether it includes any jobs identical to the one the booth is currently finishing. If it sees none, it will look for "red tag" items. If no priority job is posted, then the booth will bid—low—on any available job, perhaps prioritized by proximity to the booth or time to finishing its current job.

From the scheduler's perspective, the scenario begins with a decision point when a truck arrives and the program tells the booths, "I have a truck that needs to be black." A booth already loaded with black paint and near the end of its current job will bid very high for the black truck. A booth with another color, but almost empty, will bid slightly lower. A booth that is further away, filled with red paint, broken down, or otherwise less suited for the job will bid lower still. Based on the outcome of this virtual bidding war, the scheduler will assign the truck to the highest-bidding paint booth.

The agents operate with three simple behavioral rules: take the easy job, the important job, or any job. Of course the bidding, or what could be called an iterative sequencing schedule process, happens in nanoseconds: There is no paper involved, and the same scheduling problem would probably take humanoid wetware three to four weeks' calculation time, with no changes or interruptions factored into a very static and completely unrealistic schedule. Humanoid schedule routines would compensate for delays, unexpected changes, and setup problems by scheduling extra units or extra paint booth run times to cover disruptions, a very expensive approach to automotive cost control. Assembly lines in technologically advanced North American plants typically cost twenty-six thousand dollars per minute of downtime; scheduling assembly lines to run extra vehicles to cover for downstream problems or mix shifts is an expensive alternative to flexible scheduling.

FACILITATING FACTORS AT GM

Looking back, team leaders acknowledge that this first breakthrough system was installed under unique circumstances. They needed a plant with a benign union, they grappled with billing and cold-air problems, and they had to find a budget from which they could squeeze money. And they needed a local culture that would allow them to take time and risks: The platform design was not completed until 1988, beta test was delivered in December 1990, and the PIM (Parallel Inference Machine) was finally installed in the plant in 1991. (The Parallel Inference Machine is another Morley invention that uses cache memory to speed processing.)

And there were surprises along the way. "The difficulty is that I never knew what was going to happen," Morley remembers. Once in a while, the bidding model would actually take longer than the old scheduling program, for example. Nevertheless, the new schedule applied assets optimally overall, "Not rocket science, but it is upside down behavior," with no overriding control, *four lines* of computer code, and paint booths run by chicken brains.

Gregg Ekberg, current president of Highline Controls, Inc., a system integrator and factory floor automation and controls company, knows firsthand the benefits of autonomous agents in manufacturing. Ekberg spent fourteen years at GM in operations, maintenance, and engineering, and he describes himself as "a nerd with his feet on the ground." Ekberg is also part-owner of Falcon ColdForming, a tier-one and -two supplier to GM, Ford, and Parker Hannifin. Ekberg is the golden boy of intelligent systems, an electrical engineer with a computer science degree, an early adopter of simple approaches to what could be translated into complex manufacturing process problems.

Ekberg was project manager at the Fort Wayne operation in the pioneering 1991 installation of the paint booth and the paint application control at GM's truck assembly plant. His experience at GM led him to develop a series of similar systems for smaller operations. Ekberg's current business focus is a bridge between the pioneering paint shop applications and smaller company requirements for repetitive, flexible scheduling routines.

GM FORT WAYNE PAINT SHOP RESULTS

The Fort Wayne installation produced strong results, and it was the proving ground for intelligent systems in manufacturing. The paint shop generated $2 million in annual material savings from the feed-back control on the plant flow; the air supply house control was moved from a PLC to the PIM, with a 40 percent reduction in the number of lines of code instructions (lines of code, or LOC, were re-duced from hundreds of lines of codes to just four), and the control software was remarkable for being electrician—not engineer—sup-ported. Simplicity in the heart of complexity.

Additional project costs were minimized because the actual devel-opment of the code to control paint flow parameters and environ-mental conditions took four days, and six days were required to com-mission the installation. A paint shop is a delicate balance of factors that are in themselves difficult to control—temperature, humidity, downdraft, paint flow, atomization, and air. The control system that was in place to control the air supply house (temperature, humidity, downdraft) was complex and not very stable. The simplicity of the PIM solution allowed the process engineers to better control the paint process. Further, no solution was previously available for the paint flow rate and air pressures (atomization and fan), so just the standard feedback control of these parameters resulted in a reduction of material use for each truck body.

J. Howell Mitchell, former president of Flavors, characterized the paint shop as a combination of a typical and "traditional industrial ap-plication" and an autonomous agent scheduler—"the GM Paint Shop Autonomous Agent System was a solution to a difficult, multifactor production problem." Paint and other costing operations—such as chrome plating on Harley Davidson motorcycle operations—typically challenge auto and appliance producers because under the best of conditions, doing changeovers and running lot-size-of-one flexible schedules is next to impossible with traditional scheduling and changeover tools. Something always has to give—either cosmetically perfect quality, or economical and efficient sequencing of colors. Nis-san's Smyrna, Tennessee, plant is a showcase of high-quality, environ-mentally correct paint operations, but it does not feature chaos soft-ware of the Fort Wayne plant's type. Many industries continue to fight the conflict between maximizing schedules, with minimum changeover lost time, and meeting customer demand for every color but black. Added to the complexity is the practice of many large as-semblers of sending certain components and assemblies out to spe-cialized processing plants for specific plating or painting operations. Although contracting out these operations may have technically made sense, they tend to create chaos in the schedules. Transporting and tracking materials adds logistics and inventory costs and usually leads to some sort of quality issue.

It is difficult for humans, given the chemistry of the paint process, to design an absolutely flexible and economical system. But the Fort Wayne, Indiana, plant was a breakthrough. In GM's Fort Wayne Paint Shop truck bodies—all varieties, all colors—were conveyed in single file to the shop, where they were dispatched into one of ten booths. From there, the paint booth scheduler software determined how best to dispatch the various GM pickups.

Mitchell called this an "intelligent approach to processing time/ queue size restraints," and it was a breakthrough because it minimized blowout, changing from red to green paint barrels, for example, that are located a fair distance away. And the system cut changeover labor and material costs and improved plant productivity downstream.

Baseline code to control paint flow, fan air, and atomization air was developed in four days. This initial code was tested at Flavors Technology back in New Hampshire, with equipment similar to what would be encountered in the plant—Allen-Bradley input/output, fluid flow (water), and a robotic spray head. The code was tuned based on actual observations of the mockup.

After the system software was cleared for installation, the entire system was installed over a period of six days at Fort Wayne assembly on one line, in one booth with four paint robots. Data were collected on quality and what GM refers to as "film builds." Because of the variance in viscosity and environmental behavior, film build readings were taken and evaluated for each color. Engineers determined that the code was "doing good stuff" and the application was then rolled out to the next four robots in that same booth—eight robots per booth, four to paint and four to clearcoat.

The results were again evaluated, this time primarily for finish, and over the course of the year the program was rolled out to the other nine booths. Installation and debugging took a quick couple of days, with programming done by a union electrician on the floor. The PIM Beta Test, the first installation and verification of the PIM in an industrial application, lasted one year. The test was successfully concluded at the end of a year, when the plant chose to purchase the solution and support it internally without external support.

The electricians ran the equipment for six years without hardware or software failure, and not once did installers get called back for maintenance. The program's database, which is transparent to the user, was on disk. Written by six Flavors Technology people in four years, the package payback was 4X over a year in material savings alone.

A second function of the paint booth's autonomous agent was to control paint and air flow, real-time, for the robotic guns—four per booth, each managed to three parameters (two air and one paint). A control panel displayed the status of each run, along with some miscellaneous control functions. GM chose not to deploy the scheduling functionality as it would have cost fifty thousand to seventy-five thousand dollars in extra sensor costs.

THE PAINT SHOP BREAKTHROUGH

Ernie Vahala, a visionary president of the Auto Body Consortium and a forty-three-year GM veteran, feels that the Fort Wayne shop contributed far beyond its quality improvement benchmarks to the development of intelligent software in the manufacturing world. "Traditional, deductive engineering approaches could not have dealt with all the variables, but this system eliminated," he says, "95 percent of traditional software engineering." The control functions were done over Allen-Bradley remote input/output, and the display across the ten lines was done with Appletalk. Simple, but revolutionary.

WHY AUTONOMOUS AGENTS PREVAILED

This type of autonomous agent software application differs from other software projects in several notable ways:

1. The applications are more modular, putting the flexibility and intelligence anywhere it is needed.

2. The software and its supporting hardware are designed to juggle massive amounts of data. Storage capacities are not at issue; neither are response times for data retrieval and processing.

3. The system deals with the behavior as described by software, rather than fixed states that are described by software. This approach reduces the amount of software code—less software handles less complexity.

Second-Generation Intelligent Agent Systems

Ten years later, other simple software applications at SteelWorks and Shane Steel Processing directed by Ekberg are succeeding in taking more complexity out of manufacturing process controls. Ekberg's company, Highline Controls, designs new machines by breaking the tasks to be completed down into the smallest resource possible. He calls these discrete elements "agents," and they can be a switch or a sensor. His philosophy is to not worry about the overwhelming complexity of variables, but to do the programming one step at a time, focusing on the agents' behavior.

SteelWorks, One Step at a Time

SteelWorks is a Des Moines, Iowa, manufacturer of metal filing cabinets. The factory makes 260 units per hour, a fast chain speed. Company revenues total $100 million annual sales; products include filing cabinets for the office and home office markets. Products are two-, three-, and four-drawer, legal and letter width (eighteen and twenty-two inches deep); the typical order rate is five thousand two-drawer units per day.

According to director of operations Randy Kroh, the paint system had two paint booths, and it was difficult for production to paint three sides, the top, and some drawers, and "there was a lot going on in a small space. We could not dedicate parts of the equipment to specific parts of the process, and so we had lots of rework, and poor transfer efficiency."

How bad is "poor transfer efficiency"? Kroh remembers that rework was running at about 20 percent, a definite cost problem.

SteelWorks wanted to rebuild its two-booth paint system into a five-booth facility. Ekberg's proposal was to write the controls for the system, following SteelWork's parameters of combining old and new equipment. Following a meeting with Ekberg and Midway Industrial, the group doing the booth work and equipment setup, the concept was further defined and agreed upon. The company wanted to change how parts were identified. Previously parts had been identified one at a time; with the new system, the parts would be identified in front of each booth, an anticipated big improvement in accuracy.

Resources involved in the paint process include applicators, a high-voltage power pack, a color changer, system air pressure, conveyors, the booth, and an oscillator to move the guns.

PAINLESS CHANGEOVERS

Tony Oberman, manufacturing engineer at SteelWorks, remembers, "The change to a five-booth system was remarkably painless." Ekberg disappeared with the PLC. After about six weeks of phone calls, faxes, and e-mails between the plant and Highline, he returned and downloaded the new PLC program. He had also completed the supporting electrical engineering plan, and when they turned on the power, it all worked as planned. Small changes in the program to accommodate different cabinet lengths—Gregg used front and back adders to change the dimensions—were simple. Changeover downtime became a faint memory. Four buttons change product configuration from two- to four-drawer; in a matter of seconds, SteelWorks can make any model change. A process that had previously used two systems—one, a photo system, never seemed to "see" a part right—was also outfitted with a new Allen-Bradley PLC.

FIGURE 5.3

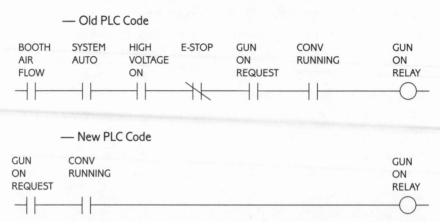

**SteelWorks's Hardware and Software Design
Reduced Complexity and Lines of Code.**

• Complete Design (Hardware & Software)

— Old PLC Code

— New PLC Code

According to Kroh, "The first two to three months were rough. We had some controls problems that had to be ironed out—some programming, and some hardware." SteelWorks did not run a pilot or a simulation before hitting the switch to start the new system, however.

SteelWorks paint application is very simple. Highline did the electrical design, wrote the code, and subcontracted and directed the electrical work. Resources involved in the process include applicators, high-phase power pack, color changer, system air pressure guns, conveyors, booth, and an oscillator to move the guns.

SIMPLICITY EXTENDED THROUGH PHYSICS

Ekberg believes that the SteelWorks application is second- or possibly third-generation PLC work. In the old PLC code, designers would have used relay ladder logic with many steps before the gun would move on. Ekberg considers that too much complexity. Instead, using new PLC code, the gun moves on request, based on a relay.

Ekberg argued for this simpler design, "It works. You are trusting the laws of physics; you didn't have to code it all in the programming." The SteelWorks application illustrates the simplicity of the autonomous agent approach in its control of the gun trigger. In a typical

PLC application the conditions on the same rung to turn on the gun would include checking for air pressure, making sure there is no emergency stop, making sure the system is on automatic, the oscillators are on, and the high voltage is on.

But the gun control with the autonomous agent approach simply becomes a gun on request, with no checks. There is no need to check for air pressure, because if there is none, the gun cannot turn on anyway—it needs air to pull the trigger. There is also no need to check the emergency stop, because if there is one, there will be no air pressure. And there is no need to check for high voltage—paint cannot come out without high-voltage; it is the high voltage unit's responsibility to have high voltage turned on, not the applicators'.

LET THE PROCESS SPEAK

So, rather than cluttering up a control program with safeties and fail-safes and sandbox extensions, Ekberg's approach is to let the simplicity speak by letting the behavioral aspects of any problem manifest themselves in the emergent solution.

SteelWorks showed results remarkably fast: The functional spec was completed in four hours, code was written in two days, and in fifteen days the system was commissioned, with only two bugs. Sixteen hours after the power was turned on, the plant went to full production, with increased ability for future improvements and changes. Further, according to Ekberg, the autonomous agent approach allows easy changes—"We were able to do a cut and paste to add two guns"—a solution unheard-of in the traditional industrial automation days. Designers used the same amount of code to generate a 450 percent increase in functionality.

Rework at SteelWorks is now down to below 5 percent; Kroh believes the target of less than 2 percent is completely achievable. Not every element of the system design, however, is perfect. Ekberg is quick to note the system's weaknesses: Scan time is too slow, causing programmers to do software tricks to get out of long loops on the PLC ("The manufacturing world works with controllers that are pretty limited"). Ekberg is pushing for synchronous parallel processors to handle the scan-time problem.

FIGURE 5.4

THE AUTONOMOUS AGENT APPROACH

• Define Resources and Their Actions
• Define Resource States and Define Variables
• Develop Software to Control Each Resource
  Through Its States and Set Global Variables

Next project on the roster for SteelWorks is in-line real-time diagnostics, supported by another Ekberg application. SteelWorks' highly automated lines will be further enhanced by using sensors to feedback position and other data before a line-down situation occurs.

Shane Steel Processing, Detroit

Shane Steel Processing performs operations in its centerless grinding facility that the steel mills and the auto industry don't want to; Shane is a processor of steel stay bars, spring rounds, and valve steel ground bars, grinding over ten thousand pounds of steel per month for such customers as Delphi Spring, Ford, GM, TRW, and Eaton. The plant straightens, shears, and grinds steel bars, generally working in the .400-inch range up to 1.5-inch—lengths vary up to twenty-five feet.

Highline designed and installed an automatic bar feeder and take-away system for a centerless grinder running bars in one- to four-inch diameters. The system is composed of:

1. A feed table that holds a bundle of steel that, based on how many bars are on the top table, will index up and load two to six bars
2. Feed arms that take the bars from the top table and lace them on pinch rollers
3. Feed side pinch rollers
4. Feed side driver roll
5. Grinder (existing)
6. Exit side pinch rollers
7. Exit side driver roll

8. Exit side takeaway arms

9. Exit side table

All the components are independently controlled and have no interlocks between them. The mechanical design of the components along with the necessary installation of sensors allows each item to operate regardless of the condition of any other component.

For example, there is no interlock between the feed side and the grinder, and thus it is possible, although not likely, that the feed side could try to drive a bar into a not-running grinder. So, to avoid damage to the grinder, the drive roll motor is a DC, amp-controlled motor that will stall out before damaging the grinder. The system will fault out on overload, and the operator will soon learn his error of placing the system into automatic when the grinder is not running.

Agents in the software control the cradle and table, feed and exit arm loading, feed and exit driver rollers, feed and exit fixture, and the grinder. When the bars pass by, the arm continues to go down, and then a pinch roller kicks in. Ekberg designed the arm "smart" so that it picks up the bar itself. He made the software uncomplex by not programming in all the conditions that could occur. "We trusted the behavior of the elements of the system, and so we didn't try to cover all possible crashes. It's not about software, it's about behavior of the elements. Fifty percent of the gains come from the hardware, not from writing endless lines of code, forever."

STEALTH TECHNOLOGY

The kicker, however, comes in Ekberg's assessment of why this system was successful. "In that design we focused on a lot of simple things—don't worry about all the interlocks. SteelWorks doesn't know we built an autonomous agent system."

Shane Steel, one of Highline's prime customers, had no interlocks on its system either. If safety is a concern, Ekberg recommends adding redundant sensors, not redundant software. Shane's software was written and installed in two hours; the customer wrote the ladder logic for an Allen-Bradley PLC.

The advantage to autonomous agent software is that it is faster to develop, easier to maintain, more flexible, and environmentally independent. Ekberg plans to take agent software into new environments, including the PIM (parallel inference machine).

The Parallel Inference Machine—PIM

Most computer system improvements seem to have focused on user productivity and ease of use. That explains Microsoft's huge success, because the software giant has provided a complete computer environment that is simple for many people, with many differing skill sets, to use.

In the world of machine and process control and modeling, the advancements of the user interfaces and ease of use only touch the surface of the complexity of the solution. The PIM differentiates itself from other system solutions and platforms by its fundamentally different approach to representing and solving problems.

In 1988 RMI designed a parallel inference machine for Flavors Technology. The system was designed to be parallel to maximize access to limited processing power. The first application drew on 128 Motorola processors, and a new language called ParaCell that circumvented the limitations of nonparallel processing. The logic was based on chaos theory to be emergent behavior–driven.

The PIM system's "brain" was created to draw inference from fundamental behavioral rules, and its approach is parallel processing based on autonomous agent modeling. The GM Paint Shop was the first application, and varieties of approaches to process problems have grown in the ten years since the Fort Wayne installation, because this way of managing complex problems is a necessary departure from complex and "fixed" software behemoths.

The PIM's hardware design and programming environment allow people to easily take advantage of a chaos theory–based approach in much the same way that Microsoft Excel allows users to quickly and easily view and edit data in ways that were previously not possible.

In the manufacturing world, the PIM will greatly improve equipment uptime and will allow continuous improvement due to the reduced complexity of the final solution.

SHANE'S PIM APPLICATION

A new application, Shane Steel, illustrates. Gary DuMoulin, Shane operations manager, says that the company wanted to get into grinding larger bars in the two- to four-inch range, a market the company could not get into because of the way its machines feed. Shane needed to develop a different feed system. Ekberg helped Shane with the software programming to get them into a new market; programming took a couple of hours.

Results from this first project have been very positive. "The process is more consistent," says DuMoulin, "and it allows greater flexibility in programming the machines." Time to change settings is minimal because of the software, and now Shane can grind material in the two-inch range. "With the speed of the programming and the number of changes that we can now do on-line—changes are not mechanically performed."

Next steps for Shane include a PIM that will do more machine controls and run more machines. Ekberg plans to run inputs and output, and laser gauges that will be controlled by the PIM. The software will read the unit's size as it comes out of the grinder, and direct feedback to control compensation in the bars.

"We're working toward lights out," says DuMoulin. The window is "probably three to six months to get there, on a pilot program with four machines."

Next steps for Ekberg include an expediting system using PIM. Ekberg sees many opportunities for new system approaches that should be simple and fast and cheaper than "mainline," fully integrated solutions.

From Theory to Application

Every successful manufacturing innovator is a bridge between the theorists and the practical applications guys. The innovator always

FIGURE 5.5 *DuMoulin Photo: Shane Steel Processing Using Autonomous Agent Software.*

wants to develop more applications with simple tools. But the operations executives hold back for full, perfect, massively comprehensive systems that usually never come. What inevitably works best is a bridge—an application like the McNeil project that quickly uses pure theory to generate quick results.

The McNeil Story, Simple Systems

Fifteen years ago, Visicalc spreadsheets ran guerrilla numbers games where elaborate central MIS systems were too slow. When McNeil Consumer Labs wanted to develop and install a mammoth complete manufacturing, planning, and scheduling system in the early eighties, it assembled a team of its "best and brightest." Usually this Johnson & Johnson subsidiary promoted team veterans of large-scale software projects into various key plant positions. The team and its project had very top-level commitment and resource support. Results were guaranteed, although specification and installation of the software in parallel with daily ship schedules was a struggle, a rigorous proving ground for future managers. The systems typically took one year or more to customize and install.

In the early eighties, when an unknown person tampered with bottles of Tylenol, the incident shut down production. As news helicopters landed on the lawns at the Fort Washington, Pennsylvania, headquarters, the company's market share and its number-one position in over-the-counter painkillers evaporated. The operation was paralyzed; no one in marketing or operations or the executive offices could predict how long the product recall would take, how long it would take to refill the pipelines, or whether the public would regain confidence in Tylenol. Within days the company's backlog disappeared, and its elaborately detailed business plans were rendered useless. Key executives struggled with tamper-proof packaging designs to be rushed through approval to packaging suppliers.

Within a month the answer to the company's market position started to trickle in as orders from distributors began to accumulate. Still, with no MIS system on-line that could deal with capacity and headcount requirements that fluctuated hourly, the company was flying in the dark with no traffic controller, no tower, and no radar.

Co-author Moody found the answer in a two-by-three-foot whiteboard and a simple spreadsheet. Moody started hourly updates of the whiteboard that was posted strategically in the hallway between manufacturing and marketing executive offices, with hourly backlog figures—unfilled orders stated in weeks of average manufacturing capacity. In a company that was accustomed to little unfilled backlog, when the number climbed from days to weeks, then to three months, with still no decision to turn the production machinery back on, the problem became very clear to everyone who walked by. Second, Moody used a spreadsheet to translate the backlog as it continued its climb, to generate quick and clear answers to headcount and materials capacity cost "what-ifs." As executives became more comfortable over the hours with the prospect of McNeil making a fast comeback, the decision to turn production back on, and to adjust to little irregularities as necessary in the pipeline, was more easily made. Her simple real-time system developed from two simple tools that completely superseded the massive manufacturing planning project, recaptured customers, and saved the company. Central, inflexible systems were too slow.

From Theory to Application: SunOpTech

In Sarasota, Chris Barlow, president of SunOpTech, a software design house affiliated with fluid valve producer Sun Hydraulics, has designed a Windows-based solution to valve scheduling. Many years back, rather than waiting for central MIS to "permit" a solution to his scheduling problems, Barlow pioneered scheduling at a food-processing plant by programming his own package on a Radio Shack desktop.

Likewise, Gregg Ekberg as a young, visionary engineer is bridging the technical worlds of computer science and engineering, with the practical result orientation of manufacturing pros. Without his sharp eyes and quick steps, the industry would be locked in big-system solutions for simple process challenges.

Localized Intelligence: The Chinese Box

When the U.S. Air Force dropped massive payloads of bombs on Japanese cities in World War II, big factories were soon replaced with small centers of activity making whatever could be pulled together—clothing, shoes, bicycles. There was a machine shop in every house. The same approach to manufacturing guided our thinking on what we have nicknamed "The Chinese Box," a replication unit whose first installation was planned for China. It's possible to put all the manufacturing equipment required to build a printed circuit board shop, for example, into a single trailer that can be dropped by helicopter into a local site—in China or on an oil rig in the North Sea or on a mountain in Nepal. Circuit board layout and production is the perfect candidate for this approach to localized manufacturing because this industry represents the heart of all in-board sensors and intelligence. Boards can be produced anywhere there is energy, satellite communications, a truck, and a few good workers. Outsourced electronic management services companies (EMS) like EFTC and

Flextronics have perfected the production process and added design and manufacturing intelligence. The smart EMS provider is a technology bridge between scattered and slower production and the Chinese Box of 2020. With global telecommunications, designs and process instructions need not stay with the equipment.

A RETURN TO "FAMILY FARMS"

"The Chinese Box" opens up the work of high-tech electronics manufacturing to subcontracting families, for example, linked to their design and process intelligence through the next-generation Internet (see Figure 5.6). With a robot positioned in the middle of the trailer floor, the intelligence goes remote. When one job is complete, the laptop worker dials up the Web and connects to their next order, for an entirely different customer, in an entirely different locale. Not unlike the globally distributed garment industry that replaced New York City's textile factories, the Chinese Box will take on plastics and entertainment devices as well as electronics.

The impact of the Chinese Box is huge. It will destroy the American manufacturing infrastructure, just as the electric motor took down water power as a business, then followed a miniaturization trend that created even smaller sources of energy.

Advanced Applications

John Marshall, director of PACT '95, and formerly head of the design team for Stars and Stripes '87, compares sailboat racing to race cars. Under heavy stress and load conditions, the America's Cup yacht *Australia One* cracked, broke apart, and sank in less than three minutes. All hands were saved, but the million-dollar hull was lost.

"If you're pushing hard at technology and you fail, you're fun to pick on," said Marshall. Critics wondered if the boat was an example of over-radical designing, but sailors and designers did not think so. "All boats have soft spots," said nuclear physicist Heiner Meler, director of technology for *America 3,* winner of the 1992 cup. "These are racing vehicles, and the odd thing is the ideal racing vehicle is one that falls to pieces right after it finishes. But sometimes it happens before."

Agent-Based Modeling

Complete systems can themselves be modeled as collections of autonomous decision-making entities, agents. Each agent individually sees and assesses its situation and makes decisions based on what it sees and on a rule set, programmed by human software developers. Agent-based modeling draws on computer power to model many possible interactions in the system that closely resembles the "complexity" of the real world. An agent can be an individual software program or a biological or conceptual entity. The agent has its own simple rules of behavior.

Aggregates, or groups of these agents, when they are assembled in a common environment, exhibit collective, explicit behavior as a group. Taxicab systems, flocks of birds, and goldfish are all examples of this phenomenon.

The real advantage to understanding agents is that we can solve hitherto incomplete problems, problems whose complexity and states are poorly understood at best. Just as Ekberg proved at SteelWorks and Shane Steel, with the use of agents, the number of lines of software code necessary to elicit emergent behavior is reduced by an order of magnitude. Agents mean less code, but they also give us the ability to solve problems we may not really understand. Agent-based solutions seem to work in situations of unexpected stimulation.

The Bios Group, a Santa Fe, New Mexico, partnership founded by the Ernst & Young Center for Business Innovation and Dr. Stuart Kauffman to commercialize the science of complexity and complex adaptive systems, has been working for several years on designing software solutions to complex problems. Using agent-based modeling makes sense for manufacturers and supply chains that want to explore solutions to difficult problems on the computer before committing resources in the real world. Bios also applies the science of complexity to finding solutions to hard optimization problems such as routing and scheduling. The software can also suggest new directions and allow the user to test hypotheses with less risk than doing it in the "real world."

Bios Group Models[1]

TOOL 1, AGENT-BASED MODEL OF THE NATURAL GAS MARKET

For a natural gas company, Bios specified an agent-based model of the futures market to assist in marketing and risk management decisions. The model, named CYMEX NG, is designed to allow a manager to test his assumptions concerning the way market forces drive price patterns in the futures market. The model addresses many variables unique to the natural gas market, including the volatility of demand, the role of storage, and the impact of regulatory constraints.

Commodity trading is a pressured, constantly up and down activity. Commodities experts, however, are not always able to explain how the variables interact to affect prices. The CYMEX model, however, embodies this understanding in an agent-based model that predicts the response of the market to a specific change. The model simulates the emergent behavior of the market by modeling interactions at the component level. And because it's a powerful simulator, managers can use the model to perform "what-if" analyses, to train traders, and to evaluate trading strategies, all relatively risk-free.

One of the first steps to developing the model is to define the agents that represent certain types of behavior. Each agent is assigned a set of attributes that represent the "real-world" behavior of that type of agent. Agents fall into two categories in this model—players and brokers—and once the simulation is running, the combined behavior of the agents cannot be controlled or predicted, because the point of the exercise is to learn what behavior emerges from the interaction of the agents that individually follow their own simple rules.

FIGURE 5.6 *Chinese Box—The Model*

There are two "layers" of modeling in the simulation. Following the rules appropriate to their types, the players pull buy or sell parcels off the Demand, Deliverability, and Storage streams at a certain price, and pass these on to the brokers. The brokers trade the orders in the double oral auction and arrive at the best possible price they can get; they pass back to the players a figure indicating the price at which the order was bought or sold. Players evaluate the success of their strategies based on their profitability. The results of a simulation run are displayed graphically in Figure 5.7.

TOOL 2, UTILITIES OPTIMIZATION

Bios has developed a prototype of a powerful optimization tool for the energy industry. The model includes agents that represent brokers, producers, generators, and consumers. The program allows a

FIGURE 5.7 *Configuration Modeling Tool*

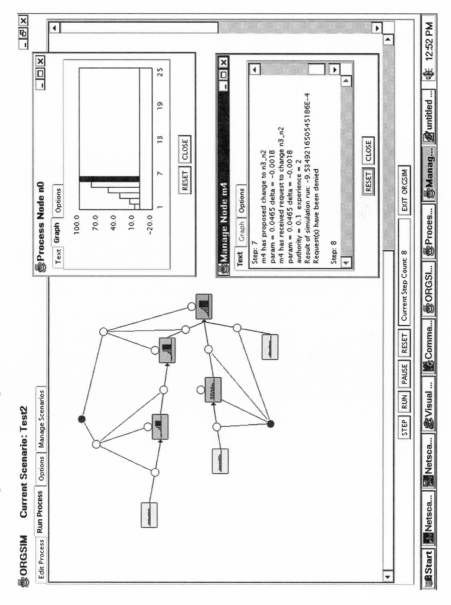

utility to model the distribution of power requirements between generating stations based on demand; the results can provide suggestions for improving operating efficiency and minimizing cost. In addition, the model can be used to calculate the potential cost of providing an additional block of power to a new consumer, to show the impact of changing operating costs on prices and profits, or to test marketing strategies. In the deregulated power industry, understanding the interaction of all these factors is vital for a company's profitability.

TOOL 3, DESIGN SOFTWARE, THE SLOW EVOLUTION TOWARD THE ONE-DAY CAR

When Toyota introduced the Three-Day Car at the 1993 Tokyo Auto Show, it launched a delayed reaction in a few U.S. observers who understood that the auto industry would not be alone in this approach to simultaneous customer design and replication. Since that show, other industries have—usually independently and unknown to each other—pioneered similar approaches, starting with parallel tooling and design (Lexmark, the printer pioneers in Lexington, Kentucky, and Minco, an award-winning Dayton, Ohio, toolmaker), to on-line design and order fulfillment (electronics component producers and eventually computer system producers). Personal items—clothing, hygiene products, recreational equipment, and geriatric and orthopedic devices—producers all are pioneering the "10X" reduction of hand-off, nonproductive / creative time.

The key to successfully redesigning the design process is intelligent use of software innovation that takes entire links out of the process, like taking clay models out of the auto design process, for example, and the design of Boeing's 777 "Paperless Airplane." The object of cutting time means performing more tasks in parallel, rather than serially, and not merely compressing specific links in the chain, but removing them entirely. The shift from sequential design to prototyping to production will be such a restructuring that distribution and logistics, long the most neglected area of operations, will become assembly and design. Technology is the absolute driver of this process.

TOOL 4, THE DESIGN EVOLUTION

The length of the design-to-prototype-to-full-production cycle in the automotive industry will become a competitive battleground because most assemblers and tier-one suppliers have learned how to take excess time out of their manufacturing processes. But huge opportunities beckon at the front end of the system, starting with the design segment. Bios is developing a user-guided evolutionary search tool that allows designers to streamline what is normally a lengthy trial-and-error design process. The designer begins with a series of points that outline an aesthetically pleasing shape. Working within general parameters—such as wheelbase length, windshield angle, and size of engine compartment—the program evolves a group of designs that meet these criteria.

6

The Big, Big Wave—
Four Software Meta-Systems
that Will Transform Manufacturing

There is a chasm

Of carbon and silicon

The software can't bridge.

Yesterday it worked

Today it is not working

Software is like that

Your system has crashed.

I am the Blue Screen of Death

No one hears your screams.

Manufacturing Moves into the
Era of Software Meta-systems

We predict that the biggest change in manufacturing will be created by software. Although most futurists would argue that their projection accuracy is about 20 percent, 20 percent is clearly better than no good projections at all, and it's hard to miss the big ones. There are a dozen "big waves" on the manufacturing horizon—meta-systems—including enterprise resource planning (ERP), Complex Adaptive Systems (CAS), MES (Manufacturing Execution Systems), Advanced Planning and Scheduling (APS), the ubiquitous World Wide Web (WWW) in its later generations, and portable, remote-controlled active replication, or distributed manufacturing. All these big waves are in the infotech arena.

Small wonder the above haiku strike terror in manufacturing execs, as they realize how little power they will exert over their own operations. Thirty years ago a party guest's advice to Dustin Hoffman's character in the film *The Graduate* was one word—"Plastics!" For the next twenty years, the word is "Software!" Or perhaps the word is "Silicon!" as science and physics take their place on the factory floor in very practical applications drawn from theoretical breakthroughs. Science and manufacturing are finding a home together in chaos theory, complexity, and genetic algorithms.

SOFTWARE GROWS UP, FROM AN ART TO A DISCIPLINE

But software itself will continue to undergo a transformation, and over the next twenty years software will become a discipline, rather than an art form. Productivity, quality, and management discipline focused on the art of software will transform the software arena into an engineering discipline. Software selection and management will cease to be a "problem" and will instead be perceived as part of the solution, a huge relief to managers struggling with no standardization in the development area. Software work—development, debugging, and growth—will move as a mature discipline under the engineering umbrella, as powerful a tool as the slide rule and the Bowmar brain were in their time. Issues of diagnostics, documentation, and compatibility will have been superseded by integrated smart systems. Further, software will accomplish what well-intended lectures and unifying themes have not—the seamless integration of disparate processes and flows into what we call the extended enterprise.

MANUFACTURING INTEGRATION THROUGH SOFTWARE

Intelligence is the next generation in the factory. The intelligence breakthrough started with simple automation of dirty, difficult, or boring work and progressed through the transformation of the PLC. Finally we are realizing the promise of machine intelligence from the very first industrial applications of Digital's pioneering PDP 8, to integration of innovative software solutions, starting with ERP, and remote-distributed manufacturing.

Enterprise Resource Planning (ERP)

Starting in the IT area, the big push for manufacturing software integration currently falls under the ERP umbrella. Although ERP in hindsight will be considered bloat ware—the cost benefit or the return on investment is not a good deal—it is the only integrated solution that offers the ability to monitor and control the food chain, an organizing window into the pipeline. Less investment and more returns will be the trend in ERP.

ERP is designed to be a management tool that allows decision-makers to selectively manipulate various contact points in the network for better overall results, to change the volume, the speed, or the direction of flows through the supply network. Changing an in-transit finished-goods flow, for example, has huge impact on inventory dollars; good ERP installations let managers simulate and review the position on all in-transit inventories, for example, as well as those ready to hit the shipping docks, before they make scheduling changes.

MES (MANUFACTURING EXECUTION SYSTEMS)

What ERP is to the management level of the enterprise, MES (manufacturing execution systems) is to the intermediate level. MES organizes the plant floor, tracks the plan, and when it is well used, improves productivity. Tied in with the third element of total manufacturing enterprise control—the PLCs—ERP, MES, and PLCs together constitute the full communication and computer integration required to run the entire enterprise, any time, anywhere, any size, at all levels.

But we are not there yet. There is a huge gap between the vision of the integrated enterprise and the reality of less-than-optimum operating performance of many members of many manufacturing enterprises. Added to simple performance concerns, the issue of software integration makes this a very explosive issue, one that will continue to be examined and worked over for the next five to seven years, until one very smart competitor (as Wal-Mart and CVS did with logistics) wrestles the diverse ideas into a single powerful tool—and the name of the innovator company will not be Microsoft.

Between now and 2020 many more smart young companies will appear armed with brilliant applications using genetic algorithms, complexity, chaos theory, and data broadcasting. Short-term winners will include agents and knowledge-based approaches, along with NT.

Other possible players include ADSL (asynchronous digital subscriber line), VRML (virtual reality modeling language), emergent systems, catalytic management, and APS (advanced planning and scheduling).

Advanced planning and scheduling, APS, is the ability to do weather forecasting, or order and manufacturing of process planning. APS implies looking to the future, rather than forecasting based on forward projection of historical data. APS means modeling the system on the enterprise, the MES, and the factory floor, playing "what-if" games, and allocating resources based on APS as a predictive technology.

CATALYTIC MANAGEMENT

Catalytic managers combine traditional approaches to industry—software, automation, and technical breakthroughs in the context of human behavior—to engineer new brilliant solutions. Gregg Ekberg of Highline Controls, Bill Fulkerson of John Deere, and Gene Kirila, founder of Pyramid, are catalytic managers. Their unique approaches to building new solutions release energy that drives the technology machine.

THE HUMAN ELEMENT

All the new approaches spring from the bottom up, rather than top down. We know, for instance, that if we want truly lasting and effective behavior change, we need to work with basic human behavior aspects, and magic happens. When a product is not selling well, for example, we raise the commission rate, and whoosh, it's out the door. Likewise, the same resulting problem and corrective action can exist with the management of software, factories, salespeople, communications, and top management. By working with behavioral aspects we can, in the short term, use emergent, bottom-up, rule-based management techniques to manipulate and improve the organization.

Winners, like JAVA and its Microsoft counterpart, because of their bottom-up acceptance, will force factory managers to put these software products in every product in every plant, and to make every network WWW and JAVA compatible. When these requirements are met, ERP and MES are enabled.

The overwhelming challenge for year 2020 managers is that to be catalytic managers they must learn to deal with whole systems—not components, slabs, pieces, or chunks of science or technology. Catalytic managers must evaluate, as did Gregg Ekberg, whole-system applications for technology breakthroughs. They must be technology experts as well as human behavior gurus. Every new technology idea—software or hardware—has whole-system implications. As stand-alone intelligence, single points of technology applications quickly reach their limits and fail; as pieces of the systemic whole, like natural systems, they have a shot at generational survival and mutations.

Technology Solutions, Meta-Systems

Disciplines derived from chaos theory and complexity show great promise, because over the past decade production systems have become too complex for human systems, and that complexity has caused an exponential increase in software code. The top-down software architectures (as well as organizational structures) have run their course, and manufacturing pros inevitably look for methods that reduce complexity and reduce lines of code. The system architectures themselves will become, therefore, more robust and faster.

Adopting nontraditional software approaches, however, will require a shift in many manufacturing operations. Some information technology professionals are unsupportive of the change; others, such as SunOpTech's Chris Barlow, Deere's Bill Fulkerson, Gregg Ekberg, and Gene Kirila of Pyramid Systems, quickly grasp and internalize the power of dynamic systems, driven by simple software. Early lessons from studying natural systems—anthills and bird flocks, for example—have led to innovative approaches in scheduling, factory control constraints management, and process modeling.

FIGURE 6.1

THE CONVERGENCE OF SCIENCE AND INDUSTRY

A sampling of conferences and seminars aimed at fostering the exchange of ideas and practical applications between science and industry

The Santa Fe Institute	A Renaissance learning process, concerned with large-scale and wide complexity issues
Bios Group L.P.	A for-profit partnership between Ernst & Young and individuals at the Santa Fe Institute
Flavors Technology	A supplier of system software and hardware to accomplish complexity solutions
NIST (National Institute of Science and Technology)	Many current NIST technology solicitations in both the private and public sector have autonomous agent technology at their core. NIST is looking for rapid prototype agent or object implementations.
NCMS (National Center for Manufacturing Sciences)	A consortium of vendors, suppliers, and users, both large and small. Ongoing agent development programs involve a number of members to bring agent technology to bear on the needs of manufacturing.
NISCI (National Initiative for Supply Chain Integration)	Founded in 1997 in Chicago, this group of leading U.S. producers — Honda, Trane, Chrysler, IBM, Hewlett Packard—is rewriting the book on partnering and extended enterprise communications protocols.

Nontraditional approaches are also changing the way software applications are conceived and spec'd, and in that area alone they provide tremendous payback, even before operating processes are switched on. Several organizations are heavily involved in facilitating the transfer of these sciences into realistic applications with competitive advantages.

Four brilliant pioneering applications of the convergence of science and industry—meta-systems— are changing the way manufacturing manages itself:

1. GM's Fort Wayne Paint Shop, an application of intelligent agents and programming in a tough, technically demanding environment
2. John Deere's Genetic Algorithm Scheduling Process
3. Pyramid's VEC Cell, an Intelligent Molding Center
4. The Net, telepresence and teleoperations

A fifth significant meta-system, the Japanese bullet train, will be covered in chapter 8.

Meta-System Number One: GM's Fort Wayne Paint Shop Software System

The GM Paint Shop in Fort Wayne, Indiana, was the first successful industrial application of intelligent machines in a technically very challenging environment, painting truck bodies. Fort Wayne holds many lessons for manufacturing managers interested in managing complexity using lean manufacturing systems. In this Fort Wayne pioneering application, intelligent agents were substituted for complex schedules, human expediting, and costly changeovers. Further, the agent software reduced complexity and allowed the paint operation to reach higher levels of cosmetic quality.

Designers experienced resistance with the first installation in 1990; blockers were opposed to the nonstandard method. The burden of proof and the burden of benefits preimplementation were difficult to present. Despite this leap of faith, the first installation achieved an equivalent product fit and finish at one-fifteenth the number of lines of code, or, one-fifteenth the amount of programming complexity. Not only did the amount of code drop significantly, but development time was cut 40 percent.

The benefits were direct and visible; more than $1 million in paint

THE BIG, BIG WAVE 165

FIGURE 6.2 *GM Paintshop. Real-time intelligent agent software changed the way the operator (and management) viewed process control.*

was saved annually and GM won the J. D. Power Award for the best fit and finish for any truck factory in the world. The system was operator-controlled and gave direct and immediate feedback. It proved the power of real-time on-line controls. It was also very robust—industrial-strength automation—but the blockers seemed fixated on the idea that it "was not standard."

THE FIRST BIG, BIG WAVE

Nevertheless, the system worked. It was a big, big wave. The software succeeded where many other approaches had been defeated by their own complexity because the techies understood the physics and the chemistry of the paint process. They respected the behavior of the process, and they built a system that respected physical parameters. Their approach reflected the convergence of science and industry because the system dealt with things—processes and materials, chemistry and physics—the way they are. *The only lasting approach is to optimize what is—the givens—not what should be.*

Co-author Morley recalls that "the system was designed upside down!" Scheduling became a pull-through process, rather than a drag- or push-through. And the paradox was that performance was truly chaotic—that is, the model/color mix was unpredictable but bounded by constraints.

The continued challenge was to actually take constraint management theory—the limits of science and chemistry that sometimes conflict with manufacturing operating preferences—and apply it against a pull-through scheduler to maximize uptime and asset use. The mathematics of the problem could only be solved with flexibility built into fourth-generation software.

It's important to remember that ERP, MES, chaos theory, complexity, artificial life, and genetic algorithms are *system* considerations, and not single-point technologies. To be successful and progress, manufacturing cannot create artificial limits by fixing only the peaks of performance. Rather, the approach is to improve the valleys and create a level playing field—overall great performance—within the enterprise. It makes no sense to be extremely good at one single skill—product design, for example—and less than best at everything else. Maturity and power come with the management not only of production (single point of technology constraints), but also of technology constraints—again, the marriage of science with technology.

Big Waves, Big Ideas, Big Time Frames

Time concepts in business prove the irrelevance of most time measurement devices as management tools. When management looks at time stamps, clocks, and watches to make decisions that lie embedded in five-year, ten-year, and twenty-year calendars, they are using the wrong tool to answer the right questions. Measures that look at next week are irrelevant—it fact, next week has already happened. There is nothing left to do but to cash out. What happens this coming year was determined by decisions made several years ago. Managers must make system decisions now so that in the next two to five years—at minimum—their enterprises will be among the winners.

ADJUST YOUR TIMEPIECES

It takes eighteen months to complete any technical turnaround—in either information technology, or a manufacturing process, or design cycles. Even the Manhattan Project actually found its roots in the work of German scientists long before World War II broke out. The Japanese attack on Pearl Harbor, and the U.S. attack on Cuba in 1898, as well as the U.S. Civil War, were all cast years in advance of their very public appearances.

There are still a few short-term "must-do" activities remaining—cost reduction, short-term scheduling, local constraint optimization, and especially, time-to-market. But over the long term, the big job is to make all elements of the enterprise compatible with all the Web aspects of enterprise management, particularly APS.

A caution about adopting a cost-reduction focus: Cost reduction assumes that there is no change, and that your only variable is reduced cost, as opposed to making better products that yield higher margins and higher value.

This shift will require managers to transform organizations—technically and structurally—and to transform the process with meta-systems. Meta-systems are big waves, systems whose impact is pervasive and global, whose workings may represent utter simplicity, but whose power is transforming. Gutenberg's press is such an engineering turning point, a big wave; so was the graphite pencil.

Total enterprise management will be a fact of life in 2020, managing discrete and distributed manufacturing elements or objects. The manufacturing object based on behavioral APS will be what the total enterprise will manage. The goal is a human-controlled computer system, not a computer-controlled mammoth. For now, total enterprise management is a competitive advantage and the bridge to meta-systems, but it is an incomplete solution. ERP requires a balanced approach to dealing with business, engineering, economics, computers, and science, all excellent, all in synch. Computers and meta-systems will truly re-form our enterprises, our customers, our vendors, and our asset manipulation. Do not forget, however, that technology loses to the market every time because the momentum of the marketplace cannot be stopped—only directed. We must learn or die.

Meta-System Number Two: Playing Darwin, the John Deere System

John Deere is a big, old company that loves innovation. The company founder was born in Rutland, Vermont, in 1804, and grew up in Middlebury, where he received a common school education and served a four-year apprenticeship learning the blacksmith's trade. In 1825, when the Industrial Revolution was picking up speed, Deere began his career as a journeyman blacksmith, and he soon gained considerable fame for his careful workmanship and ingenuity. His highly polished hay forks and shovels were in great demand in western Vermont. But in the mid-1830s, a downturn and emigration out of the East lured Deere West. He took with him a small bundle of tools and some cash, and left his wife and family behind; they were to rejoin him later.

The trip took him by canal boat, lake boat, and stagecoach, and finally, like others before him, Deere found himself in territory settled by fellow Vermonters, the village of Grand Detour, Illinois. The blacksmith was so welcomed that within two days after his arrival in 1836, Deere had built a forge and was in business.

One of Deere's first breakthroughs led to the company's founding and a long series of innovations that won the company dominance in the world agricultural equipment market. The cast-iron plows that the midwestern farmers had brought with them from the East did not work well with the rich, heavy Mississippi Valley soil;

every few steps the farmer had to stop and clear off the plow blade. Plowing became a slow and tiring task, and some farmers even considered moving on.

But Deere studied the problem and became convinced that a plow with a highly polished and properly shaped moldboard and share would scour itself as it turned the furrow slice. In 1837 he made such a plow, using steel from a broken saw blade; he tested the innovation on a nearby farm. Deere knew that this tool would be so well-received that he started making them in anticipation of farmers' orders, another departure from blacksmiths' traditional practice of building to customer order.

The "self-polishers" made from discarded saw blades were in great demand, and suddenly the blacksmith became the manufacturer. On the plains there were limited quantities of the quality materials he required, so in 1843 the entrepreneur arranged for a shipment of special rolled steel from England. The steel's journey, like the company's founder's journey before it, was long—across the Atlantic by steamship, up the Mississippi and Illinois rivers by packet boat, and overland by wagon forty miles to the little plow factory.

In 1846 the first slab of cast steel ever rolled in the United States was shipped from Pittsburgh to Moline, Illinois, the site of the company's current headquarters and the site of Deere's first big factory.

Ten years after developing the first plow, Deere was producing one thousand plows per year. Deere continued to innovate, making changes in design as he felt the farmers needed them. The blacksmith's son Charles expanded the company and incorporated more offerings—steel plows, cultivators, corn and cotton planters, and other implements.

By 1911 the company's third president, William Butterworth, had acquired six noncompeting farm equipment companies, fueling more growth by acquisition. Deere continued to fill worldwide demand for new ideas, and even during the 1930s Depression, the company achieved $100 million in gross sales for the first time in its history. By 1955 the Vermont blacksmith's company had taken a place as one of the United States' one hundred largest manufacturing businesses. The company survived the manufacturing upheavals of the 1980s to post record sales and earnings.

FULKERSON'S OBSESSION

In May, 1997, the Smithsonian Institution honored Deere & Company's use of Optimax's genetic algorithm–based schedule optimization software by including it in the Institution's Permanent Research Collection of Information Technology Innovation. On the John Deere seed planter assembly line, more than 6 million combinations of available options can be specified when the planters are ordered by the customer. With this software, the factory's daily assembly schedule is created in minutes.

The Deere & Company case study joined over two thousand other examples of innovative use of information technology. These studies are available to the public on the Innovation Network Website at http://innovate.si.edu. (Optimax Corporation, the provider of the software to other companies, including Case Corporation, General Electric and Volvo/GM Heavy Truck, announced in August 1998 that it would merge with i2 Technologies, Inc., a provider of intelligent planning and optimization software for global supply-chain management. The merger transaction was valued at approximately $52.2 million.)

Bill Fulkerson is a twenty-two-year veteran of John Deere, a trained mathematician with a biology minor. Fulkerson has the innocuous title of "staff analyst" and an uncanny eye for innovation. He had become intrigued with chaos theory after reading a couple of books during the companywide Christmas shutdown in December 1992. He absorbed the ideas of complex systems readily and became especially enamored of genetic algorithms. The company was assembling an increasing variety of new products while re-engineering their order fulfillment process to reduce time to fill customer orders. Faced with what Fulkerson calls an "infinite variety" of products with an untold number of options that were impossible to forecast, John

Deere experienced growing inventories of raw materials and unsold products.

Fulkerson had a visceral sense that genetic algorithms could help resolve Deere's scheduling problems. Perhaps genetic algorithms could be used to search for improved schedules, rather than relying on departmental schedulers with their yellow legal pads and spreadsheet templates.

It was worth a try.

In 1993 Fulkerson found a site on the Internet where scientists exchanged information about genetic algorithms. He posted a message asking if anyone knew anything about scheduling a production line, and one week later, he had a response. Bolt, Beranek & Newman, Inc., had used genetic algorithms to schedule work at a U.S. Navy lab. A prototype scheduling system was developed at John Deere to run on a PC located adjacent to the loading dock. Essentially the software played God (or perhaps more correctly Darwin), running through up to six hundred thousand schedule iterations of a month-long planning horizon of planter orders with each iteration seeking to breed an improved schedule.

The software product was called OptiFlex by its originators, the Optimax Systems Corporation of Cambridge, Massachusetts. The biological parallel is sexual reproduction; the objective is to search through strings of information (schedules) to reduce the impact of infinite variety upon assembly-line effectiveness. "In the past," recalls Fulkerson, "our challenge was volume—now the challenge has become variety."

"Planters are ideal for this approach to scheduling," says Fulkerson. "You can configure a rectangular frame to handle from four to thirty-one rows." The assembly has seed boxes and seed delivery systems, a component of the variety. "It's like building a VW bug right next to a big school bus on the same line, the same day. We had the challenge of trying to level the work requirements on the feeder lines as well. Big frames take a long time to build up and cool, and we put every constraint we had to make the software robust."

The use of genetic algorithms enabled John Deere to breed a better class of production schedule that met both market and manufacturing constraints while operating as efficiently as possible. The process starts with a population of schedules (say ten or twenty), from which two parents' schedules are selected by chance, biased by an assessment of their fitness. Two new schedules are derived from the parents by breaking them at an arbitrary point and exchanging parts as in cellular mitosis. In the Darwinian sense, these children undergo natural selection, with superior children being introduced into the original population, keeping the population size fixed. The population becomes more fit at subsequent iterations, until there is little chance of improvement and the process halts with the most fit member of the population designated as the production schedule.

What's next in the genetic algorithm factory? Fulkerson sees most manufacturing software companies racing to incorporate available-to-promise and capable-to-promise routines to take the traditional manufacturer closer to producing customer orders on demand, or mass customization. Then, successful software providers will ultimately move from these strategies to promise-to-profit strategies (PTP). The reduction of capacity coupled with a flexible and agile response to demand variation sets the stage for achieving price realization above "cost plus" formulas. Yield management strategies that reward long-range purchase guarantees with lower prices and extract premium price for short-term delivery appear on the horizon. Firms will reserve capacity for premium-priced short-term production and manage long-term purchase contracts. In the end, not all customers will be of equal value to the firm.

Meta-System Number Three: The Pyramid VEC Cell, an Intelligent Molding Center

Gene Kirila has a long history of entrepreneurship, starting at age fourteen when his father put him in charge of a thousand-acre Ohio farm with five hundred head of beef cattle. The teen successfully guided the enterprise back to profitability while he juggled school, football, and his father's other businesses. Gene had a knack for building and breaking, then fixing, things. He loved football, and like most football players, he was no stranger to knee injuries. While he was still in high school, Kirila designed and built his own custom fitness equipment, welding together benches and machines to meet the needs of various users, including a few of the Pittsburgh Steelers.

Gene went on to college at Youngstown, but he left for the same reason that he later started his businesses: "They were teaching everything the old-fashioned way." Although Gene had written a thesis on his process, just by applying what he knew—he had developed a total system that would be applicable to any manufacturing project, a breakthrough meta-system—school had no further attraction for him, so he left.

THE VEC PROCESS

Kirila created at Pyramid Composites a process—a total system for composites, called Virtual Engineered Composites (VEC). The VEC operating system enables environmentally friendly, flexible, automated composites manufacturing with low capital investment. Pyramid's mission with the VEC system is to establish an industry-standard operating system that can be used by molders to manage, develop, and mold composite parts for low- to midrange volumes. The operating system includes VEC software and hardware that manage the entire system—equipment, resins, and process. The VEC operating system runs on a Microsoft NT Network platform, and it completely integrates all the critical variables of composite production. Essentially, the system parallels the Chinese Box idea.

Pyramid's new factory near Pittsburgh, Pennsylvania, is running on the VEC operating system. This factory molds production parts and can be used for development of new customer parts on into commercial production. Once the customer's parts are made using VEC, the customer can then adopt the VEC operating system through one of the following options:

1. Joint venture with Pyramid Composites

2. Turnkey lease program called VEC/Cell can be installed in a customer's factory.

3. Pyramid can subcontract parts for customers in its Pennsylvania plant or another VEC-certified regional plant.

THE ESSENCE OF VEC

The VEC operating system enables a manufacturer to control and integrate the four key elements of closed molding:

1. The human interface variables
2. The capital variable
3. The live variable
4. The process control variable

Each of these variables is controlled by the VEC operating system for high quality and reproducible fast-cycle output of composite molded parts. Most different, compared to current system offerings, however, is the human interface feature. Human intervention is critical to any process, automated or not. Managing the relationship between human interaction and equipment/process control is essential because process engineering only works if the human factor is included.

MANUFACTURING AS A VIDEO ARCADE

Kirila designed the VEC system to cover all the variables—human and mechanical/electronic—in composite production. "In our systems, we lead the value-adding employee through the actual operations—everything from when the employee walks up to the machine first thing in the morning. It starts with a swipe of the card, just like an ATM machine. Once the person has 'entered' the system, we make the machinery and the work cell itself personalized for that individual."

This is a big wave, an industrial breakthrough that builds on human behavior to bring out the best the machine and the brain can produce. "We think it is not just our responsibility to make a part, but our responsibility to lead an employee through his workday. We want to motivate that person, instruct, and to give instantaneous feedback about not just his co-worker, but his country and the world. So we personalize the system. *We get your attention.*"

> Good morning, John. Today is Monday, and Cleveland has taken another step toward the World Series.
> Don't forget, John, tomorrow is your fifteenth anniversary. Better pick up a six-pack.

"We want to touch the personal side of the individual, and so we establish worker profiles for each floor associate. It's a video arcade game," says Kirila, and he is astonished that manufacturers would attempt leading-edge automation any other way.

> Oh, by the way, John, yesterday you scored a 200 in your production, and in quality you hit 99.6 percent—good job!—but your efficiency dropped 3 points compared to the Red Motorola Team.

Kirila's goal is to create a complete environment on the shop floor. "What we are trying to do is create a subculture within a corporate culture, like a Harley Davidson cult—on the floor. We are doing what any good manager would do, but we can do this with systems and with computers."

> Today, John, we're going to build two hundred boats, and I'll walk you through it.

SIMPLE VISUAL INSTRUCTIONS

Kirila engineered the work instructions into the system—there is little opportunity for operator error. The machine tells the worker exactly what to do, step by step, in easy, graphically clear icons and words—"Mix cereal polyester resin with gelcoat harbor green," for example.

INSTANT VISUAL FEEDBACK

After the operator has performed the work, machine indicator lights tell him if he is doing well. The machine cues the operator on pace, and when it's time to approve a part, the mold opens automatically. When the part is complete and the operator needs to perform a quality check, he simply enters the key data—thickness, dimensions, glass, weight. The beauty of Kirila's system design, called the Human Interface, is that it works *with*, rather than *on*, the operator, twenty-four hours a day, error-free—no tired feet or wrists.

THE OPERATING SYSTEM

The operating system is the brain behind the brain, guiding both the machine operations and the operator's Human Interface—the worker profile and personalized cues, work instructions, and so forth. The operating system manages the machine, but, says Kirila, "The Human Interface is the part we think is as critical as running the machine—there's human interface everywhere. If you design to be user-friendly, that's the key to the successful operating system."

APPLICATIONS

The first VEC Cell was sold to one of the largest boat builders in the world for production of all types of boats—bass boats, pleasure boats, and work boats. The company has fourteen plants worldwide. "The beauty of the machine is you don't need big volumes of any one particular product—think of it as a computer," says Kirila.

This product is a 2020 breakthrough on many fronts, even if Kirila

FIGURE 6.3 *VEC Cell*

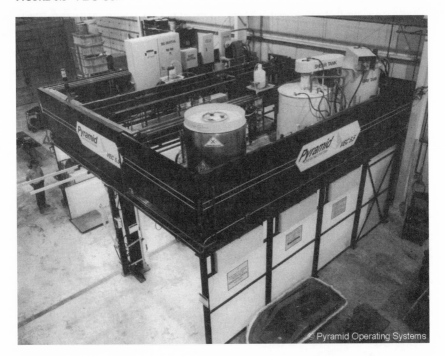

© Pyramid Operating Systems

never sells many units, because of what it proves about replication. The hardware is product independent. Manufacturers can run any kind of composite product through it—jet skis, bathtubs and Jacuzzis, or small boats. The equipment accommodates thousands of product configurations with consistently high quality and efficiency, for runs of a single part or hundreds of thousands.

This particular boat builder, however, will not run volumes on all its products of more than one hundred units in a year, and the VEC Cell allows producers to configure each and every product with an economic lot size of one.

Other applications envisioned for this composite production process extend into the automotive industry—semi-truck cabs and automotive panels. The boat application replaced a very long, multi-stepped, labor-intensive process—lay up, molding, grinding, patching, polishing—that has not changed since the first fiberglass boats were produced back in the fifties. Kirila is proud to have produced what he believes is the world's largest injection molded part, a seventeen-and-a-half-foot boat that would have taken days to produce using traditional methods, *in seventy minutes,* with ten to one labor savings.

2020 APPLICATIONS

Kirila understands the revolutionary manufacturing potential in his process. "The big gap is trying to create economic wealth in Third World countries. The potential to create wealth in new areas is enormous. Imagine, a refrigerator company will be able to drop the cell into China or someplace in Africa, and because the tooling is virtual with floating mold technology, they can build sixty different refrigeration units—double-door units, freezers, and so forth—with a single cell."

The cell ships in two ocean freight shipping containers. "In three working days we set up a factory, and people in that economy are making product." All the intellectual capital—tooling and mold design, product specs—stay back at the VEC Solution Center. "We dial in the program—the specs, the design, the chemistry—and the machinery and the software leads them through."

In North America, the implications for on-the-spot manufacturing to customer order are significant. Imagine pulling up to your local Home Depot and ordering a Caribbean-blue Jacuzzi. In less than the time it would take to pick out ceramic tiles and fixtures, the tub would be molded and ready for pickup, out back at the VEC cell.

Kirila believes his technology can handle a range of variables that typically create scheduling and process complexity and concerns about quality and operator performance. Variables that are typically programmed into the system include:

1. Quantity of parts needed per year
2. Peak demand needs
3. Product life cycle in years and quantity
4. Geometric design
5. Physical property requirements

6. Cosmetic criteria
7. Cost objectives
8. Laminate schedules

The first systems are designed with simple graphical symbols. Although workers must know how to read, Kirila is doing a language conversion. "It's visual controls and some audible cues—all we ask them to do is to basically touch the screen. We call it 'The Dual Ph.D System'—designed by a Ph.D for user-friendliness, and the user becomes the Ph.D. The Ph.D stands for 'push here dummy'!"

CAPITAL EQUIPMENT VARIABLES

The VEC Cell is a breakthrough whose results extend far beyond its Human Interface features, however. Capital equipment costs and restrictions are pretty much removed with this real-world application of Chapter 5's visionary "Chinese Box." Thermoset resins are in liquid form before the polymerization process that is initiated just before the resin enters the mold by the addition of a catalyst. By use of refined chemical engineering, it is possible to mold thermosetting composites without using the expensive capital equipment essential for thermoplastics and many thermosets. This goal of removing the capital-intensive requirement has eluded processors for years, but the VEC operating system combines the management of process control, capital, and chemistry that equates to major cost savings and drastically reduced capital equipment.

LIVE ORGANIC CHEMICAL VARIABLES

Thermoset resins are unstable organic chemicals (live) that use catalysts to cure the liquid into solid state. However, these organic chemicals change over time, even if the catalyst is not present. The live nature of the raw materials makes formulating a product mix a real moving target. Automation helps adjust and guarantee specific results.

PROCESS CONTROL VARIABLES

The variables in raw materials processing include time, temperature, pressure, volume, and physical attributes. The ability to control variables in a process is directly related to the operating cost of the process and the resources needed to manage the system. If manufacturers can control the variables of the process, they can therefore control the resource costs (the basis of statistical process control).

THE SYSTEM PULLS IT ALL TOGETHER

Kirila estimates the market for VEC Cell manufactured composites is $60 billion. The VEC operating system provides integrated control of the capital requirements, process control variables, live variables, and the Human Interface.

Kirila's idea to integrate these factors and to guarantee quality, no matter where the cell is located, and to download and control design and production remotely, is a breakthrough, a big wave whose implications for manufacturing in 2020 are only beginning.

Meta-System Number Four: The Net

Communications to customers and designers from the 2020 replication center will be enabled by solutions to the technical problems that now keep our patchwork communications systems—telephones, twisted pairs, high-speed modems, low-speed modems, fiberoptic cables, satellite links, and others—in a state of dis-integrated and limited pipelines. Managing and directly controlling processes over the Internet is a challenge, but three barriers will be the first to come down—security, response time, and bandwidth. Each factory, town, and warehouse will have high-speed fiberoptic connections. But the implied infrastructure capital costs are immense.

BANDWIDTH

Telepresence and teleoperations require each plant site to have T1 (1.5 megabits per second) performance, with interactive real-time protocol to each service location. And existing interconnect systems are preferred. Ma Bell's solution, ADSL—Asynchronous Digital Subscriber Line—is a revolutionary concept that allows high-speed interactive bandwidth in existing household installations of copper loops. It's a low-cost solution that some experts expect will leapfrog modems and ISDN.

ISDN is a high-capacity data-exchange service, the other solution to the problem that modems are stuck at 33.6 kilobits per second, before data compression. Data compression is not the same as raw bandwidth; data compression techniques can yield a virtual bandwidth of four times raw bandwidth.

The ability to have four T1 lines (about six megabits) running over copper twisted pair sets already installed in our homes and factories sounds impossible. But after tests and demos, the skeptics recognized ADSL as reliable, robust, and cost-effective. Trial deliveries over copper were impressive as tests ran ISDN, four TV channels and POTS (plain old telephone service) simultaneously without a glitch.

It's no leap to envision having T1 interactive, and ADSL with the four T1 capacity has also been tested. Motorola, Analog Devices, and others are producing the hardware.

THE GUTS

Data exchange is asynchronous; one page of text is equal to one or two kilobits and compressed graphics take up ten to one hundred kilobits. The controller takes only a fraction—estimates range from 1 to 10 percent—of the downlink. The "low-speed" capacity of T1 uses an uplink of 64 kb/s; the downlink capacity of 6 mb/s (four T1 "lines") uses 640 kb/s of control capacity, although lab tests have attempted transfer of 51 mb/s over a thousand feet of twisted pair. The basic modulation scheme uses discrete multitone modulation (DMT), a technology that seems to be the market winner against three competing technologies, Quadrature Amplitude Modulation (QAM), Carrierless Amplitude and Phase Modulation (CAP), and Vestigial Sideband (VSB).

THE PRICE

ADSL prices now running at about $2,000 will drop to $500 or less, and we will see modem-like pricing by the turn of the millenium. Typical T1 service costs are $200 per half hour with ADSL projected at $15 for the same service. By comparison, CATV and optic drops cost $2,000.

TIME TO GET TO WORK

Although the techies have "wired" every home and factory with fiber performance using phone company copper loops, no single vendor has all the bits and pieces for the phone companies, and no one has looked at systems for our renaissance in innovative replication (manufacturing). Vendors are typically small and thinly financed. Although fiber and coax are coming on strong worldwide, cultural and regulatory resistance will, as usual, get in the way of innovative technology solutions.

ADSL will change the installed copper loop capacity, and the service will quickly move from entertainment applications to data and industrial use. ADSL uses untreated twisted pair loops to yield video and T1 performance. Our factories and plants are wired today; this is a mega-system leap for industrial control and MIS needs, and it's available now. No excuses—we have sufficient computing power, memory, software, and bandwidth beyond any current needs imaginable. It's time to get to work.

Four software-based meta-systems have proven the applicability of intelligent agents and smart software to simplify and de-mystify manufacturing processes and change the way we make things. GM's Fort Wayne Paint Shop was the first big wave; from GM, software designers developed the confidence to proceed with hard industrial applications. John Deere's agricultural equipment scheduling algorithm could just as well have been applied to a computer factory, to an automotive assembler, or to appliance manufacturing where variety is the biggest challenge. Gene Kirila's unique integrated composite manufacturing system takes the intelligence required to run a fast-cycle, revolutionary process, and makes the information transportable. Kirila's innovation presages the Chinese Box. The Net—telepresence and teleoperations—enables linkage over high-speed, high-bandwith channels that will enable localized production run by remote intelligence.

A fifth meta-system, the Japanese bullet train, Shinkansen, is an application of large-scale computer modeling and software intelligence to a complex, high-speed train schedule. The bullet train will be discussed in chapter 8.

Reference

Petzinger, Jr., Thomas, "At Deere, They Know a Mad Scientist May Be a Big Asset," *The Wall Street Journal,* July 14, 1995.

7

Managing the Technology Machine

The driving ambition of the successful enterprise

ia a passion to show the world the right way to do things.

Sixty Years Ago, We Didn't Have—

Television, frozen foods, Xerox, plastic, contact lenses, radar, laser beams, credit cards, atomic power, ball point pens, air-conditioners, men on the moon, FM radio, tape decks, word processors, McDonald's, AIDS, artificial sugar, disposable diapers, Velcro, cell phones, bug zappers, CNN, cable TV, Japanese products, automatic transmission, car air-conditioning, the Internet, directional signals, the United Nations, the interstate highway system, shopping malls, the Beatles, Frequent Flyers, penicillin, jet planes, color TV, diet soda, Fed Ex, CDROMs, birth-control pills, transistors, the National Weather Service, organ transplants, polyester, nuclear reactors, color prints by Kodak, magnetic recording tape, DDT, Teflon, juke boxes, the CIA, flying saucers, the Los Angeles Air Pollution Control District, the Polaroid Camera, the first fusion bomb, scientology, 3D movies, Eniwetok, DNA, synthetic diamonds, DisneyLand, Elvis, Sputnik, Fortran, the PLC, the Singing Chipmunks, microchips, Barbie dolls, payola, the minicomputer, home VCR, the Clean Air Act, the EPA, Pinto gas tanks, floppy disks (another Morley invention), the Wang word processor, Pong video games, Cray computers, heart and liver transplants.

Ten Years Ago, We Didn't Have—

The World Wide Web, virtual pets, MS Windows, rollerblading, Snapple, the ATM, Ninja Turtles, SAP/ERP, the V-chip, privatized Internet, children bringing guns to school, shelters for battered women, four-car families, major surgery done as "outpatient," free breakfast AND lunch at school, kids watching six thousand acts of violence yearly on TV, school grief counselors, air bags.

Five Years Ago, We Didn't Have—

Viagra, flat TV, small satellite dishes, cartoon network, South Park, Olean, Amazon, www.schwab.com (on-line trading and investment tools for The Masses), wearable telephones, machines that win at chess, Beanie Babies, one-gigabyte hard drives, palmtop computing, cable modems.

The Power of Technology

Technology creates wealth and jobs and more technology. Technology is the only road to true wealth—every other manipulation is arbitrage and disbursement and redistribution. Did Compaq really create the computer business, or did it snatch it away from IBM's lost opportunity and neglected growth? The Internet, fire, the wheel, and gunpowder truly created wealth, new parameters, directions, and even freedom of choice.

Wealth means freedom of choice, not the redistribution of money. Heated rounds of merger and acquisition situations don't make much sense because they do not grow new industries or create wealth, other than funding financiers and deal-makers. When Gould acquired Modicon in 1978 for $17.8 million, for example, the stock value did not appreciably change. The combination of two medium-sized companies into one large organization did not create wealth—the merger amounted to a restructuring that shuffled the nameplates and increased executive compensation.

And sometimes technology unleashed under bad management creates complexity, too many wires connected to too many plugs with too many switches. The nuclear power industry, and the catastrophic political invasion of the space shuttle design deployment, with O-rings as a result, illustrate. No one can argue the physics of nuclear power, but clearly Three Mile Island, Chernobyl and O-rings uncovered weak management in the face of pure science.

How to Pick Technology Winners

Manufacturing professionals at all levels must understand that there are technology winners and losers, because in 2020 managers will no longer be simple handmaidens to the technology machine. They will build and manage and occasionally unplug the machine. That's a challenge that nontechnical managers are ill-prepared for, because with manufacturing and the extended enterprise dominated by advanced design, communications, and process technologies, technophobes are doomed.

One source of technology winners, and near winners, is the Massachusetts Institute of Technology. MIT technology winners create jobs that find their way into manufacturing, biotech, and energy management. According to a Special Report of the BankBoston Economics Department, by 1994 MIT graduates had started four thousand companies with 1.1 million jobs, representing a total of $232 billion in sales; the jobs created at more than eighty-five hundred plants throughout the United States equaled one out of every 170 jobs in America. And 80 percent of those jobs were in manufacturing.

MIT entrepreneurs are on a roll—"MIT graduates and faculty have been forming an average of 150 new firms a year since 1990." The earliest and best-known MIT-spinoffs include Arthur D. Little, Inc. (1886), Stone and Webster (1889), Campbell Soup (1900), Gillette (1901), Analog Devices, Digital Equipment Corporation, Progress Software, Picturetel, Raytheon.

Barbarians Within the Gate and Without

New technology management ideas and potential startups will continue to come over the horizon quicker. As information technology virtually becomes the business of many industries, such as financial service and telecommunications, computer crime and security become huge financial issues. Assets at risk draw management focus and a rush to technology solutions. Executives and managers in 2020 should understand not only how to pick technology winners and losers, but also how to manage their situation as if it were a technology investment portfolio.

Management Preparation

How can managers best ready themselves to take technology management positions in the year 2020? Preparation to understand, select, evaluate, and manage the right technology machines is scattered. Although more MBAs have technical backgrounds today, most academic institutions struggle to combine technical with business skills. And for most institutions, running a factory is still black magic.

The contrast in credentialing is puzzling. When graduate students leave MIT or Stanford, for example, unless they have completed a joint degree program, such as Leaders in Manufacturing, they cannot truly run a factory. There will be very few middle-management jobs like the ones that until the past five years were good entry-level positions. Yet when students leave law school, or medical school, they are ready to practice law or treat live patients.

We think the roots lie in a "have and have-nots" problem around technology and science. The fact that we are a republic and that policies are determined by groupthink is a technology crippler. When decision-makers don't understand either the problem or its repercussions, they inevitably will make decisions based on fashion, not logic. Bad technology and bad politics abound.

Why build an electric car with lead-acid batteries that are less effective converting wellhead energy into miles traveled per passenger?

Who makes the electricity and what fossil fuels do we burn in Nevada to make the acid rain to power electric cars that don't leave waste materials in Los Angeles?

Management blindness blocks progress in other areas—hybrid and fuel cells to power electric technology vehicles. Why install robots when cleaner processes will work? Why build a space shuttle with O-rings? What was the reason that Washington diverted millions from ARPA/DARPA into "competitiveness" local programs? Designing a multijointed structure may satisfy a political "spread the wealth approach," but it does nothing to improve structural integrity. Not only is the wrong decision bad for the industry and society, but it also blocks other, good decisions—the right ones.

Managing to Extremes

Sometimes we put our faith in fashionable software, hoping for a single solution that will solve any problem. We look at singular performance silos, instead of a broad spectrum of technology potential. We buy cars that only offer mileage performance; our hunger for SUVs has supplanted an old hunger for diesels, which followed an earlier fascination with station wagons. In manufacturing we have experienced the Factory of the Future craze, MRP, constraint management (the real answer is to remove the constraints!), and neural nets. Even the concept of the lights-out factory is blind misjudgment. The mistake of trying to get rid of everything comes from thinking, "If some is good, more is better." Remember re-engineering? Manufacturing has taken the same compulsive approach to teams, unions, MBO, re-engineering, strategic business units, cells, computer systems, even the lean crusade.

Avoidance and Technological Denial

We continue to make dangerous assumptions about change— "Change only happens to the other guy," "Somehow we'll skim by." We'll tweak a little here, and add a machine there, and we'll make do. That's the wrong approach.

Our advice to professionals contemplating the great technology tsunami that will inevitably sweep over their industries is:

Plan on putting yourself out of business.

We've worked in old companies and launched new ones; we've survived hoola-hoop management and enjoyed enormous technology successes. And we have decided that there are twelve rules about how to run a technology-smart enterprise:

TWELVE RULES FOR THE
TECHNOLOGICALLY ENABLED

1. Hire top people.
2. Have strong leaders.
3. Deliver a message from on high.
4. Have an enemy. Japanese companies frequently use big threats of market competition or technology swings to bring employees into alignment because without a shared, intense fear, the organization drifts. A story repeated within Honda about Japanese banks mentioning the possibility of Honda merging with Mitsubishi served to energize American employees when much Honda growth was shifted to the Ohio plants.
5. Ship product.
6. View work as the reward.
7. Advocate complete local control.
8. Form small work groups of no more than seven.
9. Avoid surprises.
10. Use metrics of performance.
11. Keep outsiders out.
12. Base pay on performance, not longevity.

But these Golden Rules can be further reduced to a memorable five:

1. Be the dumbest person in the place. The *New York Times* reported on a study in which researchers tracked subjects from infancy to adulthood to see if they could predict who was most likely to be successful. Their predictions were wrong two-thirds of the time. Researchers consistently overestimated both the damage of early family stress and the positive effects of having a smooth, nonchallenging

childhood and adolescence. They had failed to anticipate that depth, complexity, problem-solving, and maturity might derive from painful experiences, rather than easy successes. The message was whatever your experiences, never let past or present difficulties limit your belief in yourself or your potential for success. And when you create an organization, hire people who are specialists and smarter than the top manager, founder, or entrepreneur.

In fact, when we evaluate startup companies, we always ask if the president had a challenging childhood. Bankruptcy is a plus—not a negative—and a Ph.D is a negative!

2. Have the best tools.

3. Stay focused.

4. Don't pay very much. Good work is its own ultimate reward. Money helps, money is necessary, but money won't guarantee spectacular results.

When an employee is working exclusively for monetary reward, we predict sure failure, and the reason is that no successful companies start up just to make money. *The driving ambition of the successful enterprise is a passion to show the world the right way to do things.*

5. Tell them when they are done. When the project is over, declare it over and move on. Every project has an end point, and every successful team member develops an investment in the work. Unsuccessful projects have their own time lines as well, but the good manager's role is to call the score, ring the bell, end the game, and redistribute the resources, to keep moving.

Think of Managing Technology Like Managing Your Stock Portfolio

In your portfolio there will be a certain amount of risk that is covered by wise selection for high returns. Good investors understand where they will find the soft middle ground—little risk, small rewards—and they avoid this area. Big risks yield big rewards.

In production organizations, running the shop is something we know how to do quite well; there is little risk there. We know how to empower and train production workers, we can design manufacturable product, take costs out of inventory and bad processes, and eliminate quality waste. Our opportunities for big rewards, therefore, lie ahead of and behind manufacturing, in such areas as engineering, logistics, product design, and supply management.

By 2020 the good companies will have perfected technology that eliminates all manufacturing process risk. Such companies as Motorola, Honda, Intel, and Nypro are well on their way to perfect production processes. Intelligent systems, automation, and other very high-quality processes, combined with smaller and better-trained workforces, have taken us to Six Sigma performance, and that trend will continue in manufacturing. But, managers must expect that risk will continue to present itself in other decision areas—in systems, communications, protocols, new products, and new processes. So, the question for smart technology managers becomes "how much risk to put into the technology portfolio?"

Let's look at the lopsided aspect of the math. If we make $100 bets based on the flip of a coin, we win 50% of the time, or we lose 50% of the time, and roughly we will come out even or a little better than even. If the ability to make money on the flip of a coin with a 50% chance of gain or loss makes us roughly break even, we should expect this to hold in larger percentages. Ah, verily and forsooth, not so!

For a $100 bet, let's assume a likelihood of 90 percent or a factor of 10 times loss or a factor of 10 gain. This means that a bad bet loses $90 [($100 − 10(90)] and a gain wins $1,000 ($100 × 10). In portfolio management it's clear that for each flip of an equally balanced coin, the loss of $90 versus a gain of $900 has a significant impact on the bottom line. Approximately a factor of 10, therefore, biased toward loss per toss, will make us break even. The point is: facing bigger potential rewards, a winning bet makes us richer than a break-even or even a loss.

The manager should consider high-risk multiple forays to really substantially improve his chances of landing a winner. By continuing to seek lower risk, or no risk whatsoever, and repeatedly flipping the coin, one limits portfolio growth, because no risk in multiple tosses is quite literally no gain—the higher risk and the more tosses, the higher the eventual gain over the portfolio of forays.

The same principle applies to technology adoptions in manufacturing facilities seeking a competitive advantage. Imagine a medium-sized manufacturing facility in California that specializes in design replication—manufacturing—for the industrial controls and systems markets. There's a Catch-22 perspective at work in this modern factory, as accounting systems track costs and ascribe certain overhead charges to legacy departments, such as engineering and facilities. Even in the smallest facilities, this measurement approach leads to cost and performance silos that permit optimization of "localized" performance (Rule 7 of the Twelve Rules for the Technologically Enabled Enterprise). Reducing local costs makes heroes, but each time manufacturing "reduces" costs, engineering takes on more of the burden; the net result is a simple shift of numbers from one departmental budget to another—no better process, no more breakthrough technology, but simply a numbers game.

The further irony is that we have become so much more skilled at production that the factory floor typically accounts for less than 10 percent of costs in a modern electronics factory. And building, administration, and marketing costs run on a par with those of manufacturing. However, the costs of engineering, the engine that drives the technology machine, frolic at Dilbertish levels of more than four times floor costs.

Manufacturing runs to stringent controls, not including technology support, facility maintenance, and product design. But both evolutionary and novel development costs are skyrocketing. The budget expands each time a new buzzword walks through the gate.

Even engineering centers need to be localized and fast.

Technology management issues have become the *only* bottleneck in every agility strategy. Contrast an ultramodern automobile facility with an outsourced design center, a skunk works populated with technology experts, living and breathing the competitive market pressures. The difference in design methods, time to market, and most of all, costs, in these two competing approaches are enormous.

• Skunk works are two times faster than large-organization development departments.

- Skunk works are five times less costly than larger organizations.
- Skunk works build single-target items, not broadband products.

The Territorial Imperative

Despite its innovative platform teams' design concept, Chrysler's Farmington Hills design center, a marble monument housing hundreds of very skilled engineers, is a barrier to the art-to-part automotive design revolution, because the organization itself is a hurdle. The organizational structure itself will inevitably defeat any very lean initiative because it runs to its own agenda; expecting several hundred entrenched professionals to willingly surrender their rightful place in the design hierarchy to pursue the Three-Day Car, or paperless/clayless design, is unrealistic. These concepts require fewer engineering bodies and more innovation.

Obviously there is much room for improvement in the entire engineering function. And one approach that has been proven in other disciplines is to use metrics that reinforce the group's true objectives, because the potential for improvement in many traditional facilities ranks in the 50 percent or more range. In 1994 RMI did a study for NCMS on metrics for technology groups. Although there are many varieties of measures, the study focused on five indicators that separate the excellent performers from all the rest.

FIVE TECHNOLOGY PERFORMANCE METRICS

1. Money spent on new projects
2. Cited patents
3. Percent of revenue invested in technology compared to others in the same industry segment
4. Personnel turnover
5. Does anybody want the output?

A book that addresses the challenge of technology management and behavior change is *Fixing Broken Windows* by George Kelling. Kelling makes a Hawthornelike point about creating the right environment for success. In a case example of a warehouse in a seedy part of town, if there is one broken window, all the other windows will also soon be broken. If we fix the first broken window, others are much less likely to be vandalized, because disorder begets disorder. Kelling used this revolutionary theory to fix the New York City subway system, and it works in industrial environments as well. This approach takes advantage of a behavior that leads to an emergent property of the group—peer pressure and better individual self-esteem is used in a positive way to prevent more broken windows. In engineering, low esteem breeds low productivity. Counter that with new, powerful computers, free Coke, keys to the building, and few meetings.

Technology management concepts must be improved to speed the process in the technology machine. When technology managers learn to think like portfolio managers the winners will find and take the right risks to cover an acceptable level of losses in order to make leapfrog gains. A few smart technology managers, like Kirila and Ekberg, will understand where science, technology, and luck intersect, and will build their technology machines on the right convergence point. They will not trust the technology to grow or manage itself.

The Five-Legged Dog

Every successful research and development project or organization uses the "five-legged dog" concept, an image from an old riddle, "If you call a dog's tail a leg, how many legs does a dog have?" The answer is four—it doesn't make any difference what you call a dog's tail, it still has only four legs. Reality is what counts. Every new product and every new process design proposal must therefore consider the five legs before any other considerations—organizational preference or political style—take hold.

When even one of these five legs is neglected or missing, the likelihood of failure increases. The Lisa computer, for example, sub-

THE FIVE-LEGGED DOG

1. Management
2. Marketing
3. Production
4. Money
5. Technology

optimized its market and failed to deliver real market needs. The K-car suboptimized technology—it was a fifties vehicle wrapped in a seventies look. Note that technology is the last point, because technology is the easy part—we know how to make products. Flow manufacturing and information technology enable us to make just about anything, any time, anywhere. The tricky part is making and designing the right stuff very quickly, and moving on to the next piece.

Ask this question first: "What do people need?" not "What should we make?" There is no room for chaos in the design function, or for the creative genius who designs a product for which there is no need, or that cannot be built well or fast.

"Creativity Software"

At RMI, we have played with "creativity software," packages that offer criteria for formal R&D proposal evaluation and other supposed innovation aids. One particular package advised that the innovation section of the proposal should represent about 10 percent of the total. Other software tools promise improved new product design from collaborative software packages. We don't believe that software is anything more than an innovator enabler, the tool that helps human creativity. When co-author Morley designed the PLC, for instance, we would never had used software as anything but a second-generation improvement tool to breed PLC features into new platforms. The first big step is human—the next step is the machine.

Any technology proposal, project proposal, or technology risk should be evaluated against eight criteria:

EIGHT CRITERIA FOR TECHNOLOGY
PROPOSAL EVALUATION

1. 10X performance
2. Seven years
3. Three gurus
4. 100 percent of the market
5. Five-legged dog
6. Three rounds
7. Folding is important
8. Passion

---

1. 10X Performance

For a product proposal to be worth developing, it must be ten times better than anything currently available in some element of its functionality. One parameter of the project must deliver a factor of ten in real measurable performance—the price of your new PC offering must be 10X lower, or the performance must be 10X higher. The new engine needs to run for one hundred thousand miles with no service; or the new aircraft design needs to fly at hypersonic, not supersonic, speeds. The original Macintosh, for example, in comparison to IBM offerings, offered a 10X improvement in certain functionalities and ease of use.

Some "experts" think that Microsoft is using various strong-arm tactics to dominate the industry rather than perfecting a full range of 10X offerings. We disagree, because just as we know that taking good risks increases the probability of success, we know that a very small difference in technologies can yield a very high and very big impact when two competing environments collide. Microsoft intends to be 10X better than any other Internet access. Wal-Mart enjoyed a clear 10X advantage compared to its small-town competitors. Careful emphasis on competitive factors wins in the face of overwhelming numbers.

This phenomenon has been demonstrated best in warfare. When the Spanish invaded South America, for example, they assembled a task force of about 100 to 150 people that stood in the middle of a force of 80,000 indigenous peoples. The natives lost, and they lost because despite their overwhelming numbers, they had inferior management skills, leaders, horses, and arms. Each of these advantages, however, pales in light of the disparity between 80,000 and 150 men. One would expect that the sheer weight and pressure of bodies would quickly eliminate the Spaniards. Overwhelming odds?

Other military examples abound. In Desert Storm, allied forces lost fewer than 200 people, compared to Iraq's 100,000. Again, a very small difference—a technology advance, like the Gatling gun compared to the cannon—can yield a significant impact based on probability of success against small advantages.

The rule says ten times on *one* parameter, not several, because diffusion over several factors of two doesn't count, and carrying several items of 10X dooms the project. The basic requirement for a 10X advantage buys a startup time and distance. Apple entered the educational computer market by first capturing a niche, and from that leghold it was able to make small improvements, even while its competitors offered cheaper, more flexible products on which numerous new application platforms could run. A Boston Consulting Group study indicating that once a competitor had achieved market size, no entrant could dislodge a contender from a specifically named market is correct, because the market holder already holds tremendous advantage in distribution, connectivity, and user preference.

FIND A NEW FRONTIER, GET THERE FIRST, AND TAKE IT

It is safe to assume that the numbers of distributors, stockholders, products, pricing advantages, and customers are exponentially related, not tied in a linear way to the marketplace advantage. The only way to win is to start a new marketplace. The only laundromat or newspaper in town wins because the race has already started and the winner is ahead by many lengths. Microsoft, or even GM with its tremendous advantage, is the winner; the race is defined by Microsoft or GM, and there is "no way" any late entry into the marketplace could ever win the race. Some pundits may call this "strong-arm tactics," but we know that we are simply observing an emergent property of the interconnectivity of all aspects on the competitive landscape.

Luck plays a small part here too. The exponential relationship between small advantages that leads to an overwhelming sense of superiority, both in fact and in appearance, is what causes some observers to mislabel strong competition as "strong-arm tactics," when what they are really seeing is the properties in the math and the exponential relationship between small advantages.

Someone had to win the operating system war, for example, just as someone had to win the DC/AC power, aircraft, automotive standards, and other technology wars. The winner just happened to be Bill Gates. The situation discovered Gates.

The lesson for players? It is more important to capture and retain small gains than to craft perfect positioning of product and lose the headstart. Take a shot.

2. Seven Years

Seven years is a magic number, a long time. Further, any seven-year project must be managed into segments of three years over a five- to nine-year total life span. Nothing can work that targets the next quarter; even sustained engineering projects average about eighteen months' duration.

Seven years is the time between the back-of-the-envelope conceptual design (not the time when we first see money or the patent is issued) and significant venue, positive cash flow, or some other criterion of business success—the founder's first Porsche, or Harley, or trophy wife. It takes a very long time for the penciled designs on cocktail napkins to contribute significantly to our society. Each of the stages of investment, however, accommodate between one and three years.

HOW LONG IS A LONG TIME?

Here is the typical, average R&D/marketing meeting scenario. Marketing meetings inevitably work their way over to the time-frame question when the populist consensus of the marketeers comes to the fore. The first question they inevitably ask the techies is, "How long will the project take?"

The answer is: *"Every project takes eighteen months and a million dollars,"* although when the marketing folks hear this answer, it doesn't immediately sink in. Every marketing meeting starts at 9:00 A.M., and the techies and the managers and the marketeers continue to argue about the dollars and time needed for this sustaining project. Typically, the marketing and the engineering folks agree to seventeen months (one month less) and a reduced budget. Time passes. By 11:50 the engineers have agreed to eleven months, four days, and seven hours, with a budget of $438,974.89. The other attendees smile and congratulate each other. But as the two engineers slouch down the hall, they whisper to each other, "Those stupid bastards think they are going to get the project done in eleven months!" They only agreed to the schedule to get to lunch.

These two time-to-completion rules guide all Breakfast Club investment projects.

1. A wealth-creating program takes about seven years, independent of what it is.

2. Maintenance engineering projects take about eighteen months, independent of subject matter.

Next-quarter results have nothing to do with this quarter's R&D commitment. Seven years is the absolute time commitment necessary to birth a new product offering, and to extend the horizon well into areas that fit the process and the organization to the innovation idea, rather than vice versa.

3. Three Gurus

"Three gurus" is the number of "smart" people needed for any project—remember, this is not a Mars mission. R&D projects must be managed by small teams with clearly defined goals. Three gurus—the "smart" people—should be amplified with no more than five people each. Fewer or more humans reduces the likelihood of success and increases the time and money involved. A large team needs to be broken up into small teams with clearly defined shippable deliverables. Every project, no matter how large, needs to be broken up into groups the size of a patrol.

4. 100 Percent of the Market

Market dominance is all. With dominance in market share, the technologist has control over pricing, margins, and growth. The aggregated uncertainty and enormous costs of R&D work preclude targeting anything less than 100 percent dominance because anything less is a loser's strategy, and an indicator of uncertainty and fear that the teammates are sure to feel and react to. This is one of the most significant success parameters, because the market is defined by the outcome of the effort. Statements such as, "Eight percent of the diphthong market will be captured," are disallowed; although this philosophy applies to hamburgers, airline routing, and the cola wars, it does not apply to technology innovation.

Make this parameter so clear that it becomes your team's bumper sticker, "100% or Bust!" Consumption is the starting point for any project. Make your team understand and write the user brochure, not the technical specifications of the product. The process will raise the right questions: "What do people need?" not "What should we make?" or "What do we want to sell?" A successful market must meet future needs. Control of market is control of your own destiny. The PLC was not what that first customer knew enough to ask for, but it was definitely what he and the industrial automation industry needed.

5. The Five-Legged Dog

The five-legged dog—management, marketing, production, money, technology—must be represented, not necessarily equally, but all at the table, on every project. Marketing and engineering are typically in place for good startups, financial expertise is often missing at the scale of managing a business rather than a hobby.

6. Three Rounds

Three is a magic number in the venture capital business, and anything more than three solid rounds of money advanced to a good startup is not recommended. Round one gets the prototype, or the demo, in good engineering order; round two is used to acquire customers and build one solid product to get a leghold; round three should take the company to successive generations of products and serious production personnel, corporate growth. Too much money expended in the prototype stage is a red flag, as is too little money for stage three.

7. Folding Is Important

R&D is susceptible to the law of large numbers, because a zero-risk endeavor cannot return value. Very high risks, however, are prone to failure. Managers must navigate and choose a risk percentage or failure rate that will increase the return on the entire R&D investment.

Technology managers must think like portfolio managers, because they will be asked to very quickly evaluate new ideas, new software, new manufacturing equipment, people, and projects, and many of the ideas will come to them with high risks attached. Picking the right amount of risk and the right tool will enable technology managers to leapfrog their competition, and sometimes to create new markets. Venture capitalists choose a failure rate of 80 percent for each single investment to earn a portfolio growth overall of 20 percent per year over a decade, based on the few projects that do succeed. The rule is to choose a failure rate that leads to overall success. A suggested failure rate for personal bank loans, for example, is 2 percent, buyers' remorse for television hovers around 20 percent, and Breakfast Club angels expect about 80 percent.

Here's a story that explains why: In the days of wooden ships and iron men, an inventor could own ten sailing ships. If these sailing ships are kept in the harbor and never leave, there is low risk. If, however, the ships leave the harbor and only two return loaded with gold, the investors have taken a high risk with a high reward. The crews, the captain, and the owners want such an adventure; they want to reap their just adrenaline rewards. Route 128 in Boston and Silicon Valley in San Francisco were founded on the risk/reward ratio; no one at Hewlett Packard or Varian, for example, started with a primary goal of taking no risks.

The suggested target for R&D failure is about 50 percent. Choose each project for a fifty-fifty likelihood of failure. Looking for less risk, the "no-fail" policy that is fashionable among some investors yields the equivalent of czarist bonds in the portfolio—no risk, no reward. Small wonder large, traditional companies receive little or no real output for the huge budgets spent on what they call "R&D."

8. Passion

Every good company, technology, or project follows a natural life cycle, which requires different types of support—money and management styles—to flourish. The smart technology manager learns to read the landscape and understand the life cycle. To have a really good company, you must accept that you will never have a perfect company—go in the direction of improvement and understand that the landscape underneath you is changing. At one time, for example, reducing overhead was every company's goal; now, increasing overhead—corporate intelligence—is good. At one time hiring more people was good; now "optimization" is valued. The landscape will continue to shift as you build the base.

Basic Project Selection Rules

Once the group of possible projects is on the table, selections are in order. When the checks have been written, the next step is management. Morley's Rules of Technology Management take an iconoclast's approach to a very serious business, but they work.

MORLEY'S RULES OF TECHNOLOGY MANAGEMENT

Always be prepared to answer these questions about the project or investment:
- Who represents the investors or the customers?
- Is this a hobby or a business?
- When should we fold? What is the point of no return?
- Do the managers know everything they need to make it work? You are not a school!
- Who runs the shop? This is not a democracy!
- What's your bottom line? If you demand nothing, that's what your "kids" will deliver. Tough love works.
- Do you really want a job out of this, or just your money? Remember the differences between micromanagement, goals, and process.
- How much money did we make today? Not what equipment did we buy, or what big customer order did we pitch, but how much profit did we accumulate? It's the difference between profit and revenue.
- Do you always treat your friends this way? Remember, we are not the enemy.
- Does anybody love you? Spend time with your kids, keep in touch with your parents. Send Mom a postcard whenever you go on a business trip.

What Angels Want—$$$$$$$$

Jeffrey L. Seglin (jeff.seglin@inc.com), executive editor at *Inc.* magazine, estimates that in 1998 angel investors will sink $20 billion of their own money into young companies. Their bets on the future tell us something about where technology is headed, and Breakfast Club members (co-author Morley's gang of twelve angels) who meet twice or so per year like to "go into businesses where we're not the dumb ones."

The Breakfast Club

Co-author Morley is a member of the Breakfast Club, a group of local investors (angels) who have met periodically at the Nashua (New Hampshire) Country Club for twenty years. During that time the group has helped, watched, or pushed fifty small startups. With a success average of about 10 percent to 20 percent, the group lists lots of "living dead"—companies that survive forever but that cannot yet be written off on taxes—and once in a while, the big hit.

Breakfast Club members work hard to separate the wheat from the chaff of projects and the people who bring them over. The opening speech typically given to a room of budding entrepreneurs goes like this: "Good evening, ladies and gentlemen. I am here to tell you what *I* need. It's all about standards of living. I want you to work—I am an angel. I want you to work half-time—twelve hours a day—get a second mortgage on your house, which you'll stand a chance of losing, co-sign all notes to the company, and probably get divorced. All of this, so that I can improve my standard of living." Several wannabes leave the room.

Next, the investors set out their investment criteria on returns—they want not so much a large piece of the company as monatomic growth over a five-year period, at the end of which they expect ten times their original investment. A few more wannabes exit.

Further, Breakfast Clubbers have problems with Ph.Ds as presidents, because they represent only one leg of the five-legged dog—the technologist—and because they seem to know what the world *should* be, rather than accepting the reality of what the world truly is. Another one or two wannabes leave.

FIGURE 7.1   *The Breakfast Club, a small group of successful entrepreneurs who act as venture capitalists with an eye to picking technology winners. Seated left to right: Douglas Drane, founder of ATEX; George Schwenk, a founder of The Breakfast Club; and Mort Goulder, president of M.E. Goulder Enterprises. Standing at center: Dick Morley, founder of Modicon and Andover Controls.*

For the one or two entrepreneurs remaining, the Breakfast Club looks to dedicate from ten thousand to three hundred thousand dollars per company. Although the popular wisdom says it takes about ten million to fifty million dollars to start any high-tech business, the Breakfast Club has made commitments as low as ten thousand dollars. These angels see about 150 business plans per year, which results in three to six deals per year. Of those, the last time the group tallied results over the years, out of twenty-two investments, two were big hits (it only takes one!), five resulted in bankruptcy, and the rest are the living dead.

MORLEY'S RULES ON MANAGING THE
INVESTMENT RELATIONSHIP

---

1. Think before you jump. How involved do you want to be?
2. Beware the 50 percent hang-up.
3. Keep in touch. The one-day drive rule.
4. Get a *real* board of directors. Keep the dogs and cats
   at home.
5. Pitch in when you can really help.
6. Patience, patience.
7. Everything cycles.
8. Exits aren't clearly marked.
9. 100 percent of zero equals zero.
10. There ain't any free lunches.

As original members of the infamous Breakfast Club, Morley and partner George Schwenk have their hands (or feet) in about thirty companies that are active today. Their involvement ranges from active participant to passive investor.

Breakfast Club members do not invest in *businesses*—they invest in *people*. Steven Gaal, founding member of Walnut Venture Associates, echoes this approach: They look for "very smart people with very high integrity." Nicholas Negroponte, a founder of the MIT Media Lab involved in at least forty companies, likes electronic noise cancellation technology, on a personal, local, urban, and global scale.

Reality counts. Every company is in bad shape, but, if management can fix one problem, and then tomorrow fix another, soon there will be a good company. Plan on being old, because growth for growth's sake does not guarantee good returns. All investments follow a natural life cycle, and you must plan on your company aging.

When companies are young, they must be fed well, with lots of protein and lots of exercise. But when they age, they should have developed wisdom; they should create jobs, turn a profit, and return their gains to society. Planning for maturity means adopting bifocals before you need them, embracing the grace and the freedom that maturity brings. Middle-aged accountants who flip their thinning hair back over their bald spots, or executives who acquire trophy wives, or women who wear too-tight clothing are fighting reality, unaware of their landscape.

Recognize that consolidation is not the way to health or true growth. Adopting a common currency in Europe, for example, will not make a region that has lost its youthful agility more competitive, more like the United States. Homogenization of the trading system may satisfy the regulators, but it does not create a unified trading bloc. Consolidation is not true growth.

True growth comes from putting stress on the bone structure in animals, as it does in human organizations as well. Competition, stress, and exercise build musculature, strength, and speed. Where there is no stress, there will be no growth. European executives who form megacorporations to maintain market position are not building the next growth ring. They are playing Monopoly.

Have an Enemy

Every project needs competition, the weight of a rival sitting like a stone on the very back of the neck. Terry Maruo, the Honda Motor Company guru credited with creating the powerful supplier development method called BP, speaks of his constant awareness of the competition. "We are always thinking of Toyota. Every time. Every time." Toyota's strength and financial power are always at his back, just beyond his seeing or hearing, but, "They are always here. That is my race. My race."[1]

The ideal company life cycle curve is growth, youth, emergent success, loss of direction followed by solid growth, plateau, and death. Companies take anywhere between twenty and two hundred years to die, but they all do, and the wise technologist understands the life cycle and embraces the curve.

Making Technology Pay Off

In summers past, the living in the high-tech industry was,
relatively speaking, easy.

—S. RUSSEL CRAIN, *UPSIDE*,
NOVEMBER 1997, P. 148

Technology managers live with risk, stress, and unpredictable rewards. Conversion of some technologies to commodity businesses—
PCs, for example—can land even the best and the brightest on the
street. The challenge, therefore, is to play the game well and place
your bets on the right process run by the right professionals.

According to estimates by Andersen Consulting and Dataquest,
the computer and electronic systems industry—including computers,
telecommunications, data communications, wireless handsets, and the
industrial and consumer electronics segments (not including semiconductors or software)—is expected to reach $1.2 trillion by 2000.[2]

Huge opportunities breed huge risks and earthshaking movement
as companies rise and fall on the list of winners. Of the top 150 companies on the list, 76 dropped in rank or fell off the list by 1995. The
shift will of course continue into the new millennium, as many familiar names disappear or are swallowed by new ones.

Technology managers will undergo equally shattering changes as
they struggle to select the right technologies to win, both as implementation strategies for the process, and as innovative products. It is
not humanly possible to manage all the complexity that we have developed, and winning managers will find a balance between human
wisdom and governance and the intelligent machines that are absolutely necessary to run the 2020 enterprise.

Reference

For further readings on environmental fixes, see *Mythical Man Month,* by
Frederick P. Brooks, Jr., and *Organizing Genius,* by Warren Bennis and Pat
Ward Bedermen.

8

Two Meta-Systems:

The Bullet Train and Plastics!

Get me a ticket on an aeroplane

Ain't got time to take a fast train.

—THE BOXTOPS

Recently Yaskawa Electric (Motoman), one of the premier suppliers of motors and robot technology worldwide, wanted to talk about what role robotics would take in the twenty-first century. It is looking ahead to other applications and other definitions of robotics. Its core business, rotary motors in various killer applications, has taken it into numerous innovative "packages," and robots are one of the biggest.

Two Meta-Systems, International Plastics/Germany and the Bullet Train, Genetic Algorithms in Practice

Yaskawa has launched a meta-system—an intelligent agent system that helps run its Japanese bullet trains. Using a Flavors Technology software system, the system handles complex scheduling for very high-speed people movement. The system is used to test new control logic, test new control computers, test new schedules, and test the operation with new facilities.

The second meta-system is International Plastics/Germany (IP/G). IP/G uses the same scheduling approach, derived from emergent behavior rules, to run a complex, high-volume plastics plant that is also

FIGURE 8.1 *Bullet Train Passing Mt. Fuji*

measured on high quality and on-time deliveries. The bullet train schedules are developed for the best mix, given the number of routes, speeds, and so forth that must be managed, while the plastics schedules must deal with enormous product variety and some schedule fluctuations in a high-volume plastics extrusion plant.

The Bullet Train, Shinkansen

Seiichi Yaskawa is head of business development for Yaskawa Electric, and he is proud of the PIM (Parallel Inference Machine) used to help run Japan's bullet trains. Mr. Yaskawa calls the system a real-time parallel-processing system, and its application to simulate large-scale railroad operations is opening new, wide avenues of intelligent agent applications. The bullet trains themselves are engineering breakthroughs, especially in comparison to the United States' limited rail systems (high-speed trains are also well accepted in Europe). He recalls a series of Japanese prophecies made in the year 1901. "There

FIGURE 8.2 *Bullet Train—An Engineering Breakthrough*

were twenty-three dreams and most of them have already been real-ized—worldwide wireless telephones, advanced education, electricity, and the bullet train that takes only two and one-half hours to travel between Tokyo and Kobe."

YASKAWA'S ENTRY INTO THE RAILROAD INDUSTRY

Yaskawa had nothing to do with the railroad industry until several years ago when it started working with Japan Railways on a success-ful implementation of an agent-based application on the Shinkansen bullet train system. This system runs with a monitoring and control system called COMTRAC.

The planning or scheduling and control system is enormously complex and calls for nanosecond decision-making by humans. At the Tokyo station trains depart every three and a half minutes. There are 130 trains running at one time (the time unit is measured in fifteen-second intervals), carrying on average three hundred thousand passengers, 1 million at peak times on the Tokyo-Osaka line, at speeds of 300 kilometers (186 miles) per hour.

CONTROLS

Since the system started in 1964 there have been no fatal accidents, although the system barely escaped disaster when the 1995 Kobe earthquake struck shortly before 6:00 A.M., just before daily operations started up. Train schedules are planned to run to the fifteen-second time unit, with the result that most of the time the trains arrive at the station or leave within the error range of fifteen seconds, a factor that requires elegant and exact train schedules as well as recovery routines following disruptions.

Yaskawa calls the bullet train control center "a railroad version of NASA space control center—a room dominated by a huge panel and many terminals." The first system was developed in 1972, but the center has upgraded the computer system every few years. Currently, they are in construction of phase seven. The goal is to improve capacity—or density—per hour; twelve trains run per hour, one way, and the target is fifteen trains per hour.

"That [increasing capacity] is pretty difficult," says Yaskawa, "because it is already too busy. The key is to improve recovery time." Although most days the trains run within an error range of fifteen seconds, if it snows, or a signal breaks, from time to time there are schedule disruptions. So the problem is how quickly controllers can recover the schedule. After the Kobe earthquake, top management decided to build a backup center in Osaka to supplement the one in Tokyo that has run operations for thirty years.

THE PROCESS

The control center must test any change or improvement in the schedule, but since the system runs every day, it would be impossible to run

FIGURE 8.3 *Railway Control Center*

a test on the real system. And attempting to calculate the optimum solution for schedules is impossible. Yaskawa compares the problems to
a basic law of physics: "If the number of bodies is more than two, it
becomes impossible to analyze the motion." With 130 trains running
at the same time, and all other elements of the operation in parallel,
the only way is to run a few tests or experiments to verify any new
plan, or facility, or schedule. Previously, Japanese Railway and computer supplier's engineers attempted only a simple train operations
simulator in which they would conventionally approximate this kind
of nonlinear complex dynamic system to just a linear equation using a
predetermined average speed between stations, but this approach is
too simple. Shinkansen found itself with a simulation dilemma.

THE DILEMMA

The more we want to precisely describe a system, the more software
code must be written, but the more software that is written, the
slower the execution time will be as the computer grinds through the
solution. A simulator big enough to handle all the possible real-time

situations would be too big. For example, when a disruption like a snowstorm causes one train to be delayed, soon the incident will cascade, and you will find what Yaskawa calls "a flock of trains, like a flock of birds, or a school of fish," as one train stops at the station, and then the following trains may have to stop between their stations. Once the trains are operating off-schedule, the train drivers have no idea what would be the new feasible schedules. Every train driver knows that he is behind schedule, and each driver wants to catch up. As each train attempts to catch the leading train, the schedules change even more.

Another problem is the power surge caused when the trains are running faster to make up lost time. The incidence of trains starting up at different points on the track at the same time as the leading train leaves the station causes a power supply problem, as the pattern draws peak power within a narrow segment of the system.

Although all these patterns of chaotic behavior obviously cannot be dealt with by conventional linear scheduling programs, genetic algorithms like the ones used by the GM Fort Wayne Paint Shop, and Ekberg's work at Shane Steel and SteelWorks, as well as International Plastics/Germany, are perfect methods for developing and simulating schedules against other methods. One of the big advantages to agent modeling is the significant drop in the lines of code (loc) required to program and to run the model. And in fact, Flavors did the first implementation—the GM Paint Shop—to do just that, not to build a better paint shop, although that was certainly one of the end results.

THE SIMULATOR

The track system covers over two thousand segments, or circuits, stretching over seven hundred miles from Tokyo down to Hakata. Each segment in the simulator is one track segment on which only one train or none can exist, the basic control element that avoids collisions. Because the speed of the train is so high, and because the track contains so many curves, it would be impossible to monitor the leading trains, so the simulator runs on signal systems.

FIGURE 8.4

PIM - Theory of Operations

Cell: Time (33ms) Divided Computing Unit (125 to 500 cells)

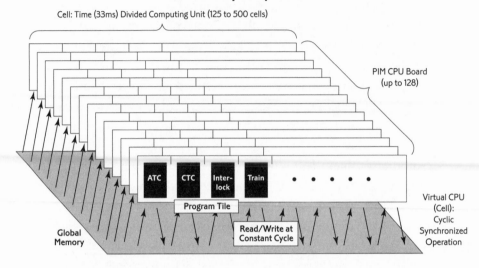

SIMULATING THE RUN CURVE

Trains must be "allowed" on the simulator to accelerate, to decelerate, which is analog (not discrete) behavior. The industry calls this pattern the run curve, and it displays distance, speed, and braking. The simulator must run more than 130 trains at a time exhibiting 130 continuous or analog behaviors.

Japan Railways chose to simulate the system using a PIM (parallel inference machine). The PIM has many virtual processors, each of which can contain many agents. The agents interact with each other through their common global shared memories (code); the net effect is the same as the real "agent" train drivers watching the speed limit generated from the track segments. The train segments are monitoring if they have a train in process; other elements of system behavior have been incorporated into the agents, including some psychology of the train drivers.

A train simulator update formula includes various factors of the operation, including the speed, whether the train is climbing a grade

FIGURE 8.5

CTC Simulator Block Diagram

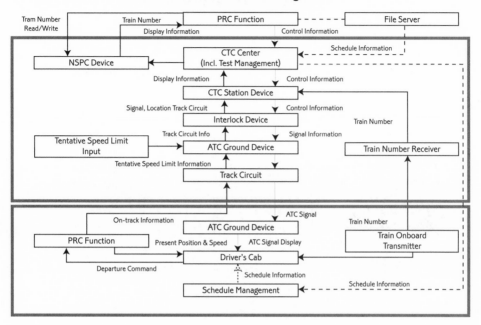

or descending, tunnels with air drag, and every other physical element that would affect speed or power consumption. The agent, therefore, can compute his own speed to the next station based on all the variables.

Controllers reproduced a schedule disruption on the simulator to compare simulator results to actual results. The match worked quite well, except for a difference at one startup point that puzzled analysts. On closer examination, however, the gap became clear. Every train driver knows that in a traffic jam, if he accelerates too much too soon to resume his schedule, the jolt will be uncomfortable for passengers. So rather than accelerating immediately to catch up with the leading train, he ramps up slowly. As a result of this discovery, technicians added another rule to the train driver agent. Although most simulations last only one hour, with this addition of this compensating factor to close the simulated to actual performance gap the simulation can run from 6:00 A.M. until midnight without big discrepancies.

FIGURE 8.6

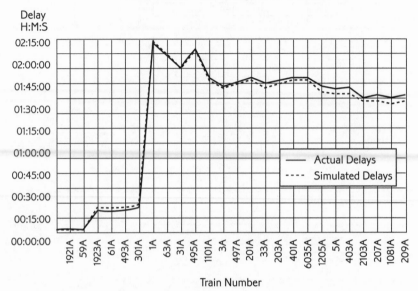

Yaskawa likes the technology and the process in part because of the "ease" of programming complex systems that were hitherto unapproachable. The science's big payback is the ability to solve complex problems within bounded budgets.

OTHER APPLICATIONS

Successful architecting of agents in the bullet train system has led to other applications of the simulator, including tests of new control computers as they are upgraded. Also, dispatchers can be trained on the simulators, a good way to prepare dispatchers to handle major disruptions. Running the control room is, most of the time, an exercise in watching rows of panels, indicator lights, and monitors—not much happens, but when it does, alarm bells, red lights, and phone calls turn the room into a war zone of heated responses. The more tools and experience offered the dispatchers, the better their emergency response.

Another application is verification of new train schedules, particularly with the addition of three-hundred-kilometer-per-hour trains. Typically it would take a team of experts months to develop a new schedule, but with the simulator, the approach is easier and faster, as new schedules are "tried out" and selected from the endless variations.

Electric power cost projection is promising to be an additional payback for simulator advocates. The simulator can help estimate electric power consumption and help shift power sources.

A very futuristic application of the simulator to road traffic and the Maglev train, which now operates a ten-mile test line, running at 550 kilometers per hour, will exercise the simulator as it has never been tested before. The plan is to build another simulator to simulate the whole line between Tokyo and Osaka for the Maglev train, before the line is built. The vision is to run the whole country's rail system on information from the model, and to eventually hook up the direct control to the agent-based system.

Other simulators are running in Japan, including an on-line simulator of 30k cells used by the Central Japan Railways, another in the Osaka backup center. The next one will be in Kyushu, a more complex, older train system.

Finally, Yaskawa is looking to use agent technology to detail auto assembly schedules and crane systems. Applications in assembly processes follow the image of assembly as the implosion (the opposite of explosion) of agents representing small parts. A car, for example, is a flight of spare parts in close formation, and the agents "want" to be near or performing a job on the full system of the car. A bolt, for example, might want to be in a bolt circle. The "bagged" bolt circle wants to be part of a wheel consisting of several independent and bagged agents such as tires, other bolts, washers, torque, and hub. This meta-bag then "crawls" over to the axle and joins the assembled community of parts!

The scheduling, the robots, the sensors, and the car are all assemblages of real or virtual agents that live in the community of the car assembly process. A wild image, but not an impossible one.

International Plastics/
Germany Plastics Extruder Plant

International Plastics (IP) has billions of dollars invested in Europe, some of which goes into new plants, and some into new ideas. The European operation dates back to the late sixties when IP chose Germany for a facility that would produce engineered plastics used in television sets, computers, automotive parts, and other high-valued-added products.

IP/G makes a plastics extrusion product completely at the site in Germany. The process mixes chlorine, air, oxygen, and other chemicals, runs the mix through high-frequency extruders into twenty or thirty thin filaments, each about one-eighth inch in diameter. At several injection points on the line color, filler, or additives are added; raw material, which is typically transparent, can be colored white, or red, or it can contain carbon or glass fillers. Following extrusion, the material is chopped into short segments, bagged, and shipped. The simple process is high-variables/high-complexity of scheduling and high-headache, an excellent candidate for a "pull-through" emergent system in which the extruders act as "customers" for the raw material.

IP/G makes plastics for a wide variety of customers who cover a variety of applications. Much of the customers' work is also high-volume, which drives large orders to the German plant. The product is highly engineered, very strong, and has good optical properties—it can be used for headlamp lenses, crash helmets, unbreakable windows; the recipe can be adjusted for many different characteristics. Other customers include toys, auto parts, plastic tubing, and even water coolers.

Customers can specify about thirty different molecular weights, as well as various colors and strengths and additives, and each of these variables requires absolute exact performance to specifications. Color control, for example, is critical. A yellow fireman's helmet, for instance, must display no color variance between batches. Or a customer might specify nonfading material, or materials that withstand oil or other chemical corrosion. The possibilities are exponential across the landscape of demand.

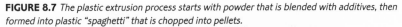

FIGURE 8.7 *The plastic extrusion process starts with powder that is blended with additives, then formed into plastic "spaghetti" that is chopped into pellets.*

THE PRODUCTION PROCESS

There are two parts to the production process. The first step is a batch process in which they cook several chemicals to produce a resin powder that resembles flour; there are a few dozen varieties of this "flour," which is stored in silos twenty feet wide and two hundred feet tall.

The next step is a mixing process in which the powder is mixed with additives in a dry blender the size of a Volkswagen. A ten-foot-wide funnel feeds in additives. Finally, the mix slides into an extruder that compresses and heats the material, forming a hot liquid that is water-cooled at the end. The spaghettilike strands are chopped by a whirling fan blade into tiny cylinder-shaped pellets that are bagged or poured into tanker trucks for transport to customers.

Project manager Gerry Jones, president of a New Hampshire–based software development house that worked with IP/G to install the new system, describes the essence of the process as the extruder line. There are some twenty lines working in parallel, some faster than others, all with different capabilities. "Scheduling changeovers is a critical issue," says Jones, because although production can change colors from batch to batch, if a customer order requires switching from a dark to a light color, the equipment must be completely cleaned out. Changeover can take hours. The line is shut down, although there are different classes of cleaning, from a simple rinse to sending a worker into the blender with a scrub brush for four or five hours.

"The problem we attacked was how to take the list of customer orders and decide which ones to schedule on which machine, in which sequence. With several weeks of orders covering thousands of different recipes, the scheduling job now handled by three humans—by hand, with a magnetic board, lots of experience, and a few basic do's and don'ts rules—was not maximizing material and equipment potential."

SCHEDULING ORDERS THROUGH A COMPLEX MANUFACTURING PROCESS

Scheduling plastics production is a complex balancing of technical requirements, costs, productivity goals, including asset use, and customer requirements. The plant in Germany runs a number of extruders and packaging lines; demand is strong, but executives felt that running their complex operation was too big a challenge for even the best human brain. So they turned to Flavors Technology (of GM's Fort Wayne Paint Shop fame) for help. They needed a process that would yield a stable operation in packaging, with better rules for planning and setting priorities, and they were hoping for better labor synchronization on the extruder floor. The operation's immediate goals—optimizing productivity, or output volumes, and output quality, as well as perceived quality of life—continued as overall operations goals. And they wanted better control over resin planning.

A SYSTEM DRIVEN BY GREED!

"So, what we did was to write an autonomous agent scheduler that produced schedules," says Jones. The package simulates the process—how long it takes and what additional operations must be performed.

The scheduler handles the lines—basically, every time one line is about to finish, it looks at a list of pending orders for its next victim. All the lines bid competitively for the open orders. Jones compares this software approach to "the old Soviet economy—everything was centrally planned and dictated. The plastics scheduler that we designed is like a free-market economy. Each of the machines is imbued with greed, and each one tries to make the most stuff it can according to its built-in rules. It works better, because you make more stuff more quickly and more predictably. In this business, the key is promising the customer delivery for a specific time—soon enough for the needs—and then delivery to the promise date, because the customer is counting on your performance."

The second phase of agent-based scheduling, linkage to the customer's spreadsheet data and translation for input to the algorithm, remains to be competed. This critical linkage will allow the massive numbers of rows and columns of data to be extracted, to be reorganized, and to run in parallel with manual, magnetic board scheduling, to see how much the software helped and where it could be modified or expanded. In any case, IP/G is fast approaching complete scheduling and simulation capability in a very complex, demanding production environment.

The problem is the metrics of benefit. How do we measure the performance of such a system? The measurement must contain the weighted parameters of desired performance, and in particular the RONAE (return on net assets employed), or asset use, of the entire process. If the local optimization for the extruders has a positive or negative effect on the neighbors in the good chain, we should know. Can we only measure the local impact? And how? Is the model good enough to use as the infrastructure of performance?

THE "BLACK ART"

Parallels to the GE Paint Shop job abounded. IP/G needed to handle great variety in order mix—color, viscosity, additives. It wanted to minimize nonproductive changeover time between orders, an opportunity to get more uptime out of the equipment, as well as to minimize materials wasted during changeover. And of course, idle time between setups tends to waste labor hours—floor personnel either are waiting for equipment to be put back on line or are shifted off to other work, an exercise that aggravates scheduling headaches. Complex structure and interactions between equipment added even more parameters to open scheduling.

Most manual or spreadsheet-driven schedules go into overload and stall out when they are used to generate rapid-fire iterations of various scenarios—increased demand, decreased capacity, changes in product mix, and different labor variables. Inevitably, the gut takes over where "what-ifs" leave off.

The state of the programming process, as above, is "brittle." This means that the intrusion of unanticipated states can upset the apple cart in strange ways. The preferred state, robustness, means that states nearby can be used without materially affecting the emergent process. The old expert systems had this problem in spades.

BIDDING

Flavors Technology gurus saw active agent technology—or intelligent agents—as the added brains that would, like GM's "chicken brain in the booth," change the way scheduling and overall planning happened at IP/G. The idea would be to use software-based agent technology to develop a good production schedule. The simulator would then compare the software's "best" schedule, given all the parameters, constraints, and variables, to actual performance history. Designers expected that the software simulation would consistently produce the better way, and they were right, although they could not prove their theory via the Newtonian method.

J. Howell Mitchell wrote the active agent scheduling code in about six months. (If it were possible to write the program using the old top-down process, it would have taken ten times longer.) The program was designed to look at three manufacturing areas in parallel—powder manufacturing, finishing lines, and packaging. Like the GM

Paint Shop application in Fort Wayne, the heart of the program ran an auction process, scheduling next steps with a bidding sequence very much like GM's.

Each extruder had an "awareness" or behavioral activity that was autonomous agent–derived. The extruder agent would look over at the main tasks to be done for particular customer orders—adding red color, for example. When the extruder runs out of work, it reviews the main task list and picks one that ideally is the same color and additive and production as it is now doing, so that there is no asset modification or changeover. If, however, the agent finds no job to be done that is identical with its current state, then it looks at what is considered to be an important, high-performance, or high-margin job; if none of these can be performed by a particular sentient extruder, then it picks any task it can do to keep its asset deployed and busy.

Bid currency changes constantly. For example, one of the bid criteria is the characteristic of "similar, but not identical." The currency of bid includes locations, run lengths, whether the product to be made is priority, whether there is high margin on the item, how long the order has been waiting in line, the order's delivery due date, and the changeover cost.

For example, for the packaging scheduler Mitchell developed these rules:

Product bins bid as follows for service of packaging:
I don't bid when I am almost empty.
I bid LOW when:
    I am almost empty and I am at end-of-lot
    Or I am almost full and other bin is not.
I bid HIGH when:
    I am almost empty *and* I am at end-of-lot *and* other bin is full
    Or I am almost full and other bin is almost full
LOW bid becomes MEDIUM when packaging does not have
to clean.

Finishing line scheduling operated with a different set of bidding rules:
Figure of merit, including:
    Cleaning time

Labor requirement (drawn from pool in time buckets)
Completion time vs. requested
Packaging penalty for secondary movement
Bid is a scalar number
Bid is zero if line is not capable of grade or additive requested

This type of software is remarkable because it represents a big departure from approaches that would develop the code to fit a previously decided solution. Architecting the system that way would never have produced these results:

Software that is not centrally planned
Aggressive bidding
Emergent behavior
Asset optimization over the group, not the individual unit

Phase One

The first phase of the project, which required a short six months to complete, resulted in a simulator for the plastic finishing process, starting with resin silos, and ending with the packaging process.

Phase Two

In phase two, the simulation was extended to resin manufacturing, including scheduling rules for the processing of customer orders. As this was extended to cover multiple extruders and the results were validated, a range of "what-if" situations were used to further stretch the performance envelope. Phase two saw ordering and scheduling added to the multiple extruder simulation. With the completion of a few more checks of actual versus simulated results, the project moved closer to actual production process control.

The development of emergent systems in this environment again demonstrated that the critical individual behavioral elements—agents—can each be identified and empowered with intelligence so that in ensemble they achieve system behavior better than traditional approaches. The vehicle for bringing this second-generation chicken brain forward is the Parallel Inference Machine (PIM), a computing

FIGURE 8.8

What is a PIM?

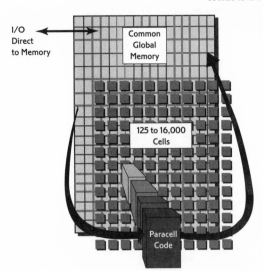

I/O
Direct
to Memory

Common
Global
Memory

125 to 16,000
Cells

Paracell
Code

- A Parallel Processor
  — expands linearly to fit the problem
- Predictable and Fast
  — well suited to real-time factory control
- Interactive and Incremental
  — programs can be modified seamlessly . . .
    while running
- Each cell reads from memory, executes
  code, then writes results to memory
- Execution is systolic, generally from
  30 to 60 Hz

platform invented in 1991 with specialized architecture that provides massively parallel operations. The system is based on VME boards, which are among the most widely used merchant computer boards in the world.

Agents identified in the phase-one model included the silos and the extruder lines, each containing these agents: virgin bin, mixes, surge bin, extruder, two product bins, and three packaging areas. Phase two added two resin lines and a scheduler covering finishing demands and external resin demands. An auction subsystem to generate a schedule for received orders was developed consisting of twenty line bid agents (one for each finishing line), and linkage to the resin-manufacturing scheduler.

The key to successfully operating this type of intelligent system is forming the right rules by which the bid agents construct their bids, and the figures of merit used to clear them. The choice of autonomous agents made sense because hierarchical architectures are inflexible and they become too complex, they are difficult to maneuver, and they are almost impossible to change. Agent-based systems are modular, and complexity is reduced through localization of information flow and control.

Modeling experts like to check out their models by a seven-step process:

FIGURE 8.9

SEVEN STEPS TO OPTIMUM SIMULATOR
PERFORMANCE

1. Develop a "KISS" model.
2. Input historical data.
3. Run a known history segment.
4. Compare actual history with model segment.
5. Evaluate gaps.
6. Repeat the process using detailed data.
7. Buy off on the model.

Simple Software Benefits

Simpler systems take much less time to develop and install. Software and systems can be improved and enhanced incrementally and continuously—add an agent, for example, when process elements change. Computer power was once a major software architecture constraint—the cause of most Y2K problems was the practice of programmers (bit miners) who scrimped on memory space by dropping two digits off their date code; by saving two digits, they frequently saved the additional expense of add-on memory. In the sixties, disk drives cost as much as a small car, but thirty years later, internal memory and add-on mass storage is commodity-priced, and software design focus has shifted from preservation of precious memory locations, to optimizing speed and massively parallel processing power. Now, systems gurus are trading hardware power for software power, and working to solve inherently complex problems. The legacy of

FIGURE 8.10

BENEFITS OF AGENT-BASED SCHEDULING

- Easily custom tailored
- Linear expansion
- Simpler, usually rule-based
- Agent behavior can be dynamic
- Robust, nonbrittle
- In the real world, assumptions and rules can change; the system is nonstationary
- Saves software lines of code (loc)
  (increases hardware entry costs, 2X on the hardware and 1/10 on loc)

"saving" hardware and memory is long gone; saving lines of code (loc) is our biggest current challenge, one that will continue well into the next millennium.

Other Meta-Systems Genetic Algorithm Applications

Complex operations—train schedules, airplane schedules, automotive final assembly, and other consumer products offering endless variety and schedule changes caused by customer demand shifts, tech-

FIGURE 8.11

GENETIC ALGORITHM BENEFITS

- Off-line schedulers simulate the execution of the schedule
- Can be run faster than real time
- Can be used to answer "what-if?" questions

FIGURE 8.12

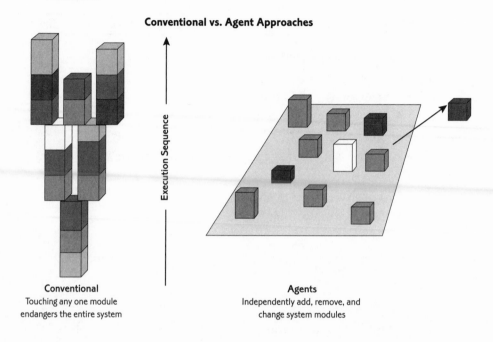

Conventional vs. Agent Approaches

Execution Sequence

Conventional
Touching any one module
endangers the entire system

Agents
Independently add, remove, and
change system modules

nology problems, supplier glitches, and other inevitable disruptions—
are ideal candidates for more applications of genetic algorithms. Up-
coming applications include:

- Engine production simulation
- Power utility management in Korea
- Baggage handling
- Cement processing
- Computer generated forces
- Battle management
- Airplane gate management
- Process control

In operations, autonomy provides fault-tolerance; debugging operations are less of a shutdown problem as agents take on real-time
on-line control and feedback loops. Bug detection becomes less of an

occasional, extremely painful exercise, and more of a constant adjustment to shifting parameters. The underlying philosophy—empower the experts to program solutions—yields on-line, on-time agility advances. Robustness—the ability to have neighbors in the landscape of operation—inevitably increases.

9

In the Land

Where the Engineer Is King

I just bought a Mac to help me design the next Cray.

—SEYMOUR CRAY (1925–96), ON LEARNING THAT
APPLE, INC., HAD BOUGHT A CRAY TO HELP IT
DESIGN THE NEXT MAC

Raising the Bar

In the land where the engineer is king, technology will be created, managed, and harvested by a special breed of cat. Although a few MBAs will still manage to slip through the cracks into technology prosperity, most professionals' credentials—managers, executives, and even a majority of production personnel—will be based on engineering degrees. After a century of capitalists and unionists, the technologist has arrived. Indeed, politically not the most correct co-author and venture capital angel Morley likes to place his bets on this kind of technology leader.

Best chances for successful start-ups are led by a thirty-five-year-old (experienced) male (knows the rules) engineer whose parents were semi–self-employed, and whose greatest joy is work—evening work, early morning work, New Year's Day work, paid vacation work, and half-day, twelve-hour work. This comer "knows" that technology leaders are never promised a rose garden. In fact, near-bankruptcy experiences count extra points in the equation. And they must remember that they stand to lose their companies when the marketing folks let them down, an experience well-known to Steve Jobs at Apple and NeXT, Ken Olsen at Digital, and Seagate's Al Shugart.

Technology Leaders

Motorola's chairman Bob Galvin is one, Andy Grove and Craig Barrett of Intel are also, as were Edison, Ford, Karl Kempf of Intel, Steinmetz of GE, the president of Sony, Edgar Land, and others whom we seem to recognize only in hindsight. All brilliant technologists who continued to face challenges dealing with their own marketing arms, they struggled to couple future needs with current technology development objectives to guarantee corporate survival, and not all of them were successful. Some companies, like Motorola, have been disappointed by manufacturing progress.

Others, like Clinton, Massachusetts, plastics producer Nypro have practiced innovation in what started as a commodity industry—plastics—so well that they have created a new industry of high-quality, precision products for only the best high-end customers, such as Gillette, Hewlett Packard, and Abbott Labs. Nypro's success is clearly tied to the vision and expertise of its leader, engineer/technologist Gordon Lankton, who married sound engineering principles with creative management ideas intended to grow strong, somewhat independent Nypro facilities. Since graduating from Cornell with a degree in mechanical engineering, Lankton's vision has been a global one, because he knew that positioning his company to live in the first tier meant competing globally. Lankton's vision further extended to building an organizational structure that fosters entrepreneurship internally. He used organizational innovation to grow more technology leaders. But the first leghold on Nypro's dream came from Lankton's understanding of technology strength acquired through perfect process.

Nypro Technology Leadership

Gordon Lankton is *one*—an industry leader with vision and a self-effacing approach to his role within the company. Lankton drives the technology machine. As current CEO/president of Nypro Corporate Inc. of Nypro, a company that got its start in the heart of Massachusetts' burgeoning plastics business, he has seen the company grow in thirty years from $1 million in sales, to half a billion dollars. After a two-year Army stint, Lankton took the first of his twenty round-the-world trips—he has logged over four million miles to date—on an NSU 250 cc motorcycle. He wasn't lost—he knew what he was looking for.

Lankton was offered an opportunity to sign on with Nypro, in Clinton, Massachusetts, a mill town (and the birthplace of co-author Morley) located in central Massachusetts, between the Route 128 high-tech area and rural small towns once supported by apple or-chards, chicken farms, and light manufacturing. Thirty years have passed since Lankton signed on, and although the company has changed very much since then, Nypro continues to make headlines and raise the bar as it invents new standards, and new organizational structures, for plastics producers and their customers.

The plastics business in the Northeast used to have the same laughable reputation that Japanese products—carnival toys and household trinkets—had before Japanese industries "discovered" Deming and Juran. Now, in a state that has largely abandoned manu-facturing in favor of money handling—investment services, real es-tate, banking, and big-bucks education—as it once abandoned farm-ing in favor of land development, plastics is a valued and respectable business. Like Nypro itself, the industry is more of a high-tech player than a commodity producer. In fact, because such pioneers as Nypro have perfected the plastics process and worked with high-tech cus-tomers, such as Hewlett Packard, to introduce new applications of new materials, plastics have assumed a healthy position in the Massa-chusetts high-tech sector. The industry provides jobs for about fifty thousand workers in the state, and customers represent high-tech (CDs and printer cartridges), pharmaceuticals, and health care (con-tact lenses, intravenous devices, and toothbrushes).

CUSTOMER SELECTION

None of this has been accidental. The transformation of an industry from making payroll by churning out plastic combs and kid toys to "clean room" production did not happen by accident. Lankton led the company onto higher ground, raising the bar to carefully select business partners—customers—that each represented at least $1 million of business. Such customers as Abbott Labs and Gillette were looking for expert outsourced help designing their products, applications, and even markets, and the help Nypro offered was near-perfect quality and predictable, fast delivery.

A Unique Business Strategy

Nypro raised the bar, and the results began to pour in. By 1998, the company estimated it had earned $20 million on sales of $450 million. Further, Lankton has followed a distributed manufacturing approach, positioning his predictably high-quality production sites next door to partner/customers, such as Abbott Labs in Chicago and Hewlett Packard in Corvallis, Oregon. In each facility Nypro establishes a very localized management team as well. Each plant runs with its own general manager and team of top managers, and each general manager sits on the board of another Nypro company. The net effect, of course, is that plant general managers are always concerned with the health of other plants as well as their own. Lankton's unique individual but integrated organizational structure has, therefore, created a balance of strong competitive focus at the local plant level, with an awareness of total company objectives—day to day, a kind of return to the concern for "the common weal" that we think will continue to grow among technology winners in 2020.

Networking these structures all together, Nypro companies are overseen by their own boards and do not report to traditional corporate executives, such as executive vice-presidents or group vice-presidents. Occasionally an executive has chosen to head off elsewhere—entrepreneurship is not feared or discouraged. In fact, a certain amount is to be expected—*it raises the bar.*

A VIEW FROM THE CLOCK TOWER OUT OVER THE *WORLD*

The Clinton site is, as were other high-tech giants Digital and Modicon, located in a renovated textile mill on the banks of a river. Visitors can climb a narrow flight of stairs to the top of Nypro's tower, originally a water tower built to hold the old mill's tin water tank fire suppressant system, and look over the mill yard to Mount Wachusett and the Nashua River flowing inevitably down to the Merrimack, another great source of innovation, and to the sea. This particular brick building once housed the Bigelow Carpet company (co-author Morley's mother was the Bigelow receptionist). It's been a good run for plastics producers, as they have rushed to move into bigger facilities that would previously have been occupied by computer producers, such as Digital Equipment Corporation, Modicon, Raytheon, Wang, and Andover Controls. From 1972 to 1996, U.S. jobs in plastics grew 3 percent while declining by 0.3 percent for all manufacturing nationwide.[1]

GLOBAL BENCHMARKING

Nypro has taken the industry where its founders might have hoped for success, but where they could not possibly have known it would go. Lankton makes six or seven global benchmarking trips every year, this time not by motorcycle, visiting the best of the best plants in the plastics industry. Lankton recalls, "When I travel throughout the world, I try to get to see the very best plastics technology, and I usually succeed. In Japan, it was through Mitsui, a partner we have had for twenty years, the largest trading company in the world—sales of $160 billion. Mitsui's function ten years ago was to bring Japanese transplants to the USA—they would do all the negotiating, the finding. And they opened the doors for me to see the best of the best."

In Europe, Lankton relied on Netsdal to help arrange visits and benchmarking trips to the best companies. Netsdal, says Lankton, is "the company that makes the best molding machinery in the world. That's what I do when I travel—I ask to see the technology centers— like the ones I have seen in India, Singapore, and Germany."

Just as Nypro raised the bar for its own industry and partners, Lankton continues to raise the bar internally. "Our intent is still to be the best custom injection molder in the world. When you say best, it includes a lot of different things. There may be some companies that are technologically better, but they are very small. As far as being large, global, and technologically competent, I think we are the best, but if you take just technology, there may be some R&D outfits better than us. Right now our thrust is to build technology centers in Asia and Europe."

THE CHINESE BOX

We asked Lankton for his impressions of the innovative Chinese Box. Does this concept seem unreachable, the way the plastics industry is going in the United States? Not unexpectedly, the thought has crossed his mind. "It comes up here all the time. If we could figure out how to put molding machines in a tractor trailer and move close to our customers—we call it 'Nytruck,' and we've joked about it for years. It's not too crazy, except we don't know how to do it. The hard part—because we like to do our business in clean rooms—would be setting up the plants. But there are also huge facility requirements, especially in power. We are one of the most electricity-intensive industries there is. We've even talked about 'Nyboat'—a container ship complete production facility."

Nypro had a recent urgent request from a customer to set up a new operation in the Philippines, a task that would typically take two to three years. If Nyboat could simply be redirected to the South Pacific, steaming along at a twenty-knot clip, pull up to the dock, connect the phone, electricity, and water lines, they would be in business, instantly.

THE *REAL* TECHNOLOGY CHALLENGE—PEOPLE

The technical execution may in fact be the more manageable of the business challenges at hand. Nypro and one of its bigger partners recently encountered a tough partnership dilemma. Nypro started up a plant in Corvallis, Oregon, to service a Hewlett Packard printer cartridge manufacturing facility, which HP suddenly converted to an R&D center, leaving Nypro with 30 percent or 40 percent of the previous year's production rate. "The economics of the molding industry is," said the disappointed Lankton, "that if you run your machines 90 percent of the time, you make piles of money. Less than 70 percent you don't make any money, and we were running at 40 percent." Big and sudden business shifts may be inevitable, but they do require Lankton to build a certain amount of flexibility into the operations, and to staff with professionals who can live with big change.

Picking the right leaders to grow the right areas of the company, particularly in an environment driven by explosive growth, abrupt changes of direction, and sudden stops, continues to take high-level oversight. When staffing up, Lankton first looks for character. "Is he honest and trustworthy, that's what you have to establish. Good family life, whether they treat people right. Then we check out their background and see what they've done." Surprisingly, not all managers he has chosen are engineers, but "most would come from some kind of plastics background."

The $470-million company has twenty-four molding plants, three assembly plants, and several mold building plants.

LOOK TO THE EAST

Every profitable technologist feels the presence of the competition at the back of his neck—sometimes the competitor is Goliath, and sometimes it's Wall Street, and sometimes it's a newly industrialized region, but they never go away. When Teruyuki Maruo, the Honda supplier development guru, was asked where his personal challenge was, he answered, "We are always thinking of Toyota. Every time. Every time." Maruo is not worried about other competitors. Toyota's strength and deep pockets are always at the back of his head, just beyond his seeing or hearing, but "They are always here. This is my race. My race."

For the U.S. plastics industry, China is its biggest competitor. Lankton believes that for the U.S. producers, pricing is being established by China, "And we have to beat it, and if we don't, then the business is going to China or Mexico. These are the two hot spots. A supplier tells a story about Xerox—the landed price from China on a variety of copier components was quoted at 50 percent of the U.S. price. Xerox contacted their suppliers, and told them that in order to compete, they would need a price of 30 percent less than current quotes. 'If you can't do that, we intend to move the business to China.'"

And it's not all efficiency. Raw material costs are lower in China, because the raw material suppliers—the chemical processors that have to run continuously all year long—dump product in China. When there is a slow time in some markets, processors dump the excess in China. "China is the big one, where the real competition is. We hear it day after day after day."

Nypro's response to the Chinese giant looming on their horizon? With two plants in China, they have just opened a mold-making plant in Hong Kong, and are thinking of opening a third plant in Shanghai. They are "seeking the challenge," one of Maruo's guiding principles, and a key component of Honda's Racing Spirit philosophy. (Be ready on time, and seek the challenge.)

BEING FAR-SIGHTED *BEFORE* AGE SETS IN

Nypro's founders never had small ideas about their company's growth. Plastics producers must be flexible and alert to avoid being locked into low-margin commodity business. Just as Foster Grant in nearby Leominster, "The Plastics City," found a new business—sunglasses—when women started cutting their hair and killed the comb business, so have other far-sighted young companies well understood the temporary nature of the products they manufacture. The survivors migrate their core intelligence through various media.

The Nypro Institute

One strategy Nypro has leveraged to deliver big-company education and training with smaller-company resources is the Nypro Institute. The institute was started about sixteen years ago as a small training program. It evolved to offer noncredit and college credit courses. The Certificate in Plastics Technology includes courses in the company's bread and butter areas—injection molding, mold design, polymeric materials, blueprint reading, hydraulics and pneumatics, industrial electrical maintenance, SPC, and principles of supervision.

Courses are populated with Nypro employees, customers, suppliers, and even competitors, most of whom are small regional molders for whom Nypro provides resources they cannot afford. Offering courses to outsiders raises the bar. By working with local institutions—Fitchburg State College, the University of Lowell, and Worcester Polytechnical Institute (Lankton sits on their board)—the company has been able to assemble a very focused range of courses that fits its needs. Pioneering Web-based learning, the institute offers to employees and others training delivered on the Web that can accumulate up to thirty credits toward a four-year degree. Courses of instruction include plastics technology and mold-making. As the institute expands, more courses are added, as well as a unique offering on Nypro's business structure, its decentralized plants, and the board governance. The institute captures and disseminates very technologically advanced plastics and mold-making technology, and offers it in a standard, documented form that helps Nypro and its partners retain its technology lead. It's a way of maintaining corporate technology intelligence.

Honda's intelligence, for example, is making engines. In fact, some observers believe that the company makes cars to sell engines. Honda's technology leadership is its engine, and they are the "only" engine technology company. Honda is the winner in engine technology, but Toyota is king of process, and despite what Honda may feel, Toyota does not compete with Honda on the technology side, because Honda builds anything with an engine in it, while Toyota builds cars. The U.S. Post Office sells delivery, and Federal Express sells time, a day for fourteen dollars. Each of these stars lives for technology leadership—not cost or revenue enhancement.

Other technology leaders, like Honda, have leveraged a singular obsession into a company, and sometimes even an industry—Motorola, 3M, Bolt, Beranek & Newman (BBN), and Hewlett Packard, for example. Sony's intelligence is consumer entertainment technology, while GE excels at management science. Microsoft sells operating system intelligence; one of Microsoft's most aggressive growth strategies is acquisition of smaller, smart engines, more than thirty in the last few years.

Time Warner sells communications, just as Pixar produces entertainment simulation, Pratt & Whitney produces engines, and FedEx really produces scheduling technology. Frito-Lay is expert at materials handling—the commodity product just happens to be snack foods. Phillip Morris is in the addiction business—tobacco, chocolate— and had they been quicker and smarter, they could have been in Nintendo.

Polaroid used to sell pictures in time, Amazon sells the village technology, and Flavors is the leader in Complex Adaptive System technology.

IBM

IBM, for example, started in business machines and migrated information processing to big computers, then to medium-sized computers, then to networks, and then to human wetware (consultants). If the medium for intelligence transfer were Necco wafers, IBM would be making candy and distributing it on street corners.

Motorola

In less than fifty years, Motorola migrated another information carrier technology vehicle from radios into computers, satellites, and mobile phones. Motorola's innovation edge has long bolstered its less productive, divisionalized, and internally competing manufacturing sectors. Motorola's product is innovative communications vehicles, and if Motorola could package compact, mobile communications in an ankle bracelet, we would all be sporting engraved copper leg rings.

Xerox

Xerox, "the document people," has enjoyed mixed results as it chased various fluttering pieces of paper down long corridors filled with competing technologies, cut-throat price competition, and less than visionary leadership. Xerox is in a fight for its life with Canon, and if Xerox could bring back Gutenberg on a cheap chip, and transfer the reproduction hardware technology to the user, leaving the technology core—intelligence—to its R&D folks, it would have a shot at survival.

GM

GM, long the easy target of Lopez jokes, and now the butt of dozens of columns citing "Why GM Just Doesn't Get It," and "GM's Guide on How Not to Make Friends with the UAW," and "Why GM Thinks 96 Percent Quality Is Just Fine," despite its recent shortsightedness and episodes of sheer blackout blindness, always knew it was in the people-moving vehicle business. At the company's beginnings strategists concocted a plan to force trolley cars out of operation, leaving the road wide open for its products.

Nucor

Nucor Steel, the maverick that redesigned a mature, big-money industry with a single electric furnace acquired in Germany, was guided from day one by iconoclast Ken Iverson's image of small, local minimills that would quickly and with greater efficiency supply a commodity market with a completely different product—scrap steel, the cast-off hulks of Detroit's planned obsolescence, junkyard gems, crushed and melted, then poured into pure finished metal. Iverson's struggle to find the right technology machine had a few failures, but in full view of an unseeing and disbelieving Goliath (USX), Iverson was able to sneak under their line of sight to capture small, valuable pieces of market share. When USX stirred and awoke to find it had been raided by a new technology, its response—mini-mills of its own—came too late to save the giant from divestiture of most of its basic assets, including the building in downtown Pittsburgh that housed headquarters. Its vision was nearsighted and narrowed to a thin line that blocked views of the technology guerrillas. Further, pre-occupied with labor and union issues, and mistaken forays into unfamiliar territory, such as its acquisition of Marathon, the company diverted resources from technology to sheer, mature management "challenges," just as GM and Caterpillar nearly went down with long strikes before them.

Solectron

When Winston Chen and Ko Nishimura took over two-time Baldrige winner Solectron, they envisioned a company that would carve a path straight into the hearts of customer designs and end-customer needs through their smart packaging of high-quality printed circuit boards with design and engineering intelligence and good service. Although the culture of Solectron is somewhat gray and stressed, there is no doubt that the founders' dreams of a first-tier company rising from a third-tier industry came true. Solectron's growth-by-acquisition strategy has supplemented its distributed manufacturing power as, like colleagues Nypro and Nucor, Solectron discovers the advantage of speed and proximity to major markets.

Flextronics

The $1.1-billion global electronics supplier Flextronics, another company dedicated to remaining on the top tier while many of its competitors struggle with commodity margins, has taken the new product introduction cycle one level beyond its competition. The fourth-largest supplier of electronic management services, Flextronics understands that its business is electronic solutions—not just hardware. It has migrated its high-quality, contract manufacturing expertise to an even faster custom approach to meeting customer design and manufacturing challenges. The overall goal is speed, and by establishing seven Product Introduction Centers (PICs) in the heart of major customer sites, Flextronics has found a way to serve both customers and the company's global manufacturing operations. Nicholas Brathwaite, vice-president of advanced technology and engineering services, calls it "managing chaos." With approximately twenty locations in the United States, Mexico, Brazil, China, Malaysia, Austria, Hungary, Sweden, and Scotland, the global enterprise is taking a very distributed approach to manufacturing and design. The electronic manufacturing services industry represents a nearly $76-billion machine with an average annual growth rate of 30 percent or more. The industry's compounded annual growth rates through the end of the decade are projected to be approximately 25 percent. Each of the seven PICs is armed with significant RF expertise, all the software engineering a customer could ask for, the usual layout and analysis services ("one stop shopping"), and *speed*.

Flextronics has, by expanding its innovative offerings to customers, transformed itself from a contract manufacturer restricted by economies of scale to big orders from big customers, to a more flexible operation capable of taking on even very small orders. There is no purchase order, and the preparation of the launch package allows customers to take the work anywhere—they are not tied to a particular factory, including other contract manufacturers.

Flextronics global manufacturing operations include three industrial parks located in each of the major low-cost markets, colocating key suppliers on-site for speed and lower costs. Products that have done well in this strategy include Barney, an interactive multimedia electronic toy, and a new and very innovative Web-connected system for Audible, Inc.

AUDIBLE, INC.

Audible, Inc., has created the first top-end system for secure delivery and management of premium audio content via the Internet. The

Audible MobilePlayer™ is a 3.5-ounce, hand-held player that holds two hours of audio for mobile playback. The AudibleManager™ is a software system that manages access to, scheduling, and automatic delivery of audio programming. Audible.com is a Web store offering almost fifteen thousand hours of spoken audio programming from more than eighty-five different providers. Listeners use the Audible-Manager to download audio from Audible.com and onto the Mobile-Player for playback wherever and whenever it is most convenient. Audio downloaded to the MobilePlayer can be played back through headphones or via any stereo system, including car stereos (drive time).

The MobilePlayer's digital format is designed to be more durable than tape-based audio, and the player also permits indexing for quick access to specific content segments and audio status reports for "eyes-free" content navigation. Audio content can be downloaded quickly over the Internet, with one hour of programming available in as little as six minutes using a 56k modem.

The Audible MobilePlayer is a breakthrough product for the industry, because it moves information from the Web to other applications. Its heart is basically a molded plastic body and a board, a simple but very innovative product easily produced in local manufacturing centers. It was given a Gold Award by the Industrial Designers Society of America, and it was recognized as "The Breakthrough Product for 1998" by *Business Week* magazine. Time from design through manufacturing full production, including prototyping, was approximately *ten months.*

MANUFACTURING SPEED COUNTS

Flextronics' innovative approach to the electronics business cuts out most of the purchasing time that typically slows new product introductions by one or two months. It's a land where the engineer is truly king—the new Product Introduction and Engineering services organization has one of the largest groups of engineers in the EMS industry.

Michael Marks, Flextronics chairman and CEO, is a Harvard MBA who understands the uniqueness of his position. "If you look at industries, very few graduates from HBS ended up in manufacturing, particularly in electronics—it's not a driver to success in the business. The CEOs of Sun, Silicon Graphics and Hewlett Packard did not come up through manufacturing. That's an opportunity for us, because we contract manufacturers are really good at manufacturing."

FLEXTRONICS' INNOVATION STRATEGY, "SELLING TIME"

Contract manufacturing is a crazy business. Its unusually high growth attracts companies that have tried to take a position with no fundamental understanding of or interest in the business. Many OEMs that have historically been well-run in other areas have encountered no success when they tried doing contract manufacturing—IBM, Amdahl, Texas Instruments, Lockheed. And some financial players are attempting to take a major piece of the business, but, says Marks, "They have not been very successful cracking top-level customers." Marks understands that what Flextronics does, assembling circuit boards, can be done by many people. "It's not hard. The service is what the customers want—*we are selling time.*"

Marks believes that there is a difference between being a service company and being a product company, and he credits their success to service, compared to OEMs' emphasis on products. "What we have done is to structure our company around the way our customers work. What the customers have been saying for years and years is logical—cost is a major element—tells us we must build in low-cost locations. When you add the cost of logistics—over the past ten years time to market has become a dig deal—you can see why we have low-cost locations on each continent. China serves Asia, Hungary serves Europe, Mexico for North America. The formula is: high volume, close to the market, low cost, supported by some regional facilities."

The last piece of the three-pronged strategy, the Product Introduction Centers, Marks plans to expand to forty or fifty, because, although customers want their high-volume manufacturing in some low-cost center, they don't want to travel there. After the engineers have designed the product, it will get built in a low-cost location— Hungary, for example—"And what the customer really wants is a program manager. . . . They want the right interface. They want to talk to those guys every day—they want project support on prototyping, engineering support, circuit board layout, test, etc., etc." The company in essence is taking on a very important new role, the engineer as a bridge.

NEXT STEPS

Next steps include moving product from the factory to the customer, logistics management, and the decision of where is the best, not just lowest-cost, place to build. "We have to develop new expertise— doing distribution, building warehouses on-site with big manufacturing," says Marks.

FOLLOW THE MONEY

Marks believes the other next step for his industry is information management. Flextronics now builds the product and warehouses it, but customers want to know—realtime—what happened. When did the product ship, through what routes, when will it and the invoice arrive? End customers ask these questions, and Flextronics needs to be able to answer them, not just for its OEM customer—Hewlett Packard, for instance—but for the end user, as well.

"We need the information real-time, and that requires building information structures between the companies that have never been built before. We ship to Ericsson's end customers—Ericsson will never see the product. We have a Cisco system in our place; after we build their product, we receive it on the Cisco system, it 'becomes' available in their warehouse, although it is on-site at Flextronics. It's all about money flow. Cisco becomes an air traffic controller—we, build it, pick up, and drop it where they want to ship it."

EMC

EMC is a fascinating billion-dollar technology machine that didn't start out that way. In 1979 the company was a board shop making add-on memory boards for the prevailing computer companies, including Digital and Prime computer. The opportunity was to make boards at a significantly lower price than the computer companies' internal board shops could. At that time, computer customers had little choice of board suppliers, and EMC seized the opportunity to build its market niche on a commodity product. It was a tough business, but it sustained the young competitor until the industry started to open up.

EMC's watershed breakthrough came ten years later, in the late eighties, when some engineers developed an idea for a disk storage system. It was another niche opportunity, a much bigger one, with more technology potential than commodity-priced PC boards. The disk storage business drew on EMC's memory board roots to extend the company's expertise in an R&D area somewhat neglected by IBM, Digital, and Hewlett Packard.

Although mass storage devices were offered by computer companies as part of a system configuration, it was not their main R&D focus. Digital, for example, preferred to concentrate on the microprocessor; memory and storage were offered to customers as "add-ons," peripherals that customized a system. EMC's technology breakthrough—stringing together cache memory and software—proved to be more reliable and faster, and cost half as much as their competitors'.

The company targeted the IBM mainframe and midrange market, and later (in the nineties) the open systems area. Within ten years EMC occupied the number-one spot in sales and market share, capacity, and revenue, becoming the world leader in one decade.

INDEPENDENT DECISIONS SUPPORTED TECHNOLOGY GROWTH

Technology upstarts achieve dominance at a price, however. Although Digital sued to retain ownership of its fat annuity business, deep pockets did not drive this competition under. By the beginning of its second decade, EMC's Symmetrix, its first disk product, had changed the storage industry forever.

Storage is no longer an automatic purchase when a customer buys a system. What had been the big computer manufacturers' "dirty little secret"—by not competing on storage devices, they protected revenues that would have represented an automatic 40 percent to 50 percent of the system—was uncovered when EMC handed the decision-making over to the customer and moved the choice on mass storage out into the open. In effect, it changed the variables in the configuration equation—suddenly, the storage device itself became as important as the computer or server, which was fast becoming a commodity. EMC's technology breakthrough meant that it was the first to build a mass storage system that could attach and hold data no matter what server, PC or CPU. Customers could make the storage decision first, use EMC tools to retrieve and protect data, and then contemplate whose server they would buy. In effect, because the server market contains competitors that leapfrog each other from month to month, the customer was freed to play server vendors against each other. None of these aggressive approaches to raising the bar would have happened had customers been technologically locked into a single storage supplier. The lesson? Technology and the market, like life, will always win out.

THE MONEY *IS* IN SOFTWARE

As equipment margins continue to shrink, EMC leverages its product mix of low-cost hardware supported by high-intelligence software. Some experts believe that in the disk drive arena, technology advancements have outstripped Moore's law.

Preparation to Be in the Land
Where the Engineer Is King

There used to be a rule of thumb about the shelf life of the average engineer: It was expected that seven years after receiving his degree, the half-life of his core education would have passed, and by fifteen or twenty years postdegree the changes in his discipline would have rendered him technically obsolete. If, however, he had chosen to take the management track, his corporate longevity would have thereby been extended another forty or fifty years or more; technology was superseded by political skill.

We think that there is truth to this bit of oral history—and oral history is the most accurate of all records—that although specific technologies will mature and die, just as core memory was replaced by chips, so will technologists who migrate their basic core competence into new media be king. Physicists who become software engineers, naval architects who migrate vehicle study to aircraft design, biochemists who become DNA slicers, and inventors who become venture capitalists all make sense. These are uncharted routes on the career path, but they make sense and signal a winner.

The transitions we describe—evolving from a physicist to a software engineer—may superficially look like a stretch, but below the surface, they come from the same roots. Basically, the technology king will possess a certain number of useful technical skills—computers, drafting, numbers, visualization—and he (and occasionally she) will be most distinguishable by an aura, tracings of hyperactivity, and sharpened focus in areas missed by marketing, finance, and other superficial contributors. Don't just sit there, build something, bill somebody!

Think of the engineer/technology manager as a consultant, selling wisdom, instant gratification, hope, and energy. None of these skills can be attributed specifically to a B.S. in mechanical engineering, or an MBA, although these degrees may be a first step for a few managers. Instead, fill your calendar with trips to the Santa Fe Institute and participation in other conferences and seminars. Night school for seven years to learn C++ won't do it. Buy a package and teach yourself programming; go play with your simulator. Build a car, design an airplane, but don't come home until you have made something.

For technology stars looking to dominate manufacturing in the year 2020, these are the hot areas that will continue to be very important to manufacturing:

Software: artificial intelligence, intelligent software, agents, modeling
Machines and processes
Computers, in all forms—parallel processing
Robotics, embedded and stand-alone, and machine vision
Standards
Communications
Business
Auto manufacturing
Enterprise management and maintenance

The Engineer as a Technology Bridge

But what . . . is it good for?

—ENGINEER AT IBM COMMENTING ON THE MICROCHIP,
1968

Tesuro Mori, a Yaskawa Electric executive, coined the term *mechatronics* in 1969. The idea is to combine the concepts used in electronics, mechanics, and computers, into a single system. This hybrid system can be applied to everyday products that themselves are combined applications of separate disciplines. For example, mechatronics applies to cameras, cars, planes, robots, copiers, cellular phones, and ATMs. A formal definition might be the "application of embedded complex decision-making to the operation of physical systems."

But the word mechatronics, as much as it is recognized and understood in Asia, is unknown in the West. That's OK, because the real issue is the shifting of disciplines, the cross-pollination of engineering and manufacturing training—Gordon Lankton's obsession with control systems applied to a plastics process; EMC's application of software to what had been a high-end hardware business; Nucor's application of electrical engineering to solve a new steel processing problem; Flextronics' breakthrough blending of design with manufacturing.

Yet engineering enrollment is far behind demand. And few engineering schools offer a "degree in integration" of computer science with mechanical engineering, for example. Don't look to established educational "institutions" to offer the answers, because we don't give out letter sweaters to nerds, although we continue to celebrate athletic ability. If a kid is bored or rebellious in class, he is told, "Don't be a wise guy," or he is put on a steady regimen of Ritalin. The energy and the intelligence have to go somewhere.

And what does a practicing engineer end up doing, anyway? Meetings, Dilbert, budget discussions—living in a cubicle and speaking up in meetings is not the creative engineering that breeds technologists.

Learning to Hear the Music

More of the engineering curriculum should be devoted to subjects such as the history of technology, business issues that emphasize the goal of profit, and the who, what, when, where, and how of technology (today we do mostly the "how"). For more technology success stories, we need an education that will ensure that at least some of us are unreasonable.

Manufacturing in clustered companies, what some of us now call the extended enterprise, will require additional manufacturing process flexibility. Flexible assembly, and change on the fly, especially machine changeovers that are eliminated by intelligent agent scheduling like the software used in GM Fort Wayne and the International Plastics/Germany plastics plant. Multipurpose machines, and multitasking product lines, along with end-of-cycle product configuration, will increase flexibility from both product design and tooling flexibility. Either route, the technologist must direct creation of these flexible, changeable product pipelines. Manufacturing in MMXX will be volume, as well as model mix flexible.

Charlie Baker, the head of R&D for the breakthrough Acura CL, the first high-end Honda luxury vehicle designed and produced in North America for the North American market, has explained his unique approach to staffing for fast-cycle R&D. Baker looks for a very special breed of engineer, and they don't come from automotive. Charlie looks to aerospace, because he knows that such techniques as simulation and the design rules that can be used to build an aircraft— you don't model them in clay, take measurements, transfer the metrics to software, and repeat the cycle—are the departure from the traditional process that is just what a leapfrog competitor needs in automotive. There is a new breed of cat, trained in basic mathematics, capable of some amount of hand-drafting, so skilled in software manipulation that he can make the damn things dance. Further, the rules of approximation that allowed Oppenheimer and his Manhattan Project's wild-eyed band of physicists, mathematicians, and "technicians" to "know" when they had reached a certain mathematical level of correctness, the art of approximation, is a fast-disappearing skill that most innovation machines badly need.

There are six disciplines or virtues that make an engineer or technology manager a professional in the same sense that an athlete, artist, or soldier is considered a professional:

1. Physical rectitude
2. Moral forbearance
3. Temperate habits
4. Correct behavior
5. Magic and an ear for the ineffable
6. Dedication

Physical rectitude. Stay in shape! Exercise until you can't think about anything except stopping. Chess players prepare for a big match by exercising, just as boxers do. You are tuning the power supply for the wetware. It's called preventive maintenance.

Moral forbearance. Think only about the work. It is the only thing worth thinking about. Great athletes think about the next game all the time, as do artists and writers and scientists. A master stonemason thinks, dreams, and works in stone, not wood. Work a problem over and over until it snaps into place. Focus on the calling and ignore the distractions. Don't worry about being politically correct or well-balanced by anyone's definition. Create your image in the shadow of someone you admire. Your calling is music that only you can hear.

Temperate habits. Recognize and correct bad habits. Every task is different, and you must learn to adapt behavior to the task at hand. The idea is to take risks, make mistakes, and experiment. Most of us still take courses or attend seminars, which is fine, but don't get credentials, get educated. Don't get caught up in technical drool—stick to the basics and analyze history for the future. Know where you are on the timeline.

Correct behavior. As the fundamental underpinnings of emergent objects, individual behavior patterns determine overall performance. Some of the rules are: don't brag; it's okay to look bad or foolish; be an egoist; dream; don't fight it; never hit the brakes; never be satisfied; and get over it.

Magic and an ear for the ineffable. You get zero points for just doing a good job. As an NBA coach once said, "Everyone's got to have an angle." Magic and flash generate confidence in you and the customer. Go fast, be hungry, and act as if you're the oldest inspired adolescent in town. Store up your bag of tricks and attack. Think of the big athletes and their hair color!

Dedication. Live the trade. You can do nothing less. Be loyal, not to your company, but to the music. Work with the best tools, whether they are computers or brushes or people. Eat Ramen and drink Jolt.

Don't get comfortable. Find the challenge and choose your parents well. (When we evaluate technology managers, we ask, "Do you remember your children's birth dates?" If the answer is yes, their credentials are suspect.)

Is This Teachable?

Can one be taught, or learn somehow, to be a technology king? Probably not—it must be in the genes. If you have it, let it out; otherwise, go into marketing.

10

Silicon Life on a Carbon Planet

This "telephone" has too many shortcomings to be seriously considered as a means of communication. The device is inherently of no value to us.

—WESTERN UNION INTERNAL MEMO, 1876

Computers in the future may weigh no more than 1.5 tons.

—POPULAR MECHANICS, 1949

I have traveled the length and breadth of this country and talked with the best people, and I can assure you that data processing is a fad that won't last out the year.

—PRENTICE-HALL EDITOR, 1968

If people do not believe that mathematics is simple, it is only because they do not realize how complicated life is.

—JOHN (JOHANN) VON NEUMANN, 1903–57

Technology Leaps and Bounds

The challenge to all technologists and manufacturing visionaries is to see enough from a distance to make the right choices about process, products, and people. With few signposts and too much interactive stimulation, distractions abound, because the world—unrestrained— is flooded with visual and audio stimuli, messaging systems, and noise. If each of us could learn in our few early years in school the twelve or so guiding rules for successful and profitable carbon life on a silicon planet, we would not be making repeated forays into technology fads. And spiritually we would have found peace.

But as the flawed mathematics giant John von Neumann told us, life is too complicated for easy serenity. Von Neumann's life spanned theory and application. His early work with computers opened the field that will take manufacturing and other disciplines into the next big transformation, although some areas and some disciplines will move faster and more smoothly into the application stages. Like DaVinci, Doc Edgerton at EG&G, and other geniuses whose technology interests appeared to be far-flung and all-encompassing, von Neumann had knowledge of many other engineering fields—ordnance, submarine warfare, weapons, weather prediction, ICBMs. Combined with his incredible math ability (at age six he could reportedly divide eight-digit numbers in his head), his vision of the possibilities of computers—he saw them not just as giant adding machines dedicated to specific problems, but as a bridge into deeper applications—set him apart from his peers, of whom there were only a handful.

Von Neumann was a bridge from the theoretical to the practical. By his pioneering work in computer architecture, he laid the foundations for expansion of computer arithmetic processing into stored memory and shared data concepts. His work on the EDVAC machine epitomized this giant leap from known theory to advanced, visionary applications, the same kind of leaps-and-bounds thinking that will carry technology winners successfully into 2020.[1]

Look to the East

In some respects, we are already there. China, for example, whose capital city, Beijing, houses 12 million people, is a world of opportunity for advancement and profit—in leaps and bounds—a curious blend of early industrial and postmodern eras. Travel door-to-door from Morley's Barn takes twenty-nine hours; a long time to be packaged with three hundred other souls in an aluminum tube. Travel times and other infrastructure networks are being stretched to their limits in China as double-digit development and thousands of foreign investments take hold. One factory, a chocolate candy joint venture, gets an allotment per week of five days' power; the company wants to run seven and twenty-four, however, so the solution is motor-generator sets. But how will the diesel fuel get there—no gas stations, no pipelines, no monthly tanker deliveries, and no roads that can handle tankers?

In the cities, bicycles and cell phones are everywhere. The country is leapfrogging from an earlier era of industrial structure past modern utilities directly into the postmodern industrial age via the microprocessor and the Internet. There are no copper wire or telephone poles—communications systems are all satellite links instead.

Clearly, for the next twenty years in China, the challenges are enormous, and by working on any one of them investors can expect a good chance of high yields. It's a matter of picking your spot and raising the risk.

A Warning About Junk Science and Sham Technology

It will be difficult for carbon life forms on a silicon planet to pick their way through the exploding pockets of junk science and sham technology. The kind of science that happens when what is nothing more than opinion is dressed up in the credentials of a recognized expert is called "junk science" or sham tech. The resulting nonsense assertions have several distinguishing characteristics: They mysteriously appear, they spread rapidly, they tell a good story, and they fade like a water diet.

Unfortunately, this is how science and technology begin to be a "world explanation" as magical as any ancient mythology. After all, no one of us is able to confirm that the world actually is made up of subatomic particles, and precious few will ever learn how quantum mechanics works. Yet the success of scientists in predicting and controlling atomic events means that many people must have faith in what science asserts, and sometimes that has led to blind acceptance of some pretty sloppy thinking. Take Social Darwinism, for example, or the belief that the cure for cancer is just around the corner.

Techies are a debunking bunch. Or so we think. As engineers and managers, knowledge workers and software developers, we—who have faith in progress and the rational—have our own fetishes, just like any communal tribe. We have our own "lite" version of junk science: a kind of "junk wisdom." You can evoke the parameters of our fables by interjecting any of the following words or phrases into a conversation with any of us: cellular phones, diesel exhaust, the transputer, Lisa, 68060, NASA O-rings, iron in spinach, computers and productivity, travel is glamorous, "nobody" uses Macs, a paperless office, sexless engineers, ramen soup and Jolt, Unix wins–Unix loses, paradigm shift, or linearity.

Too often, engineers and managers take actions based on the assumption of competence, and they are surprised when they don't get results. Since we are the experts, we avoid scrutiny. We state to anyone within JAVA range that the data speak for themselves, and that all data are wisdom. Ergo, since computers are data manipulation devices, computers can solve all our problems!

Whoa. We know that data don't speak—not really. What we see always is based on our preconceptions—"Seeing is believing" should read "Believing is seeing," ultimately what we all want. At the beginning of this century, Ernst Mach and the Vienna Circle tried to come up with a science based solely on empirical facts, but they soon found that without theories to provide a provisional ordering of facts, no knowledge is possible. What's frustrating is that once we admit this, we are forced to wonder if we really ever make contact with the "objective" world.

Dilbert is probably the supreme unmasker of management's unstated assumptions, including these manufacturing fables:

- Lowering costs is the key to prosperity.
- Mass production lowers costs.
- Lowering overhead decreases costs.
- Individual behavior can be modified by the corporate culture.
- Management science exists.

Y2K, a Technology Sham or a Gateway Technology Event?

During the closing years of this decade, thousands of consultants and bit miners have racked up millions of frequent-flyer miles and billed hours finding, fixing, and killing the Millennium Bug. And it is indeed true that many systems and embedded software programs have been infected with this small but powerful glitch that causes ATM machines to stall out, messes up your pension records, and generally maintains an attitude of fear in MIS departments.

But the crisis is not all-encompassing. Think of the Y2K fever as a gateway technology event, another big test of our technology management ability, rather than the end of the world . . . again. Sure, thirty years ago some bit miners saved precious memory space by abbreviating the way they coded dates, and yes, the year 19XX was assumed to be in place for almost "forever," but the money and anxiety that this Chicken Little technology problem has generated is almost laughable.

Small and medium-sized companies were reportedly especially vulnerable to millennium problems. Big companies with deep consulting budgets may think they are immune, but money, as all manufacturers who have tackled twenty-five-year MRP I/II/III software implementations know, doesn't cure every ill.

The Stamford, Connecticut–based GartnerGroup, an information technology house, reported that as of 1997, 88 percent of all companies with fewer than two thousand employees had not yet started Year 2000 remediation projects.[2] "Many companies that are addressing problems with their computer systems may be overlooking potential problems embedded in other systems such as machine controllers and telecommunications," said Kevin Carr, director of NIST's Manufacturing Extension Partnership.

Further, because some mechanisms for electronic currency exchange and data maintenance use the year 2000 in advance of its actual happening—expiration dates on your driver's license, for example, or your ATM card—the problem started to appear years in advance of the midnight hour.

Companies included in *Information Week*'s September 1997 500 list reported being at varying stages of completion:

Johnson Controls	80% ready
Texas Instruments	40%
Eaton	75%
Allied Signal	25%

TRW	50%
Rohm & Haas	85%
HB Fuller	15%
Procter & Gamble	16%
Lennox International	95%

One bug fixer from data information experts Datastream has been working with some alert clients since 1996; she believes that "this is not black magic. All the code will get fixed by 2000." But it is going to cost you.

HOW BIG IS THIS TECHNOLOGY BUG?

Chris Barlow, president of SunOpTech, a developer of manufacturing-decision-support and supply-chain-applications software headquartered in Sarasota, Florida, believes that Y2K really is a problem. "Programmers took shortcuts and tried to save space on forms, disks, databases, etc. by using only two digits for the year . . . yet they often say something like ^ if expire_year ^ this_year then Expired [to check if a password, contract, lease, etc. has expired]. Bingo! The code will fail when the year is '00!"

"To make matters worse," warns Barlow, "many programmers used year '99 as a special year. For example, some order entry systems say that if an order's year is '99 then the order is 'on hold'—this means that the problems will start toward the end of 1998, not the end of '99!" As Alexander Graham Bell said to his assistant "Come here Mr. Watson, I need you."

SunOpTech is not working much on Y2K, reports Barlow, "except to make sure our software is OK." But Sun Hydraulics, the sister company that manufactures precision hydraulic valves, is trying to replace its in-house-developed system with a new one before the end of 1999 partly to make sure there is no Y2K problem.

Barlow agrees that this is a costly problem to fix, because if you have it in your system, it's everywhere. "It involves making room on the screens and databases for two more characters. Picture a library with thousands of books stacked together and you need to fit in two more books on each shelf. It means shifting everything, moving books to new shelves, adding shelves, changing the index signs at the end of each aisle, etc.—a librarian's nightmare."

"WHAT HATH MAN WROUGHT!"

Electronics manufacturers should be on top of this problem, we might think. And many of them are, including Flextronics International, the San Jose, California, producer ranked fourth-largest EMS (electronic management services) provider in the world. Cecil Koupal, worldwide director of information technology, believes that Flextronics is being proactive. The company has embarked on "an aggressive two-year legacy conversion of its major enterprise MRPII systems standardizing on Baan worldwide." And the company is replacing older hardware and software with year 2000 implications. Further, Koupal says that they are also using the latest desktop management tools to ensure that all floor and desktop systems are compliant.

Milt Gregory, president of Gregory Associates, a breakthrough design and manufacturing outsourcing expert, also based in San Jose, believes that their problem "is minimal, because virtually all the software we use is off-the-shelf. Microsoft is our largest software vendor. To the extent that they have taken care of the problem in Windows 95 and related applications, we are OK."

But some manufacturers are worried about bugs outside their domain. Larry Olson, president of K*Tec Electronics, Sugarland, Texas, thinks that most of the focus has been on computer systems' internal and external businesses. "Until recently there has not been as much focus on the peripheral items that could be affected—areas such as telephone system and security are also impacted by Y2K, and I'm not sure that people are spending enough time on those areas. K*Tec has in place a formalized Y2000 process designed to review every aspect of our readiness, our suppliers' readiness, and our customers' readiness. Imagine going through the process and being absolutely prepared internally and with our suppliers, only to find out that our customers cannot place purchase orders or pay invoices? It could be devastating."

ANOTHER EXAMPLE OF RISK MANAGEMENT

For most suppliers and first-tier producers, downtime caused by undetected Y2K bugs or any other technology failure could be financially a disaster for them and their customers for whom consistent and uninterrupted product flow is as important as Six Sigma quality. Don Blumer, IT manager of EFTC Corporation's new Oracle system in Denver, Colorado, understands that, "As a seven by twenty-four business, EFTC's internal systems must support the reliability and efficiency of product delivery—even a short down period means significant loss of revenue."

Like many other electronics manufacturers, EFTC is using software to solve any potential problems. Blumer notes, "Year 2000 compliance has been one of the driving factors leading to the implementation of EFTC's new Oracle system. Our legacy systems would have required significant upgrades and customization to become compliant." Blumer says that all EFTC Oracle systems have been tested to ensure correct storage, presentation, and date calculations before and beyond year 2000.

Despite all the careful planning and, in some cases, modification of current software, or installation of young packages, events outside the producer's control could still be "problematic." Blumer is concerned that despite EFTC's confidence in its own systems, risk management ranks high in priority because "our systems or those of our business partners may be affected by events outside of our control. A stand-alone software which runs a piece of machinery on our floor may not belong to EFTC but if it stops working, our business may be shut down. EDI data will also be of concern as data from all trading partners will need to be validated before being loaded into EFTC internal systems."

A BIT MINER SPEAKS OUT

Al Krever, a Los Angeles–based productivity consultant, and one of the original Digital Equipment Corporation large-systems software designers, thinks there is a lesson in this whole Y2K bug scam. When he was in high school back in Hackensack, New Jersey, Krever took a summer job at a company that made clothing labels—"Blooming-dale's," "Fruit of the Loom," "100 percent cotton." His job was to count the orders for these tiny banners, adding them up and verifying the count against available inventory. He was apprenticed to a hard-working, twenty-three-year veteran of label counting, Max.

Max was among twenty-four others of varying longevity who sat in three rows of eight desks per row. Each counter had an electro-mechanical adding machine; Max tallied up columns of numbers across and down, checking to see whether the totals of the resultant row and column sums matched.

After twenty-three years, Krever's mentor could add in his head a column of twenty or so four-digit numbers in the time it takes to read this sentence out loud. Speculation said that Max could recognize the sets of numbers and their totals through long familiarity, and he may not have had to add them at all.

Max told Krever that he had been doing crossfoots without the aid of a mechanical adding machine in the beginning, and that these new machines were the *dernier-cris* in his line of work. During breaks he complained bitterly about his boss as he praised the company for always keeping up with the latest advances.

TECHNOLOGY CREEPS UP ON THE GARMENT INDUSTRY

These newer machines, of which there were only five given to the lucky tenured employees in the department, upped Max's throughput 10 percent or more. The machines were flesh-toned, fifteen inches deep by ten inches high, with forest green keys, gray, red, blue, and white for functions, stamped with a silver placard that read Remington Rand. This was 1963, and eighteen floors below, in a two-storied, environmentally controlled space in the Sperry Rand Building, and using enough power to light quite a few homes back in Hackensack, was the UNIVAC. It did crossfoots, too. Almost as fast as Max.

Krever finished high school and started college in a drama program. His day job, however, was—you guessed it—business machines. He was enchanted by the machines he was learning to guide—loved flowcharting—and programming became his passion. By 1968 he had learned to program a crossfoot on the IBM 402.

Programming this box was done by plugging wires into a board. The wires set switches that directed columns of digits on punched cards to print locations and instructed the machine to give totals. The process produced an accounting system that looked like a wall of five-pound trays filled with multicolored spaghetti. The machines took up a small room. Krever learned to do his next crossfoot in Autocoder, a type of assembler language, on the IBM 1401, a much larger machine with magnetic core memory of 4k characters. Although there was a Cobol (second-generation software) compiler for the 1401, it was so slow and cumbersome that almost everyone using this machine wrote all their applications in the Autocoder Assembler.

Later, on the IBM 360–30, Krever learned BAL (Basic Assembler Language), RPG, a higher-level simulation of a rotating drum accounting machine, and Cobol, Grace Hopper's remarkable Common Business Oriented Language. His first job—in a bank, naturally—gave him the opportunity to branch out and do Cobol on an NCR 315, a system that used rod memory instead of core, and random storage. His first assignment—a general ledger package—led him again to crossfoots.

By this time, everybody on Wall Street wanted a machine that could do crossfoots in record time. Although Krever realized that it was more likely that he would spontaneously learn to speak Chinese by eating dim sum than come across a crossfoot error in a program, nevertheless, each company that he and other early programmers worked with insisted, when converting from manual routines to automated batch systems, on crossfoot checks. Just to be sure there was no errant bit throwing the calculation off.

Maybe all this crossfooting made the accountants, the guys who wanted the systems in the first place, feel better, but they also insisted on printing the entire database on hernia reports, even when only 2 percent of the records were affected. The shredded paper made for perfect tickertape parade ammunition.

By the time Krever hit Digital, computers had grown beyond the 4k memory stage to huge banks of memory and on-line storage. Transactions and data flows became more complex, heavier, and they started to move into different applications. The first work he was called upon to do was, of course, a conversion of an archaic business system to the top-of-the-line monster computer, the DEC 10. But rather unexpectedly, clients still wanted exception reports and most specifically, crossfoots. Further, clients insisted on printing user records in their entirety—more ticker tape. The actual data had not changed in look and feel from the original data punched into cards only fifteen years before.

Krever says the source of the Y2K panic is the typical programmer's frugality and an unwillingness to fix something that wasn't, or didn't seem to be, broke. Precisely the same mind-set that required him to code all those ridiculous crossfoots in every generation of programming language, and to print all those detailed transaction reports, caused the Y2K glitch. Programmers discovered a simple method to abbreviate date codes in the programs, and ever the bit miners, they seized the opportunity.

Programmers and their bosses knew about the problem, and the simple solution. Most bit miners recommended the solution every time they upgraded systems. But making the changes, like Chris Barlow's stretched library shelf, would have required more space for dates, bigger records, more storage space, more money, and more paper, a management nightmare.

So the word came down from the suits to the techies: "Just move the application over to the new machine." It took less manpower, less overhead during system upgrades, and less money. Besides, nobody would still be working in the computer room by the time the calendar clicked over, so who really cared?

Here we are, awaiting the stroke of midnight, stuck with the same code more or less that we were running almost forty years ago, but pretty soon the computers are going to stall out. "You can blame the bit miners, of course," says Krever, "We did it that way, but hey, you asked for it."

AIN'T THAT ALWAYS THE WAY . . .

Michael Maynard, president of Azimuth Partners, Inc., of Stowe, Massachusetts, thinks that the more he sees, the more it all seems familiar. The following lines were written in anticipation of the coming millennium—*in the year 999:*

> As love waxed cold and iniquity abounded among mankind, perilous times were at hand for men's souls. For by many assertions of the ancient fathers we are warned that, as covetousness stalks abroad, the religious Rules or Orders of the past have caught decay and corruption from that which should have raised them to growth and progress. From this (covetousness) also proceed the constant tumult of quarrels at law, and frequent scandals arise, and the even tenor of the different Orders is rent by their transgressions. What then can we think but that the whole human race, root and branch, is sliding willingly down again into the gulf of primeval chaos?

> —*EXCERPTED FROM WORLD WIDE WEB SITE OF PAUL HALSALL, FORDHAM UNIVERSITY, HTTP://WWW.FORDHAM.EDU/HASALL/SOURCE/GLABE-1000.HTML., RALPH GLABER,* MIRACLES DE SAINT-BENOIT

One thousand years later, Maynard believes many of us are approaching the second millenium with the same dread and confusion. This generalized anxiety is not necessary—maybe we do have a little more control over our technology than we think. Indeed, Maynard cites that in all his research on computer hardware vendors, the two who have reported no Y2K problems are the dinosaurs Digital Equipment Corporation (now part of Compaq) and Apple.

Where Technology Has Taken Us,
the Devil's Advocate Position

Every technology breakthrough is pitched to glowing scenarios of improved productivity—"labor-saving devices," more free time, long-distance messages transferred immediately at no cost, and so forth. The atomic bomb announced the birth of cheap, immediately available nonfossil power. The internal combustion engine would allow us to go anywhere—almost—without a train schedule. The washing machine was a labor-saving device—no mention of all the other electric gadgets that, having removed household servants from the home, were to be replaced by overworked and isolated houseslaves. The 747's promised big cheap rides—no one knew that to reach maximum load efficiency, passengers would be queued and batched for endless hours on plastic sixties-era benches in airless glass boxes.

A dyslexic friend has learned the power of the spell checker to spew out daily reams of memos, most of which should never have been put to paper. Maynard quotes a venture capitalist colleague who felt that the worst change to happen in his industry was the invention of the PC and the accompanying word-processing and spreadsheet software. Too many entrepreneurs found it too easy to write too many business plans, and he felt that only the really committed entrepreneur would write a business plan without the availability of these tools. Indeed, Civil War historian Shelby Foote authored his histories by hand, in pen, page by page, line by line—each word was considered before it appeared on the page.

The first profitable use of electronic bulletin boards was pornographic. The biggest and best monitors inevitably sell on their entertainment value. The fastest cars with the most features are not necessarily the safest. The real crisis of the year 2000 fever is that it has distracted our attention from asking the questions about why we have let technology pervade our lives, says Maynard. In manufacturing, we have gained an ability to capture more data about more products and processes than Francis Cabot Lowell and his entrepreneurs might have ever foreseen or wanted.

"There is no sadder commentary on my life than the fact that I'm able to reach my neighbor across the street more easily by using e-mail than by going over to his house. . . . What's so important and urgent in both of our lives that we can't find time for one another? I'm concerned that the tools we've created to bring us together are driving us further apart since we no longer are required to meet in person to communicate. I'm concerned that the world community created by telecommunications has caused us to lose a sense of community in the world closest to us. I'm concerned that an industry legacy based on the quality, integrity, and compassion imparted by Ken Olsen, Dr. An Wang, and other industry founders has been replaced by a fool's gold rush to get rich quick through IS. And I'm concerned that the visionaries who dreamed that computers would improve our lives have been replaced by sociopaths who are using the technology as a means to gain more and more control over our lives."

Maynard doubts the end value of technology, saying that "as we enter the third millennium, it seems we haven't learned a damned thing in the past one thousand years. We're still worshiping false gods that will only betray us in the end. We just have more technologically sophisticated ways of doing so."

Take a Hiatus from Silicon Life

Sometimes we seem to emphasize computer control of systems to the detriment of the human side of the equation. The Morley's Barn in rural New Hampshire used to harbor real farm animals, and for the twenty-seven or so foster children who found themselves "down the road," the way the animals lived had many lessons.

The first lesson comes from the dumbest but one of the most vicious of all farm animals, geese. Geese are programmed to cluster in groups, a gaggle; once the gaggle has formed, it is impossible to change the aggregate. One of The Barn kids once tried to form a single gaggle from two geographically separated flocks, a very difficult and only partially successful project. Inevitably, the dominant geese attack the smaller, less aggressive fowl and drive the losers away until the farmer intervenes. A single goose as a rogue can never be assimilated into the pack.

In business, suits tend to show the same behavior. The pack instinct is a human trait that is immune to the advances of what we
call technology, hardware, and silicon. A corporate merger between
two entities, for example, elicits a response similar to the goose gaggle. The dominant species drives out and suppresses the weak, and
the rogue, unless it is very strong, will be destroyed. New ideas in-
jected into the matrix of the system will be pearled; the new idea is
considered an irritant, and covered with a hard shell and discarded.
Apple Computer was a young, immortal, and very vigorous rogue,
and like many rogues, Apple did not feel the need to join the existing packs or even form one of its own. Looking back, anyone can
see that Apple could have formed a robust and very competitive
gaggle with itself as leader. But as the rogue aged, the need to join
became apparent even to the most avid fanatic. Too late. The Gates
pack will not let others join its mature group, even if the logic is
correct for such a technology move. Our animal instincts form the
action plan.

The second animal lesson is from Willie, the deceased Rottweiler and general security system at The Barn. Willie weighed in
at about 110 pounds and he was ably equipped with just three neurons: threat response, food, and sex, in that order. Willie believed
that he was part of the overall farm pack, and the adults at the top
of the pecking order were only one small step above him. In fact,
that sequence meant that Willie was programmed to take over
when the top dogs were away; his leadership algorithm was to deny
motion to any other person or animal—no defaults, no loops.
When Matt, one of The Barn waifs, took the dog for a trip to the
local recycling center, Willie kept the kid out of the truck cab after
they had dropped off their load. Willie's program read "No entry,"
and all neurons and their algorithms were engaged. Password de-
nied. No entry. The kid walked home. Willie held his position in
the truck cab, a slave to the command structure and his procedure
manual.

The corporate human pack can behave like Willie and the geese
sometimes—many decisions are made in the name of "procedure."
Although the successes of the past form procedures that are no

longer valid for today's marketplace, the mature organization never leads, and it never leaves the home area unless it is forced out. The territorial imperative is evoked to the overall detriment of the common good, and in effect the basic management structure is distorted to serve only the set of Willie neurons.

Carbon Animals Managing Silicon Farms

We are carbon animals running silicon farms. Our responses to stress and organization derive from a pack instinct that is almost a million years old. Remember Willie and the geese when your organization goes into a decision process; lead the group and form the pack.

Manufacturing managers aren't the only ones that practice self-deception. Marketing has its own fables:

- Product features and product benefits are the same thing.
- Packaging is the product.
- Ignorance outranks intelligence.
- Lower prices sell product.
- If you don't know what you need, you don't need it.

These themes have a longevity and vitality beyond all understanding—perhaps the human spirit seeks to expand its mastery even at the expense of truth. We must rationalize and improve products and performance ad infinitum. It's a treadmill, not Dickensian, but a treadmill just the same. Our training says we are logical, and the Newtonian clockwork is the alpha and omega of our existence. But few of us question the day-to-day morass of legacy prejudices. The bosses are idiots. Smart people are weird. Work is dehumanizing. The old days were better. *There is no end to what technology can achieve.* We are at the top of the food chain.

These fables sound familiar—even scientists and technologists slip a few into their conversation. But occasionally we should try to question the a priori assumptions that spawned them. Can't we all just be a little more honest with ourselves?

Know When to Fold

Remember our discussion about portfolio growth and risk management. Success in poker is knowing when to fold, not when to bet. Establish a failure rate and know that it's the way to maximize return—it is reasonable to establish risk as a parameter of management, but too often the culture of companies, even startups, penalizes failure for each endeavor, rather than total success.

R&D investment planning should be centered around failure. Increase risk and the likelihood of success increases across the board. But not for the individual project. We cannot predict individual stars or losers, but we can predict the group behavior.

As zero risk yields zero return, infinite risk also yields an R&D benefit of near zero. What is the optimum? An 80 percent failure rate will optimize portfolio return for an angel. Do deals that have a greater than half likelihood of failure. A friend of ours who tried and failed to become a successful venture capitalist has the problem that he tried to reduce, rather than increase, risk. George tried to cut his losses by concentrating on lowering risk across the breadth of the portfolio. And by doing so he decreased the value of his entire portfolio.

Imagine that you have $20 million to invest. Where do you put it? In a portfolio of twenty companies that have a 50 percent chance of being worth $2 million for each $1 million invested, and a 50 percent chance of being worth $1 million? Or in a portfolio of 95 percent chance of zero return and a 5 percent chance of returning one billion dollars? At the end of ten years, you have about $35 million in the first case for your $20 billion investment. And in the second case you have a 64 percent chance of becoming a billionaire. Think Bill Gates. The greater the risk, the greater the reward.

Closing Predictions

Mike Kaminski, a manager in GM's Manufacturing Center in Warren, Michigan, shares his predictions for manufacturing twenty years out, and they reflect interests that he has developed in more than thirty years of engineering and consulting work. After making numerous twelve-hour trips to Europe and Japan, where he delivered one-hour slide shows, Kaminski has a dream that expanded bandwidth will enable business technologists to see their audience in 3D. Holography and communications bandwidth speed are moving rapidly, and Kaminski thinks his dream may be not that far off, another contributor to the inevitable decline of business travel.

Kaminski's second dream involves the expansion of communications into another dimension. Our communication to and through computers is still limited—voice recognition systems and other sensing devices will advance, but like the keyboard, these amplification devices are one-way input and output utilities. What Kaminski wants to see is contextual communication, the kind of discussion one might have with a lab assistant: "Beaker, get me the square roots of these factors," or, "Bunson, find us everything Frank Lloyd Wright designed and built that suggested water running over granite boulders," the kind of communication that separates understanding from calculation and clearly limited searches. Multidimensional communications will enable enterprisewide decisions and remote manufacturing, just as genetic algorithms have localized shop-floor intelligence.

It won't be long before fifty-gigabyte databases are fairly common, and because it is easy to be buried by that amount of data, search engines, WWW published sites, terabyte memories, and T1 communications bandwidth on every desktop create problems as well as solutions. In parallel, new tools will be available that will reduce the data to a small quantity of usable information. Knowledge data decision (KDD) automates data analysis by identifying valid, novel, useful, and understandable patterns in the data being examined using data heredity and parentage tracking techniques that have themselves been available for two decades. The technology base for KDD is also available now, but many of the applications envisioned for KDD presuppose an ability to access a variety of data formats and procedures. This implies either a single standard for all databases or using a technology for heterogeneous access. Expect the latter, starting with JAVA.

All the World on a Phone Jack

Remote manufacturing intelligence—running a machine center in Germany over the Net from a laptop in Michigan—is close. Kaminski believes that simulations based on the current operations of the machine and the ability to make in-process adjustments will free maintenance and plant engineering monies, as well as keeping plants on-line, a move toward twenty-four by seven. On-line remote diagnostics and repair are part of this picture because the capability of putting tiny microprocessors in literally every moving part on the machine enables the 2020 vision of the intelligent factory, directed from the United States, operating in Japan or Antarctica or the Channel Islands. The control and maintenance of designs, machine processes, and other intellectual property will continue to be a growing companion to technology.

Real-time capabilities—fast, robust, and repeatable—must be part of the decision-supporting process, because it is clearly better to make a less than optimal decision at the right time, as opposed to a potentially better decision too late. This applies to a surgeon in an operating room or a planner trying to formulate the next day's production schedule.

Imagine a system that operates by connecting diverse databases to a variety of search engines. Interfacing is done via memory-mapped blackboard systems across several embedded PCs with a rules-based, scalable management operating system coupled to it. Further applications in manufacturing will include:

- Understanding complex purchasing behavior
- Demand management and forecasting
- Sales channel analysis

Additional applications in transportation, automotive, semiconductor, pharmaceutical, and food industries are not far behind.

KDD is more than a search engine—it is a knowledge-based repository that helps decision-making by identifying trends, behavior, and patterns too evanescent for humans to handle. With the

Web being the de facto standard for databases of the future, we'll be able to put the execution system, and even the tire enterprise, on a phone jack.

Onboard Manufacturing, Replication on Wheels

EFTC'S ALLIANCE WITH FUJITSU AND LOGISTICS PROVIDER

Jack Calderon, president of Denver, Colorado, EMS (electronic management services) supplier EFTC, has plunged his company into Web-based manufacturing and repair of boards and electronic devices in a partnership with transportation providers and component distributors. The result is a unique build-to-order infrastructure that runs to advanced information links and that minimizes logistics time and costs by locating in transportation hubs. EFTC's innovative logistics partnerships inevitably minimize supply inventory throughout the network. In this case, information and time are truly replacing silicon and iron.

Calderon knows he is on to something—he has localized board manufacturing and repair. By taking on the computer assembly work for Fujitsu, remote to Fujitsu and his own Colorado headquarters, he is leading the way in breakthrough distributed manufacturing. Further, by forming a partnership with a logistics provider to handle customer contact and logistics details, he has cut two more links out of the supply chain, including preassembly warehouses so common in electronics and automotive extended enterprises, as well as cut acquisition, movement, and tracking material costs.

The costs that accumulate from in-process, repair, and finished-goods inventory are considerable. If your company runs at a $100-million rate per year, and there is one month of finished goods on the floor, you are carrying a permanent $8.33-million investment ($100 million divided by twelve), at approximately $1 million per year in interest lost costs. Running any company at one inventory turn per year is irresponsible; running at ten turns starts the pipelines. Time really is money—if a product, or pieces of product, or even a portfolio of jobs are delayed an average of one month over one year, the carrying cost reaches one hundred thousand dollars. Systems and engineers that "clear the floor" amplify their good works across the enterprise as they practice lean manufacturing and beyond.

Anything—device, protocol, human hierarchy—that gets in the way of "clearing the floor" is a problem. Less is more.

A Recipe for Slow Death

Technologists and managers make choices every day—when to make a changeover, who runs the new product schedule, when to staff up for the next deluge. Technology managers can be sure that they will not suddenly find their organization suboptimized if they retain and grow the skills they currently hold. Sara Beckman, a University of California at Berkeley researcher and former member of the board of directors at Hewlett Packard, now teaching at MIT's Sloan School, warns of these four steps to immediate technology decline:

1. Stop making the most difficult things—parts, components, and equipment.

2. Allow your workforce to lose its skills, especially machinists and tool and die makers. Manufacturing in 2020 will not be devoid of human intelligence and experience.

3. Allow your technical skills to atrophy. Beckman sees at least four categories of heavy engineering that will be needed in factories: manufacturing engineers, new process engineers, materials engineers, and new product engineers. There will be a dozen more, and each of these groups of engineering expertise preserves the information and intelligence capabilities that 2020 enterprises will thrive on—commodity cost intelligence, process intelligence, and technology intelligence.

4. Learn that you have no special expertise to offer, to a potential partner, or to a customer.

Human Factors, the Power of Emotion to Affect Closing Predictions

Our predictions focus on technologies that will be broadly accepted in use, not designs and not prototypes or concepts, or even ideas that have been patented but not implemented, because there is a twenty-year lapse between concept and earliest use. Bar code patents, for example, are being licensed by GM thirty-five years after the event, and patents in manufacturing from the sixties form the basis for fees today. Watch out for the time lapse.

One big category of predictions centers on the human factor of emotion. The stock market, for example, runs on emotion, as do wars and marketeers. In the mid-nineties, analysts watched the market climb like a roller coaster that started out slowly, accelerated, reached a peak, shuddered, and continued to climb with occasional heart-in-the-throat moments. Everyone on the ride "knows" that the fun will end, and they will have the choice of getting off or getting back into the car for another ride. The thrill factor attracts everyone. When the stock market begins its drop, we are triggered into a fear reaction—unless we are bear investors—and because fear suggests flight for survival, we sell and convert to cash. We have relieved the "emotion," but by this very action, the individual who now feels better has caused the market to crash further.

If we are in a narrow industry segment, high-tech for example, our actions will spread to other areas, just as downturns in some electronics markets inevitably spread to the capital equipment and wafer production plant sectors. The cycle looks like a pile of sand: When we gently dribble sand onto a single location, the buildup occurs in a linear pattern; when the pile becomes steep enough, however, it collapses to a shallower core. We call this the power law, or the $1/f$ slump. A large slump occurs less frequently than a minor slump, and to our surprise, the line relating frequency of occurrence and severity of slump is dead straight on a log plot—dead straight as in earthquake dead straight, and venture capital dead straight. The big deals *will* occur, but less often than the little ones, and they will appear in a straight line.

The parallels are everywhere. We humans are like the grains of sand on the slope. As stability builds up, it must inevitably come down, and emotions are the slump material that allows us to behave for survival in animal mode. Our emotions are part of the universe; they truly help us survive, and they are a big part of the driving force in human interaction. The stock market won't slump only because of emotional reactions, or only because of financial forces or political problems, but the combination of the three is apocalyptic.

The story of the bull market and how it was perpetuated, and historically how long it can be expected to perform at such heights, is easy to listen to. But what really drives that type of aggressive market is emotion—sometimes fear, sometimes greed, and always excitement. Further, the importance of perceptions in reacting to market swings is worthy of attention—when the *perception* of failure in the Southeast Asian markets, for example, is broadcast globally, suddenly Wall Street and other markets react. The ticker takes on a mind of its own as we start to personify it—to give it a personality and a brain— "The market tried to recover today," or, "Wall Street found itself on the floor today."

And ironically, whoever or whatever organization constructs the best story gets to control where the market moves. Statistics and trend reports become a function of emotions and human energies.

Think about the implications of the following scenario.

The Stock Market Viewed from Forty Thousand Feet Up

The combined GNPs of Japan and China are smaller than that of the United States. But the United States is not the size of the world, and if Asia drops like a rock and Europe is stagnant, a not surprising possibility, the United States cannot hold up the perceived value of the world. Arbitrage exists in many forms, but leveling of some kind will occur, it's an inevitable rippling process. Emotional reactions, hence perceptions, hence real adjustments will occur when the discrepancies in valuation differ so greatly from one global area, Asia at half value, to another, the United States at 2X. If the United States does not adjust, then Asia *must* rally, or we (the Unites States) *must* fall. We can talk endlessly about the points of difference—balance of payments, computers, cash reserves, currency conversions, International Monetary Fund, labor unrest—but the real economic imbalance between the two regions translates to a simple fact of physics: Water flows downhill. The United States cannot grow any more through increased exports or other advantageous currency tricks until rallies occur elsewhere, because the North American economy does not exist and grow in a vacuum.

Microsoft does $12 billion a year in revenues and has a "greater fool" market value bigger than General Motors or South Korea. The correction will come, and it will be large-scale. The arguments of traders and some press observers is that "it cannot happen here," "six thousand ain't bad, at least it's six times the valuation of several years ago," and so forth. Morley's dad used to meet the financial Turks visiting The Barn, and they often bragged about how smart they were— by being lucky enough to be born investing in a boom market—or they would complain about the recession "caused" by local politicians, as if the Rhode Island governor or Maine's secretary of commerce could control the global recession. After the Turks left, Dad would say, "Don't they realize that the last seven recessions (booms) were deeper?" So soon we forget.

So human factors engineering, especially the areas relative to brain systems and emotions, senses, and feelings, will be a greater concern for all businesses from a profitability perspective, and for manufacturers as part of maintaining very high quality and innovative performance. Changing culture or creating or modifying technology will be enabled or stopped by human factors—not the technology itself—and larger successful enterprises will quickly break down some of their more puzzling human factors issues into manageable problems, just as they conquered teams and compensation issues in the past.

Emotions—specific agent behavior—can be ascribed to corporate entities as well, or cause the success of a marginal movie, or cause the Y2K Chicken Little slump. If the cone is already fairly high, emotions will "shake the table" and help chose the timing of the next event. Apple Computer, Netscape, and Microsoft all have emotions, and emotional behavior, and these same emotions—passion, fear, terror, aggression, and love—all serve us well. The key is to allow the emotions to aid and build us, rather than to destroy the body. Anger destroyed Willie the Rottweiler. And it may destroy Netscape.

The Landscape of Survival Consists of Our Actions

Within any organization or system the culture or atmosphere of the place itself determines how it functions, whether the group succeeds or fails, and whether its inhabitants know and appreciate their successes. Simple indicators include answering the question, Is this organization in an atmosphere of fear and survival, or one of trust, opportunity, and inspiration?

Human factors engineering will take on a new definition as organizations—businesses and schools especially—move beyond a nineties focus on drugs as mood levelers and "containment aids," to total environments that evoke powerful and effective emotions. Indeed, this human engineering breakthrough will answer many of our questions and problems about motivation and reward systems as we learn to look inward for triggers.

Closing Predictions from The Barn

2020 WILD CARDS

Human factors attributes in MIL design with modeling; modeling of corporate organizations according to tasks and resources; the Internet as a commodity evolves from intoxication to the hangover stage; encryption solves the problem of an Internet that is not trusted in the world of commerce as well as working well for simple information exchange and entertainment; designer drugs; communities of intellect; 10k CPUs; the moon becomes an economic satellite to the earth (finally); working at home becomes respectable (again); Dick Tracy video conferences go live; the New Microsoft is born, and the technologies that win will be biotech applets, satellite launchers, uplink communications, embedded operating systems, GE Capital, fuel cell innovation; "smart" structural materials, especially in bridges and cars; information technology dominates manufacturing; questionable mergers stop; intelligent agents run airports; Chinese Boxes everywhere; manufacturing at the point of consumption; flat screens everywhere, in lighting and on wallpaper and as windows; art attributes in Autocad packages; power distributors market and sell based on cost, quality, uptime, stability, power factor, and surge immunity; some enterprises move to extremely localized power (self-contained plants); China remains a threat to the world economy; every motor and appliance is JAVA-compatible; new RT operating systems for embedded systems; twenty thousand satellites in orbit; no landline phones, all communications run through satellite uplinks; 59 percent of the U.S. population will not work in large companies; a new Internet will become the industrial Web; populations will be more dispersed globally; permanent residents in Antarctica; political correctness is reversed, and crime and insurance problems won't be solved by wishes; the stock market lowers to six thousand and then accelerates to the equivalent of thirty thousand points by 2020; NASDAQ accepts and solicits foreign companies; engineering productivity triples (it's not an art form any more); art galleries appear on the Net; consultancies become a large sector of the economy; every factory contains only the equivalent of a CNC machine, WWW connectivity, AGV (auto guided vehicles), many control systems; ink jet printers produce auto, boat, and bike custom paint jobs; Recaro seats for autos everywhere; university degrees describe all the new technology curricula available for completion on the Web; tree huggers become realistic and capitalistic; silicon books, demo'd today, fall into the production and distribution structure, and take off, starting with kids; newspapers continue to print daily; ADSL in all businesses; remote control houses wired to run TVs, autos, heat, light, and food preparation; money available in IPOs to support social manipulation; "education" and chemical behavioral modification and control; marketing becomes a true science, data-driven and specific, predictable; DNA applets; space communications enjoy renewed financial megasupport, this time not from government, but from economic entities with money to support big systems projects; all product prices (commodities and custom products)—are value-determined; semiconductor foundries at individual companies—("bake your own chips"); generic discrete factories form chains and franchises; mechatronics gets respect; movies and music composed "on the spot"; remote control houses; U.S. postal service offers small fast alternative; spamming is good; the return of atomic power, clean this time; extreme sports get more extreme; more private schools, and much more adult education; silicon books; hypersonic jets; 100 mph corridors for limited use; extremely privatized transportation corridors, with electronic tollgates, "belong to" powerful enterprises, the United Maritime States of the Atlantic, for example, or, "You are entering the Federated Midwest Automotive Transportation Corridor, no minivans or personal vehicles allowed"; the supply chain flattens and becomes Amazon; Wal-Mart and e-mail merge; real estate goes global and gets simple; one hundred screens per household, and five thousand TV access channels, all reruns; PLCs have ears and eyes; make your own juice (local electricity generation); Hong Kong acquires China; Italy defaults on the Eurobuck; South Africa overrun (again); North and South Korea recombine; global, global, global.

Out of the Forest Come the Winners . . .

Manufacturing technologists polled in a recent automotive study named thirteen core technology areas in their enterprise for which high-level needs had been identified. The list included a mix of practical operating improvements and advanced technology. Their immediate concerns reflected stiff competitive pressures that will cause some of them to drop out of the race to consolidation experienced by the losers. The winners will of course continue to aggressively pursue cost and time advantages, which they are hopeful will be facilitated by meta-systems. Don't expect the current automotive industry, however, to find the final solution to its cost problems, because franchises and primitive design protocols, along with entrenched bureaucracies, will interfere. The thirteen core technology areas are:

1. Flexible process and equipment
2. Optimized stamping process
3. Casting using lightweight materials
4. Modeling in paint application and other centers
5. Global logistics modeling
6. Materials flow optimization
7. CAE modeling tools
8. New materials, including structural glass
9. Dry machining to reduce pollution
10. Modular electrical designs
11. Lean manufacturing methods
12. Reliability/maintainability techniques
13. Product information management

Security, Emotional and Otherwise

Encryption and security systems are a wide-open area that will be fully explored and resolved with technology. Although there may be indications that a merger is happening between commerce on the Net and Net business, these transaction systems are not the same. The financial community has been able to deal with the problem, which has two aspects—emotions and security. Today, we call our broker and commit to a ten-thousand-dollar trade over the phone, no problem. Our stocks are held in street names, and not only do we do the transaction ourselves, we never actually really own anything before or after the phone call. In fact, our "money" is just a number in a computer, because paper money and gold, a relatively useless metal, are only used because of the need for trust in the system, and as a tallying mechanism. Money has no intrinsic value; it is simply a medium of exchange that eliminates barter. For credit card transactions, customers give numbers by phone where no security exists, but the system works, and if fraud is discovered, the credit-card company is the holder insurer within a respectable fifty-dollar limit.

But we still don't trust the Internet, so encryption technology will be more pervasive. The technology involves the concept of trap doors using prime numbers and exponential representation that allows the sender and the receiver to both have keys that only work on the ends assigned. Users work mostly with passwords (PIN) and code references, and in fact the most common password is "Password." ATMs are really secure, but losses for the card company amount to less than 3 percent, easily financed and cheaper than a complicated nonworking encryption system. The thirty-two-bit trap-door code takes several hours to hack over the Nets using coordinated unused Net computers. The same computers that are being protected are used to break the code because *no* code is unbreakable—it's a Catch-22. If security can be made transparent to both ends of the line, it will take off, but, like NASDAQ and the U.S. Post Office, the liftoff depends on the trust of the community.

RMI tried to sell a new code system for identifying the person in a card transaction, because about 30 percent of supermarket transactions are signature-based, of which 10 percent are questionable, but the problem is only valued at about a $500-million loss spread across thousands of banks. Credit-card companies decided it was cheaper to self-insure.

Building controls are multilevel password secure, but the feature sells well and is never used; we seldom use the parity (check) bit in computers, but it's still there, and who ever reads his phone bill? Manufacturing tends to think that ideas will be stolen over the Net, but we forget the people who walk out every night, hit the bar, and talk, talk, talk.

By the year 2020, look for the new automotive killer apps to appear from an unexpected source, rental car companies, for example, or transportation intensive producers themselves—private fleets—or other commodity providers for whom sensible and cheaper transportation must be available. With factories running seven by twenty-four, logistics providers are likely sources of information systems design-to-volume speed, as well as innovation in commodity shipping areas to feed a network of Chinese Boxes.

Cash Farming

Dick Schonberger, Tom Johnson, Robert Kaplan, and Dan Dimancescu have all studied and attacked the burden of corporate accounting systems. Indeed, the powerful innovation of computing development has pretty well tagged the needs of accountants for the first fifty years of the computer as important above all other applications. And reasonably so, considering the origins of what was orginally "the business machine."

In the Lowell, Massachusetts, textile mill complex, visitors to the Boott Mill can enter the mill through only one gate after they have passed over the canal (the moat). One hundred and fifty years ago, at ten minutes after the morning startup bell, nineteenth-century mill workers who were late were further diverted as they rushed to their spots. The iron gate was locked shut, and latecomers on the way to their posts were forced to detour through the superintendent's office, where the ledgers were updated in meticulous detail to exactly record their lateness. Transaction processing was immediate and accurate to the penny, and weekly cash disbursements reflected perfect time keeping.

Somehow our money-capturing systems have evolved from that same image. Extremely accurate posting of discrete transaction history—from one customer or supplier or worker or client to another—has formed the basis of money measurement, not the true statement of value creation or movement, but the static valuation of the numbers. Dan Dimancescu, author of *The Lean Enterprise* and *The Seamless Enterprise*, calls it "revenue farming" management.[3] In fact, he predicts that managers will use the word manufacturing less and less, not because the making of "things" is vanishing into virtual space, but because specific concerns—"factory floor" and "delivery efficiency" (management areas)—are being quickly superseded by a much larger agenda. Manufacturers are becoming more aware of door-to-door objectives, rather than merely discrete production goals. They want to see the cash move through their plants and they want to convert raw material to money immediately, and they want money to flow directly to their operations. In other words, they want to skip the middlemen, and the middle steps.

We aren't just talking about plastic transactions over the Web, we are redesigning the money flows, and manufacturing becomes the printing press for currency generation. The medium changes—steel in one plant, plastics in another—but the fuel is the manufacturing transformation process. And unfortunately our current accounting and even corporate financial systems do not recognize the transition that is coming. It's the difference, in manufacturing terms, between process and discrete flows; typically, process flows describe chemical processing or oil refineries in which volumes, rather than discrete parts, and rates, or single units, are measured, usually by sensors. Discrete manufacturing, however, like discrete currency tracking, focuses on single units, following the progress of that single unit from creation through a series of steps until it returns to the bank.

Dimancescu cites Nortel's focus on downstream activities, including cost accumulation and reporting. In fact, terminology changes—from work-in-process to orders-in-process—more clearly highlight the necessary systems shift that will enable manufacturing to see and capture the money flows. Other innovative organizations, such as EFTC, Dell, AST, Cisco Systems, Flextronics, and Pitney-Bowes, are pursuing the same flows by attempting to manage the "cash-to-cash cycle." When cash is released from in-process inventory or capital equipment, manufacturers see immediate profitability margins move up.

Dimancescu also points to another technology boom that comes quite naturally as a result of this renewed focus on currency: encryption. On-line consumer transactions, for example, or cell phone transmissions that are entirely unprotected, exemplify the kind of systems solutions that must be made to fully realize the electronic cash management possibilities unleashed by ATMs and the Web.

Dell Computer's supply-chain approach—selling off the Web, almost directly into its supply base, and filling customer orders faster than most other computer providers—is the most likely pioneer application in the computer world. Where Gateway struggles with maintaining supplier quality, localized warehouses, and retail outlets, providers like Dell in the United States and AST in Europe are taking product revenue generation in another direction. EFTC's pioneering collaboration with Fujitsu and logistics providers to repair, return, and even assemble electronics devices, without the Colorado plant ever touching the product, makes the point that innovative logistics solutions are not all about where to put the warehouse, or which air freight company gets there the fastest. It's about who does the work, and who captures the money. Dell's order-to-cash-in-hand cycle is reportedly one day; Compaq's is thirty-five days.

One Pitney-Bowes executive sees the implications of the change in his role. "We are broadening our view of 'asset management' as a driver," he says. "It's the cash that flows out of the order-to-installation-to-billing process that is now treated as the measure of our effectiveness as 'manufacturing' executives." As a natural result, the talk at Pitney-Bowes has less to do with "work-in-process" and a lot more with learning to manage "orders-in-process."

Executives at Lotus's headquarters in Cambridge, Massachusetts, and in its software distribution center in Woburn understand this challenge quite well. In fact, Lotus uses its own product, Lotus Notes, to run its software operation like a high-speed assembly and billing operation. When manufacturing managers update their production schedules and daily order rates, they know that they are, without setting foot on the production floor, moving money.

According to Dimancescu, Lotus wants to cultivate, or farm, its revenue potential and to ensure that monies owed for software licenses, upgrades, documentation or other paid services—all the combined intellectual capital wrapped around software media—are all collected as promptly and accurately as possible, direct. "There's the growing danger of electronic transactions falling into some great big black hole," says one manager, "or even prey to hacker fraud." These are concerns that—at Lotus—are grouped into the responsibility of "manufacturing." What's going on in all these companies has significant organizational implications. Not the least is an increasing emphasis on treating "manufacturing," or "innovative replication," even if it's an intangible like software, as a team-managed end-to-end process with stringent performance standards. This is a game played by the manufacturing personnel, for the benefit of the company, that may not necessarily be managed by the people who always kept score, the accounting and financial people.

Process counts, and companies are turning their focus to fixing, perfecting, and better understanding their entire process. Given the right sensors and metrics, most managers will find the right way to maximize the game score. Dimancescu cites Paul Allaire, chairman and CEO of Xerox: "We realized our organization had to be redesigned to reflect our strategy, and that's when we began focusing on processes. . . . You can't redesign processes unless you know what you're trying to do. What you are after is congruence among strategic directions, organizational design, staff capabilities, and the processes you use to ensure that people are working together to meet the company's goals."

As the metrics shift, managers begin to perceive a possible transfer of power that is unnerving and professionally a challenge. Terms like "head-counts," budgets, and overhead accounting become less powerful as process teams study and improve key processes. Inevitably, applications packages from other disciplines will step in to help make the change.

The Death of Software

In the late 1800s every respectable manufacturing company boasted a vice-president of electric motors. Electric motors were precious; companies rushed to work with standard and the challenges of central single versus distributed power motors. Electric motors, like software, have not gone away, but they have certainly been deglamourized, as software will be. Within twenty years the care and feeding of software will be such that software engineering will not be extensively taught in universities.

Manufacturing at the Point of Consumption

Historically, villages located manufacturing sites at the point of raw material—smelters at ore deposits, arrowhead factories at the site of quartz deposits, refineries at oil fields, and pottery kilns near sources of clay. Later, large manufacturing facilities were located based on labor availability—location at the source, not the point of need, was the rule.

Recently, however, our society has become consumption constrained, as opposed to production-constrained. The result is that the way we think about production and consumption will change. We will locate innovative replication facilities at the point of consumption, in quantities of one or one hundred, with zero defects, with zero inventory in process. Desktop manufacturing, virtual prototyping, and the Internet are the primary enabling technologies. Further, teleoperations will allow companies to ship a virtual product—the process and other technical information needed to manufacture—rather than the real thing.

Extending this image into 2020, strawberries will be grown and harvested in the supermarket, autos will be assembled on demand at the dealer showroom, and custom jeans will be cut and sewn on-site. The manufacturer of the next millennium will either have distributed physical facilities at points of consumption, or will make extensive use of specialized express services in combination with assembly and reman, as has EFTC. Assembly at the airport, or onboard the orbiting satellite, will be commonplace and cost-effective. Product design and assembly layout will be partly determined by replication and distribution considerations; Hau Lee at Stanford has studied the design process of various printer products at Hewlett Packard and other electronics assemblers that have modified their parts design and assembly sequence to facilitate better throughput. Even pharmaceuticals will be tailored to the individual—the automated drugstore on the Web.

Computing. We can decode, calculate, word-process, and work in color over long distances, with movement and sound. Computers now have, for most purposes, infinite capacity, but the wire connecting the two computing devices is narrow and constrictive—transmission of all the code from one computer to another takes an hour or two. That too will change with an increase of one hundred times in the channel width among computers worldwide.

The PLC, back in the factory where all our interest in reliable and fast control systems still resides, will continue to dominate over PC-based systems that have yet to demonstrate cost savings, increased reliability, or reduced time to implementation. Customers continue to demand integrated production solutions—"one butt to kick"—and with micro PLCs at two hundred dollars compared to most desktops at around one thousand dollars plus software and programming, the technology direction is clear.

Despite all these changes, we predict that in 2020 or sooner manufacturing will represent less than 5 percent of the GNP, with 50 percent asset use the norm and doubled R&D productivity with thousands more local, small Chinese Boxes. Dilbert awakens.

Back at The Barn

We started our journey at the mouth of a small river—the Nissitissitt, or the Blackstone, or the Nashua, or the Merrimack—and we followed it downstream until we came to a dam that powered a group of brick mills where we saw spinners and weavers working in cotton and copper, and we heard the noise of metal hitting metal, gears and treadles clacking in a rhythm that gradually dropped to a whisper. One hundred and fifty years into our journey, we peeked around a test bench as a hung over engineer fumbled with yet another wiring diagram and sketched out a new $5-billion industry, the PLC.

Meanwhile, software and silicon pioneers worked furiously at schematics and toggle switches, and as we watched the pattern of on-off, on-off lights, we came to see the beginnings of a new machine. A generation of managers and analysts marched into buildings where tired factory hands wordlessly emptied their pockets and cashed out. Out in the millyard, trucks delivered boxes of new machines, gray painted cabinets with indicator lights—machining centers on wheels, voice-activated process controllers, audio/video teleconferencing from remote sites. The landscape of manufacturing technology moved out into the countryside again, alongside the same rivers, as Web sites and e-mail addresses dumped decades of manufacturing intelligence into the waiting arms of storage devices.

The machine began to hum as robots and clean rooms magically sculpted autos and cameras, telephones and music players from small pellets of plastic and metal. Sometimes, we caught a glimpse of the alchemist's process, the transformation that inevitably produced hot-molded parts.

Where colors and smells once marked the end products of full-tilt production runs, we see plants, clustered work stations, and land-scaped vistas to outside meeting areas. We have described the technologies, the managers, and the knowledge workers that will make manufacturing work in 2020, as well as the fuel that drives the technology machine—money, ideas, and risk.

We gave you some ideas on how to get there, how to prepare, and who to pick to make the journey. Don't expect that they all will—Moses wandered in the desert for forty years. He wasn't lost—he was waiting for "the old ones" to move on.

Don't waste too much time on moving mountains. Let the process run itself and you will make the journey. Expect that some people will choose not to go. Identify them, pick the new players quickly, and keep moving. Count your money, place your bets, choose the right technologies, and keep your vision uncluttered by distractions—standards controversies, limiting financial ploys, and other shams. Make mistakes and have fun, celebrate the marvelous power of the technology gods, who made connections where none were imagined before, who mixed sand and copper to make words appear on a glass screen.

When co-author Moody's father lifted her up to see the heart of the paper-manufacturing process, he could not have guessed that his daughter's interest in machines and things would carry her out of the machine age into the uncertainties of electronics and the birth of new industries. He could not have known that on the site of the dam that he carefully and lovingly rebuilt, on the river where he learned to swim and where he built his home, there would be a revival of the manufacturing village that surpassed all his financial limits.

When one of the last vestiges of water power converted to steam energy, the penstock, a high-pressure conduit that carried water from the upstream dam to the downstream power plant, exploded, and the sound traveled across town and upriver. These same brick buildings will house a different kind of alchemy, one connected through wires and antennas and satellites to mobile replication centers whose route schedule—Beijing this week, and São Paulo next—parallels the itinerant jobbers who rolled into town with tools and tinware clanging to announce another visit.

When we lived "up the river bankin'," our families were served by a score of portable resources—a fish man, an apple man, a bread man, a dry-cleaning man, the newspaper boy, the rag picker, and of course the milkman. The parallels to 2020 manufacturing and delivery systems we predict will not be that strange in comparison to fifty years ago: The process will have changed, but the strategy of producing and delivering customized localized products on-site still makes sense. And money. Technology is about money.

Hardwired Intelligence

Technology has redefined intelligence. We are putting microscopic brains in the skins of composites and robotic arms; there are chips on the back of shampoo bottles and movie tickets. Different forms of intelligence—organizing data, collecting, retrieving, and other database functions—are dwarfed by the possibilities of Bios's intelligent agent models, and the pioneering GM Paint Shop application that proved how simple genetics really is.

Shane Steel and SteelWorks process intelligent software, the second generation of simplicity in heavy machining, are further clues to big industries like automotive and capital equipment of the power of small software dynamos. Simplicity reigns and thrives in all these applications.

Bill Fulkerson, the woodcarver at John Deere who used his mathematics training and restless curiosity to unleash the first and biggest genetic algorithm, is a breakthrough technologist, as are Gregg Ekberg and a succession of brilliant programmers at Flavors Technologies.

International Plastics/Germany and the Japanese bullet train simulators, meta-systems derived from a Darwinian approach to modern plant scheduling, proved what scale intelligent agent and complex adaptive system software can encompass.

But these industry applications of schedulers and simulators are second-generation tools. The next generation that is closing fast on pioneering systems and innovative process approaches will take the process real-time, by taking the principles of real-time on-line control systems and running the manufacturing centers that will instantaneously churn out custom jeans and personalized video machines. We won't be watching simulated train runs over a high-speed rail network, we will be watching dispatchers send trains out to Tokyo and Osaka, real-time, running to software-managed and -developed schedules. We will see chaos theory and simplicity enable true lot size of one production in challenging businesses, such as automotive and computer manufacturing.

Look for a new generation of enterprise leaders to rigorously train and prepare to design and run the Technology Machine. Software engineers, physicists, biogeneticists, materials engineers, communications engineers, analysts, writers, process designers, transcultural traders, thinkers, and brokers will gradually supplant the MBA ranks as history and static performance metrics give way to real-time on-line closed-loop feedback and variance adjustment.

Expect the 2020 factory to look more like an air traffic control center, a laboratory type environment, than a bricks-and-mortar structure. Look for wheels under every workbench and every piece of machinery. Where clean-room technology dominates a handful of industries—some pharmaceuticals, certainly chip-making, and some chemical processing—expect the clean-room environment to take over all 2020 excellent performers.

Do not to expect to see, hear, or smell much. Look for ripples on the surface indicating steady product movement as it passes from raw materials clear through rows of quiet workers and humming equipment, down to the waiting express truck. This machine doesn't stop for sundown, nights, holidays, or birthdays. The 2020 manufacturing facility will be a twenty-four-by-seven-capable operation and staffs will be lean and superbly prepared to keep the machine running.

Expect technology leaders to be scientists, chemists, physicists, engineers, and other knowledge intensive workers. Understand that if you plan on being one of them, you will extend the longevity of your young technical training with "age-appropriate" seminars and video training experiences. And you can put away your road warrior gear, because teleconferencing and portable manufacturing combined with aligned customers and suppliers, and well-documented process controls, will simplify the whole business of making things.

Get ready to spend more time thinking about money—how to plant, water, and very quickly harvest this short-shelf-life product. Study money pipelines and flow rates as you would a wiring diagram, because the competitor who discovers how to capture the money as it pours through the pipeline reaps the highest interest recovery rates. Put your best programming power on the money-generating machine. And the innovators, primarily springing from the electronics business, who get to the intellectual property finish line first, with the highest number of money transactions, win.

Think of your career and your management challenge like a winning portfolio—you will pick a particular industry or technology focus, understand its underlying processes very well, and fill your portfolio with fifteen or twenty winners. You will shoot for high risk and even higher rewards, and your expectation is that if one of your picks is a winner, you get the market. You will expect to—on some occasions, but certainly not all the time—"lose." But with an expectation that picking the overall winning portfolio—either of skills, or processes, or new products, or venture capital business plan funding proposals—you will create a healthy return. The individual winners and losers will tend to blur into an overall picture of prosperity.

Work to create a renewed sense of the common good. Your best single-point technology winners will falter in the depths of human pain and neglect. Think about how to use technology to energize elderly lives and free children from the addiction to yet another electronic eye. Understand that the money that you invest in technology winners should trigger a cascade of small improvements that you will be proud to remember and talk about with your peers.

Play the game hard and well, and play to win, eyes ahead, knowing that you will sometimes lose the race. Know your competitor, memorize the rules, and when the race starts, don't look back or down: Accelerate!

References

"Advice for Millennium Watchers," Patricia E. Moody, *Target*, Third Quarter 1998.

"The Year 2000 or so. . . . Of Crossfoots and Bit Miners," Alfred J. Krever, *Target*, Third Quarter 1998.

NOTES

Chapter 2.
One Hundred Twenty-seven Wild Cards—Who We Will Be, and What
We Will Do.

1. *AOL Online News,* May 12, 1998, Washington, D.C.

2. Gilder, George, *Telecommunications Policy Roundtable, Forbes ASAP,* December 5, 1994, p. 162.

3. Mansfield, Howard, *In the Memory House* (Golden, Colo.: Fulcrum Publishing, 1993).

4. Ibid., p. 278.

Chapter 3.
WHACK, Why You Can't Get There from Here

1. Kerschner, Edward, CFA, *Morning Notes Research Reports,* May 11, 1998, p. 1.

Chapter 5.
Intelligent Systems That Will Get Us There—Chaos, Complex Adoptive
Systems, and Other Enabling Technologies

1. "Artificial Ants and Technological Graphs" copyright the Bios Group LP. Printed with permission. Other Bios materials on simulations used with

permission of the Bios Group LP, 317 Paseo de Peraita, Santa Fe, N. M., 87501, 505-992-6700.

Chapter 7.
Managing the Technology Machine

1. Nelson, Dave Rick Mayo, and Patricia E. Moody, *Powered by Honda—Developing Excellence in the Global Enterprise* (New York: John Wiley and Sons, 1998).

2. Craig, S. Russel, "Making High Tech Pay Off: Ten Ways to Build a Better Technology Company," *Upside,* November 1997.

Chapter 9.
In the Land Where the Engineer Is King

1. Diesenhouse, Susan, "Remolding an Industry," *Boston Sunday Globe,* July 26, 1998, pp. G1, G5.

Chapter 10.
Silicon Life on a Carbon Planet

1. Cabrera, Barney J., "John von Neumann and von Neumann Architecture for Computers (1945)," a paper presented on June 2, 1995, University of California, San Diego. Cabrera cites the following bibliography: Aspray, William, *John von Neumann and the Origins of Modern Computing* (Cambridge, Mass.: MIT Press, 1990); Hayes, John P., *Computer Architecture and Organization* (New York: McGraw-Hill, 1988); Heims, Steve J., *John von Neumann and Norbert Wiener: From Mathematics to the Technologies of Life and Death* (Cambridge, Mass.: MIT Press, 1980); Macrae, Norman, *John von Neumann* (New York: Pantheon, 1992).

2. *U.S. Department of Commerce News,* May 11, 1998.

3. Dimancescu, Dan, "A New Landscape," *Target* magazine, September/October 1997, pp. 6–8.

BIBLIOGRAPHY

Barnet, Richard J. and John Cavanagh. *Global Dreams—Imperial Corporations and the New World Order.* New York: Simon & Schuster/Touchstone, 1994. A dense and visionary (though unfortunately little-read) pioneer in the area of globalization.

Bios Group. "Artificial Ants and Technological Graphs." Santa Fe, N. M., 1998.

Cabrera, Barney J. "John von Neumann and von Neumann Architecture for Computers (1945)." Paper presented at the University of California, San Diego, June 2, 1995.

Crain, S. Russel. "Making High Tech Pay Off: Ten Ways to Build a Better Technology Company," *Upside.* San Mateo, Calif.: Upside Media Inc., November 1997.

Croswell, Ken. *Planet Quest.* New York: Simon & Schuster/The Free Press, 1997. A book to take us out of this galaxy, a star search.

Dalzell, Robert F., Jr. *The Enterprising Elite: The Boston Associates and the World They Made.* Boston: Harvard University Press, 1987.

Dimancescu, Dan. "A New Landscape," *Target* magazine, AME, Wheeling, Illinois, September/October 1997.

Gilder, George. Telecommunications Policy Roundtable, *Forbes ASAP,* December 5, 1994.

Gleick, James. *Chaos: Making a New Science.* New York: Penguin, 1988. The chaos "Bible."

Hamel, Gary, and C.K. Prahalad. *Competing for the Future.* Boston: Harvard Business School Press, 1994.

Hareven, Tamara K., and Randolph Langenbach. *Amoskeag: Life and Work in an American Factory-City.* Boston: University Press of New England, 1996.

Kerschner, Edward. *Morning Notes Research Reports.* New York, 1998.

Mansfield, Howard. *In The Memory House.* Golden, Colo.: Fulcrum Publishing, 1993. A magic look at the past from an urban historian—reflections on how people saw their lives.

Maynard, Michael. "The Real Year 2000 Crisis," newsbytes, Minneapolis, 1998.

McRae, Hamish. *The World in 2020—Power, Culture and Prosperity.* Boston: Harvard Business School Press, 1994. A different perspective on what makes countries and economies change.

Oresick, Peter, and Nicholas Coles (editor). *Working Classics: Poems on Industrial Life.* Chicago: University of Illinois Press, 1993.

Petzinger, Thomas, Jr. "At Deere, They Know a Mad Scientist May Be a Big Asset," *The Wall Street Journal,* July 14, 1995.

Popcorn, Faith, and Lys Marigold. *Clicking—16 Trends to Future Fit Your Life, Your Work, and Your Business.* New York: HarperCollins, 1996.

Poss, Jane. "Angels of Capitalism," *The Boston Globe,* November 13, 1990.

Robert, Ralph. *Zone Logic—A Unique Method of Practical Artificial Intelligence.* Radnor, Pennsylvania: Compute! Books, 1989.

Sherden, William A. *The Fortune Sellers—The Big Business of Buying and Selling Predictions.* New York: John Wiley and Sons, 1998. A somewhat critical (jaundiced?) look at the business side of telling the future.

Target magazine, a publication of the Association for Manufacturing Excellence (AME). Wheeling, Ill. AME pioneered just-in-time in manufacturing and has been among the leaders in adopting other newer approaches, including teams and kaizen blitz. *Target* is a good source of small- and medium-size company manufacturing implementation stories. Phone: 847 520-3280. Website: http://ame.org/

Womack, James P., and Daniel T. Jones. *Lean Thinking.* New York: Simon & Schuster, 1996.

ACKNOWLEDGMENTS

We have good memories of touring hundreds of factories, good and bad, and of meeting thousands of inhabitants of the manufacturing world—engineers, designers, entrepreneurs, bureaucrats, workers.

But not too many accountants.

Between the two of us, our combined consulting and teaching experience stretches over sixty years. Holder of twelve patents and creator of the device that revolutionized the way factories run, the PLC (programmable logic controller), co-author and partner Dick Morley celebrates the thirtieth anniversary of that breakthrough with new and equally exciting innovations in new technology areas, including his Next Generation Vehicle, the Blackbird, and the Javahoe.

But long before, and along the way, and as Dick is wont to say, "in the days of wooden ships and iron men," we were blessed by a powerful legacy of other engineers who built the Technology Machine:

- Farraday.
- Paul Moody, the young engineer who transformed Francis Cabot Lowell's "industrial espionage"—stolen images of fully integrated cotton mills that he had memorized on visits to English factories—into iron, the first fully integrated textile machine on the banks of the Charles River. That prototype's profits soared to over 200 per-

cent in two years, and spawned the first industrial city in North America: Lowell, Massachusetts, on the banks of the Merrimack.

• The Amoskeag, Manchester, New Hampshire—profits and economies of scale bred to extremes until 1937 when this Tyrannosaurus rex, the nineteenth-century descendant of Lowell and Moody's 1814 pioneering vision, stumbled and collapsed, taking thousands of workers' lives and pensions with it, a lesson in the dangers of extremes.

• Ken Olsen, the founder of Digital Equipment Corporation, father of the minicomputer. Ken ran his good ideas into helpless paralysis. He proved that even the purest technologist, faced with the challenge of staffing up to support massive growth, could easily fail to hire the right people, could easily prove the weakness of visionaries run by "the suits."

• MIT—if it is possible to acknowledge the contribution of an institution, our most productive technology machine, the hands-down winner, racking up more companies and more ideas per year than any other institution, we honor the Massachusetts Institute of Technology. We enjoy each and every trip we make to the Dome, and we treasure each connection and each carefully worded suggestion from our many MIT friends:

• Dan Whitney, who continues to combine theory and application on the factory floor

• Robert Solow, Nobel prize–winning economist and grand teacher who proved that growth and wealth are produced by the Technology Machine, and whose generous conversations continue to lead

• Patti Maes, whose Media Lab and Firefly work is moving along the concept-to-profit continuum

• Nicholas Negroponte, another very bright, dyslexic kid who specialized in memorizing European train schedules, and later became head of MIT's Media Lab, where he continues to feed the Technology Machine

• Michael Schrage, a brilliant industry analyst and writer for *Fortune*, for the moment lodged at MIT, whose phone calls from airports around the world continue to inspire us, and whose foresight reaches for miles and miles

and alumni:

    • Jim Womack, founder of The Lean Enterprise Institute and coauthor of *The Machine that Changed the World* and *Lean Thinking,* a young voice in the wilderness who continues to confront corporate blindness

    • Doug Currie, president of Flavors Technology, one of Morley's bright young Barnicles who got roped into fixing some "problematic" code and ended up building a railroad

• Ben Priest, '56, a dear friend and engineer fallen off the path

• Joe Alsop, founder of Progress Software

• Bob Galvin, a classically trained third-generation giant, now tackling tennis at the age of seventy-two. His wisdom, vision, and sharp determination continue to inspire us.

• The Breakfast Club, Morley's gang of twelve who meet somewhat irregularly to ponder and gift and to occasionally attend at the birth of another technology player. Club members, including the founder of Sanders Associates, continue to feed the Technology Machine. Amazing testimony to the gift of hard work and genius, not one of the Breakfast Club was born rich, but each of them has achieved a very comfortable life.

• Gordon Lankton, CEO of Nypro, headquartered in Clinton, Massacusetts. Nypro could have become another marginal player in the commodity plastics industry. Instead, Lankton's global vision has taken this company around the world; his clear understanding of the value of real-time on-line feedback and control systems render his factories wonders in the plastics community; his fearless sharing of power and decision-making has created an entire generation of young presidents at every new Nypro installation. Lankton fuels the Technology Machine.

The authors acknowledge the generous and energetic sharing of their technology visions with thousands of hours of interviews and on-site visits, by the following executives, entrepreneurs, and visionaries: Kevin Landry, TA Associates, Boston; Ray Sansouci, president of Modicon; Robert Booth, GM; Mike Kaminski, GM; Ernie Vahala, Auto Body Consortium; William J. LaPointe, president, Andover Controls; Seiichi Yaskawa, Yaskawa Electric Corporation; Albert H. Shiina, Yaskawa Electric; Robert R. MacDonald, Chairman of Bios Group, a for-profit partnership between Ernst & Young and Santa Fe Institute; Karl Kempf, Intel Corporation; Ross Little, Ernst & Young Center for Innovation; Chris Meyer, Ernst & Young Center for Innovation; Steve Ricketts, NCMS; John Decaire, NCMS president; Professor George Markowsky, University of Maine; Michael Damphousse, vice president of Pangaea, Inc.; Greg Ekberg, president of Falcon Cold Forming, etc., etc.; Morton Goulder; George Schwenk; Harry Healer; Kenneth Crater, president Control Technology Corporation, founder of the Industrial Computer Society; Professor H. van Dyke Parunak, University of Michigan; William Fulkerson, John Deere, Inc.; Larry Hill, DBI; Steven Bomba, Johnson Controls; Rich Ryan, president and CEO of Rockwell; Garry Berryman and Greg Smith of Harley-Davidson; Joe Yacusa, head of worldwide procurement at American Express; Bill Schaefer of IBM; Jerry Hirshberg, founder of the Nissan Design International in San Diego; Joe Rizzo, director, program management, Nypro; Brian Tracey and Jack Calderon, president, EFTC; EFC; FTC; Mark Ruettgers, president, EMC; Walt Wilson, president of the Americas, Solectron; Stefan Mitman, Intracomm Communications; Mike Peak, president of Peak Public Relations in California; and the Barnacles—Pat Letourneau, Karen Simpson, Bob DeSimone, Scott Russell, Kris and Kate Heikkila, Amanda Lapierre, and, as always, Shirley.

INDEX

Abbott Labs, 237, 239

Abell, Bruce, 124, 125

Advanced Planning and Scheduling (APS), 158, 161

AEG Schneider Automation, 121

Aerospace industry, 46

Agent-based modeling, 150–52
benefits of, 231

Airbus, 70, 114

Allen-Bradley, 101, 136, 137, 139, 143

Allied Signal, 266

Amazon, 245

Amoskeag complex, 8, 82–84

Analog Devices, 181

Andersen Consulting and Dataquest, 210

Andover Controls, 121

Apollo Computer, 10, 109

Apple Computer, 10, 199, 276

Appletalk, 137

Arndt, Bob, 115–16

Arthur D. Little, Inc., 188

Asea Brown Boveri, 18

AST Computer, 19, 36, 292, 293

Asynchronous digital subscriber line (ADSL), 181–83

Audible, Inc., 248–49

Automobile industry, 39

Autonomous agents, 22–23
software, 137–38

Baker, Charlie, 257

Baldrige Award, 11, 75, 90

Balsams Resort, 110

Barlow, Chris, 148, 162, 267–68

Barn, The, 120, 121

Barrett, Craig, 237

Beckman, Sara, 282

Bedford Associates, 100, 107

Benchmarking, 90

Bios Group, 150–55, 163

Biotech, 48

Black and Decker, 19

Blumer, Don, 269

Boardman, Bruce, 101

Boeing, 70, 114, 154

Bolt, Beranek & Newman Inc. (BNN), 171, 244

Boston Consulting Group, 199

Boston Manufacturing Co., 82

Bowmar, 10

Brazil, 39

Breakfast Club, 201–9
Briggs and Stratton, 77–78, 79, 92
Bryant Chuck and Grinder, 108
Bullet train (Shinkansen), Japanese, 213–21

Calderon, Jack, 281
Campbell Soup, 188
Carr, Kevin, 266
Carrierless amplitude and phase modulation (CAPM), 182
Case Corp., 170
Cash farming, 291–94
Catalytic management, 161
Chaos, defined, 123–24
Chen, Winston, 247
China, 39, 263–64
Chinese Box, 148–49, 241
Chrysler Corp., 39, 76, 195
    SCORE, 18
Cisco Systems, 292
Cities, 53
Clothing industry, 54
CNN, 32
Communication, 40–41, 51, 180–83
Compaq Computer, 75, 79, 110, 293
Compensation, 24–25
Competition, role of, 209–10
Complex adaptive systems (CAS), 158
    agent-based modeling, 150–52
    attributes of, 125
    defined, 122–24
    design rules, 130–31
    examples of, 124–26
    GM Paint Shop, 2, 129, 130–37
    programmed behavior and, 129–30
    SteelWorks, 138–42
    SunOpTech, 148
    utilities optimization tool, 152, 154
Complexity, simplicity versus, 89–93

Computer industry, 43, 46, 47, 50, 51, 52
Coolidge, Thomas Jefferson, 83
Copernicus, 128
Copyright, substitution for, 28, 43
Cost reduction, 167
Crab skin, 45
Critikon, 72
Crosby, Phil, 75
CVS, 160
CYMEX NG model, 151–52

Dalzell, Robert, 82
Data General, 10, 109
Datastream, 267
Davis and Furman machine shop, 97–98
DEC, 10, 19
Decker, Al, 19
John Deere, 76
    genetic algorithm scheduling process, 164, 168–72
Dell Computer, 292, 293
Design evolution, 155
Digital Equipment Corp., 105, 110, 188
Dimancescu, Dan, 291–92, 293, 294
Discrete multitone modulation (DMT), 182
Doyle, Mike, 75
Drew Santin, 32
Drugs, 48, 58
DuMoulin, Gary, 145

Eaton, 266
Economies of scale, 81–84
Education, 50
EFTC Corp., 148, 269, 281–82, 292, 293
Einstein, Albert, 128
Ekberg, Gregg, 20, 134, 138–44, 145, 148, 161, 162

Electronic management services (EMS), 148

EMC, 252–53

Emergent properties/behavior, 127–28

Emotions, role of, 283–84

Employment opportunities, 47

Encryption, 289–90

Energy industry, 50, 57

Engineers, role of, 255–59

Enterprise resource planning (ERP), 158, 159–60

Ernst & Young Center for Business Innovation, 150

Ethics, 31–32, 48

Excellence
    role of, 13–16
    value-chain models of, 18, 19

Falcon ColdForming, 134

Federal Express, 244, 245

Financial industry, 49, 55, 57

Five-legged dog concept, 196–97, 203

Fixing Broken Windows (Kelling), 196

Flavors Technology, 121, 137, 163, 226, 245

Flextronics, 36, 149, 247–52, 268, 292

Ford Motor Co., 109

Forrest, Stephanie, 123

Frito-Lay, 245

Fulkerson, Bill, 161, 162, 170–72

Future
    anticipating the, 64–65
    industries of the, 41
    resistance to the, 40
    Wild Cards, description of, 40–60, 287–301

Gaal, Steven, 208

Galvin, Bob, 19, 237

Garment industry, 270–73

GartnerGroup, 266

Gates, Bill, 38, 86

Gateway, 75, 79

Gell-Mann, Murray, 122–23

General Electric (GE), 170, 245
    Factory of the Future, 4, 109

General Motors (GM), 11, 41, 81, 92, 108, 109, 170, 200, 246
    compared with Honda, 124–25
    Paint Shop, 2, 129, 130–37, 164–68

Genetic algorithm scheduling process, 164, 168–72
    applications of, 231–33
    International Plastics/Germany (IP/G), 212–13, 222–31
    Japanese bullet train (Shinkansen), 213–21

Gilder, George, 60

Gillette, 188, 237, 239

Global competition, 36–37

Governmental issues, 55

Gregory, Milt, 20, 268

Gregory Associates, 18, 20, 268

Groupe Schneider, 100

Grove, Andy, 237

Harley Davidson, 75, 76

HB Fuller, 267

Health issues, 49–50, 51, 55, 58, 60

Hewlett Packard, 36, 37, 237, 238, 239, 244, 295
    calculator wristwatch, 4
    deskjet printer plant, 18

Highline Controls, 20, 138, 139, 140, 142, 143

Hobart, William, 20

Hobart Brothers, 20

Honda of America, 18, 36, 44, 70, 72–73, 76, 77, 193, 244
    compared with General Motors, 124–25

Housing, 56, 60

Human factor/emotions, role of, 161–62, 283–84

IBM, 245
Imai, Maasaki, 114
India, 39
Indonesia, 39
Industries
    of the future, 41, 45
    marginal operators, 41
    mini, 43
    Wild Cards, description of, 40–60,
        287–301
Innovation, 61, 63
    problems, 79–81
Intel, 193
Intellectual property law, 43
Intelligence
    factory applications, 128–29
    localized, 125–26, 148–49
    second-generation intelligent
        agent systems, 138
    systems, 52
    technology and, 298–301
International Plastics/Germany
        (IP/G), 212–13, 222–31
Internet, 84–87, 116
In the Memory House (Mansfield), 64
ISDN, 181
i2 Technologies, Inc., 170
Iverson, Kenneth, 19–20, 43, 246

Japan
    bullet train (Shinkansen), 213–21
    as a financial center, 43
    kaizen, 71–73
JAVA, 162
Jobs, Steve, 31, 84, 236
Johnson, Tom, 20, 291
Johnson & Johnson, 72, 146
Johnson Controls, 266
Jones, Dan, 114
Jones, Gerry, 223–25
Junkyards, 43
Just in time, 81

Kaizen, 71–73
Kaminski, Mike, 278–79, 280
Kaplan, Robert, 291
Kauffman, Stuart, 150
Kelling, George, 196
Kempf, Karl, 237
Kerschner, Edward, 84, 86
Kirila, Gene, 5, 20, 161, 162, 172–80
Knowledge data decision (KDD),
        279, 280
Knowledge workers, 27–29
    characteristics of, 31
    models, 32
    transitional, 30–31
Koski, Ed, 21
Koupal, Cecil, 268
Krever, Al, 270–73
Kroh, Randy, 138–39, 140, 141
K'Tec Electronics, 268–69

Ladder List, 110
Land, Edgar, 237
Landis, 108
Languages, 57–58
Lankton, Gordon, 19, 20, 237–43
Lantech, 72, 113
Leaders, visionary, 19–20
Leading edge technology, 9
Lean Enterprise, The (Dimancescu),
        291
Lean manufacturing, 113–15
Lean Thinking (Womack), 72
Leather, 45
Lee, Hau, 295
Lennox International, 267
Lexmark, 19, 154
Lisa computer, 196–97
Localized intelligence, 125–26,
        148–49
Lotus, 10, 293
Lovrenich, Rodger, 89, 91–92
Lowell, Francis Cabot, 8, 81–82

Machine That Changed the World, The
  (Womack and Jones), 72, 113
Manhattan Project, 167
MAN MAN, 79
Mansfield, Howard, 64
Manufacturing
  invisible, 45
  lean, 113–15
  locally produced, by global com-
    petitors, 36–37
  opportunities for technology,
    9–11, 38–40
  at point of consumption, 295–96
Manufacturing Execution Systems
  (MES), 117, 158, 160–61
Market segmentation, 43
Marks, Michael, 250–52
Marshall, John, 149
Maruo, Teruyuki, 73–74, 114, 209,
  242, 243
Mass production, 41
Materials, of the future, 45
Maynard, Michael, 273, 274–75
Maytag, 113
McNeil Consumer Labs, 146–48
Mechatronics, 255–56
Meler, Heiner, 149–50
Meta-systems
  Deere genetic algorithm schedul-
    ing process, 164, 168–72
  GM Paint Shop, 2, 129, 130–37,
    164–68
  International Plastics/Germany
    (IP/G), 212–13, 222–31
  Japanese bullet train (Shinkansen),
    213–21
  Net, 180–83
  Pyramid Virtual Engineered Com-
    posites (VEC), 172–80
Microsoft, 41, 86, 144, 160, 198–99,
  200, 245, 268
Midway Industrial, 139

Mill villages, 87–89
Minco, 154
MIT (Massachusetts Institute of
  Technology), 188, 189
Mitchell, J. Howell, 129, 135, 136,
  226, 227–28
Mitsubishi, 101
Modicon (MOdular DIgital CON-
  troller)
  competitors of, 101
  description of, 96–97, 99–101,
    107–8
Moody, Paul, 97, 98
Mori, Tesuro, 255
Motorola, 19, 36, 37, 61, 181, 193,
  237, 244, 245
  Iridium project, 3
  Quality System Review (QSR), 90
  Six Sigma, 11, 75, 90
MRP, 79, 80

National Association of Purchasing
  Management, 76
National Center for Manufacturing
  Sciences (NCMS), 163
National Initiative for Supply Chain
  Integration (NISCI), 75–76, 163
National Institute of Science and
  Technology (NIST), 163
Natural gas market, agent-based
  model of, 151–52
NCR (National Cash Register), 11
Negroponte, Nicholas, 208
Nelson, Dave, 18
Net, 180–83
Netsdal, 240
NeXT, 10, 31–32
Nishimura, Ko, 247
Nissitissitt River, 87
North Andover, Massachusetts,
  97–98
Nuclear power, 43, 64

Nucor Steel, 9, 18, 19–20, 43, 246–47

Numalogic, 105

Nypro Corporate Inc., 18, 19, 20, 36, 193, 237–43

Nypro Institute, 243–45

Oberman, Tony, 139

Ohno, Taiichi, 71

Olsen, Kenneth, 19, 84, 236

Olson, Larry, 268–69

OPT, 4

OptiFlex, 171

Optimax Systems Corp., 170, 171

Oracle, 79

Organizations in 2020, 21–24

Outsourcing, 46

Paint Shop, 2, 129, 130–37, 164–68

Pakistan, 39

ParaCell, 144

Parallel Inference Machine (PIM), 134, 135, 137

International Plastics / Germany (IP / G), and, 228–31

Japanese bullet train (Shinkansen) and, 213–21

Shane Steel Processing and, 145

Parker, Bob, 76

Parker Hannifin, 72

Partnering, 16–17

Pasadena Design Studio, 31, 32

Pella, 113

Performance

hyper-, 59

metrics for tracking, 20–21

for technology, 195–96

Phillip Morris, 245

Picturetel, 188

Pitney-Bowes, 292, 293

Pixar, 245

Polaroid, 245

Population Reference Bureau, 39

Postal system, 44, 244

Pratt & Whitney, 109, 113, 245

Procter & Gamble, 267

Productivity, 47, 55

Profit margins, future, 44

Programmable logic controller (PLC), 97

challenges facing, 109–11, 296

development of, 101–7

purpose of, 100, 108–9

reliability issues, 110

software implications from, 108

SteelWorks, 139, 140–41

versus personal computers, 111–15

Progress Software, 188

Promise-to-profit (PTP) strategies, 172

Pyramid Systems, 20

Virtual Engineered Composites (VEC), 172–80

Quadrature amplitude modulation (QAM), 182

Quality, problems with, 81

Raytheon, 44, 188

Reformation Generation, 15

Reich, Robert, 27

Relevance Regained (Johnson), 20

Religion / spirituality, 53–54

Remanufacturing, 43

Research and Development, role of, 203–4

Rewards, 24–26

Richter, Gene, 17

RMI, 144

Rohm & Haas, 267

Ross Valve, 32

Rule-based languages, 110

Sailboat racing, 149–50

Santa Fe Institute, 163

Satellite manufacturing, 46
Scheduling, pull-through, 132
Schofield Blacksmith Shop, 98
Schonberger, Richard, 20, 291
Schwenk, George, 208
Science, junk, 264–65
Seagate, 41
Seamless Enterprise, The (Di-mancescu), 291
Sears, 124, 125
Second-generation intelligent agent systems, 138
Security/privacy issues, 52, 289–90
Seglin, Jeffrey L., 206
Shainin, Dorian, 20
Shane Steel Processing, 142–43
    parallel inference machine at, 145
Shewhart Award, 20
Shingijutsu, 113–14
Shugart, Al, 236
Siemens, 101
Simplicity versus complexity, 89–93
Smith, Jack, 16
Social classes, 53
Software
    See also Complex adaptive systems (CAS)
    Advanced Planning and Scheduling (APS), 158
    application programs, problems with, 79–81
    autonomous agent, 137–38
    creativity, 197–98
    death of, 294–95
    design, 154
    enterprise resource planning (ERP), 158, 159–60
    human element, 161–62
    Manufacturing Execution Systems (MES), 158, 160–61
Software industry, 39
Solectron, 18, 36, 37, 247

Sony, 245
Specialization, 32–33
Springfield Manufacturing, 20
Stack, Jack, 20
Standardization of work, 71–73
Steel manufacturing, 39, 45
SteelWorks, 138–42
Steinmetz, Charles, 237
Stock market, 284–86
Stone and Webster, 188
StorageTek, 41
Story's Boatyard, 32
Sun Hydraulics, 21, 31, 32, 148, 267
SunOpTech, 148, 267
Supply America, 76
Supply chains, 75–76

Taxicab system, 126–27
Taylor, Frederick, 39
Technologically enabled, rules for, 191–92
Technology
    avoidance and denial of, 190–92
    Breakfast Club, 201–9
    competition, role of, 209–10
    core areas in, 288–289
    decline of, steps to, 282
    false promise of, 63–64
    five-legged dog concept, 196–97
    how to pick winners in, 188
    human factor/emotions, role of, 283–84
    intelligence and, 298–301
    investment relationship, rules on managing, 208
    leaders, examples of, 237
    managing, 192–95
    pack instinct, 275–77
    performance metrics, 195–96
    power of, 187–88
    preparing management for, 189–90
    rules for breakthroughs, 4

selection rules, basic, 205
sham, 264–67
Technology proposal evaluation, criteria for
five-legged dog concept, 203
folding, 203–4
100 percent of the market, 202–3
passion, 204–5
seven years, 200–202
10x performance, 198–200
three gurus, 202
three rounds, 203
Television, 47
Texas Instruments, 266
Textile industry, 8–9
3M, 244
Time travel, 46
Time Warner, 245
Toyota, 37, 39, 109, 154, 244
Toyota Production System, The (Ohno), 71
Trane, 76
Transportation industry, 54
TRW, 267

Unions/guilds, 48
University of Chicago, 76
U.S. Post Office, 244
USX, 9, 10, 20, 246–47
Utilities optimization tool, 152, 154

Vahala, Ernie, 137
Valley Logistics, 18
Value-chain excellence models, 18, 19

Value-chain management
use of term, 16–17
vision, 17–18
Variables
capital equipment, 179
live organic chemical, 179–80
process control, 180
types of, 178–97
Vestigial sideband (VSB), 182
Virtual Engineered Composites (VEC), 172–80
Voice recognition systems, 51
Von Neumann, John, 262–63

Wal-Mart, 50, 124, 125, 160, 199
Wars, 54
Watson, Greg, 90
Weather forecasting, 51
Wild Cards
description of, 40–60, 287–301
use of term, 39–40
Williams Technologies, 43
Wiremold, 72, 113
Womack, Jim, 72, 113–15, 116
Workers, in the future, 44, 46–47

Xerox, 41, 246

Yaskawa, Seiichi, 61, 213–16
Year 2000 problem
fear of, 265–67
how big is, 267–69
impact of, 274–75
lessons from, 270

Zimdars, Leroy, 75

ABOUT THE AUTHORS

PATRICIA E. MOODY is a well-known manufacturing management consultant and writer with over twenty-five years of industry and consulting experience and a client list that includes such industry leaders as Honda, Selectron, Motorola, Johnson & Johnson, and Mead Corporation. As the editor of *Target,* the magazine of the Association for Manufacturing Excellence, she created and developed breakthrough work on the future of manufacturing teams, kaizen, new product development, and supply chain issues. Her consulting practice, Patricia E. Moody, Inc., has for fifteen years helped bring leading-edge solutions for manufacturing and supply chain challenges to a wider audience through teaching, seminars, articles, and books. She holds degrees from Simmons College and the University of Massachusetts, is certified by the Institute of Management Consultants, and has published eight books—including *The Kaizen Blitz, Powered by Honda,* and *Breakthrough Partnering*—and dozens of articles. Ms. Moody lives with her engineer husband and beautiful daughter, an old cat, and one wild-eyed white dog on Boston's North Shore, seven miles from the spot where her predecessors dropped anchor in 1634. She can be reached at <pemoody@aol.com>.

RICHARD E. MORLEY is CEO of Flavors Technology, Inc., and is the founder or co-founder of more than ten companies, including Modicon, Andover Controls, Chaos in Manufacturing, Lightsync Inc., R. Morley Inc., Graeme Publishing, Eloquent Systems, Termiflex Corporation, Bedford Associates, Functional Automation, RemTech, and FASFAX. A nationally recognized expert in the fields of computer design, artificial intelligence, and factory floor automation, and a leading authority on the application of chaos theory in manufacturing, Mr. Morley holds more than twenty United States and foreign patents, including one for the Programmable Logic Controller, the key tool of factory control architecture, now housed in the Smithsonian Institution. A recipient of the Automation Hall of Fame's 1996 Prometheus Medal, Mr. Morley is recognized as one of the giants in the field of factory automation by the Engineering Society of Detroit. Mr. Morley publishes a monthly column on leading-edge technology in *Manufacturing Automation* magazine. He lives in rural New Hampshire and can be reached at <morley@barn.org>.